THE NATURAL HISTORY OF TASSEL-EARED SQUIRRELS

THE
NATURAL
HISTORY
of
TASSEL-EARED
SQUIRRELS

Sylvester Allred

UNIVERSITY OF NEW MEXICO PRESS
ALBUQUERQUE

THIS BOOK WAS MADE POSSIBLE BY A GENEROUS CONTRIBUTION
FROM NORTHERN ARIZONA UNIVERSITY.

The author would like to express his grateful appreciation
for the support of the following organizations:

Library of Congress Cataloging-in-Publication Data
Allred, Sylvester, 1946–
The natural history of tassel-eared squirrels / Sylvester Allred.
    p. cm.
Includes bibliographical references and index.
ISBN 978-0-8263-4655-1 (cloth : alk. paper)
1. Abert's squirrel.
I. Title.
QL737.R68A375 2010
599.36'2—dc22

2010022654

TO DONNA, MY LOVE—YOU KNEW ME
WAY BEFORE I ENCOUNTERED THE TASSEL-EARED
RASCALS AND YOU HELPED ME TELL THEIR STORY.

CONTENTS

CHAPTER THREE: HABITAT, HOME RANGE, AND DISTRIBUTION   21

CHAPTER FOUR: FOOD AND FEEDING ACTIVITIES   38

CHAPTER FIVE: NESTS   56

CHAPTER TWELVE: CENSUS AND MONITORING METHODS AND TECHNIQUES   144

CHAPTER THIRTEEN: MANAGEMENT AND CONSERVATION OF TASSEL-EARED SQUIRRELS   157

ILLUSTRATIONS

Figures

Tables

Plates
[Following page 130]

Acknowledgments

Acknowledgments for their assistance in this book project are given to the following individuals and their affiliations and institutions, in alphabetical order.

Ms. Ellen Alers, Smithsonian Institution

Dr. D. Barnosky, University of California, Berkeley

Ms. Kim Beckwith, Registrar, Intermountain Region Museum Management Program, Museum Collection Repository

Mr. Daniel Boone, Bilby Research Center, Northern Arizona University

Dr. Chris Conroy, University of California, Berkeley

Dr. Allen Dart, Old Pueblo Archaeology Center, Tucson, Arizona

Mr. Tony DeLuz, Bilby Research Center, Northern Arizona University

Dr. John Denboski, Denver Museum of Natural Science

Mr. Tom Denniston, Bureau of Land Management, St. George, Utah

Mr. Norris Dodd, Arizona Game and Fish Department

Dr. Lee Drickamer, Professor Emeritus, Northern Arizona University

Dr. Darrel English, Professor Emeritus, Northern Arizona University

Mr. Andrew Edelman, University of New Mexico

Dr. William Gaud, Professor Emeritus, Northern Arizona University

Dr. H. T. Goodwin, Andrews University, Maryland

Dr. Joe Hall (died September 2005)

Ms. Elizabeth Hickey, Associate Collections Manager, Anthropology, Museum of Northern Arizona, Flagstaff

Dr. Richard Holloway, Professor, Northern Arizona University

Dr. Laura Huenneke, Vice President of Research, Northern Arizona University

Mr. Bill Hurst, Regional Forester, U.S. Forest Service (Retired), Southwestern United States

Ms. Diane Iverson, Illustrator

Ms. Bernice Keith

Dr. Jim Keith (died May 2006)

Dr. John Koprowski, Biology Professor, University of Arizona

Ms. Leslie Kostrich, Alexandria, Virginia

Dr. Richard Miller, Arizona Game and Fish Department

Mr. Steve Mull, Photographer

Dr. Bill Newmark, Museum of Natural History, Utah University, Salt Lake City

Dr. Bill Noble, U.S. Forest Service, Coconino National Forest

Dr. David Patton, Professor Emeritus, Northern Arizona University

Dr. Gilbert Pogany, Professor Emeritus, Northern Arizona University

Staff of the Document Delivery Services at Cline Library, Northern Arizona University

Staff of the Special Collections, Cline Library, Northern Arizona University

Dr. Jack States, Professor Emeritus, Northern Arizona University

Dr. Michael Steele, Biology Professor, Wilkes University, Wilkes-Barre, Pennsylvania

Ms. Melissa Swain, Librarian, Arizona Game and Fish Department

University of New Mexico Press Staff

Ms. Colleen Wade, Special Collections at the Grand Canyon Museum, Grand Canyon National Park

Dr. Andrew Wallace, Professor Emeritus, Northern Arizona University

Dr. Maribeth Watwood, Professor, Northern Arizona University

Ms. Deborah Westfall, Curator of Collections, Edge of the Cedars State Park Museum, Blanding, Utah

---

A special acknowledgment to Ms. Jill Root, the copy editor of this book.

A special acknowledgment to Mr. Clark Whitehorn, editor-in-chief, University of New Mexico Press. Thank you, Clark, for taking this project for the UNM Press.

AUTHOR'S NOTES

Their ears are their most marked peculiarity, being ornamented in a grotesque fashion by tufts of long hair. Colorado seems to be particularly favorable to the growth of ears. Please don't take I mean disrespect to the new-fledged State. I only state a fact. Donkeys flourish there; so do mules. And those squirrels' ears, aside from the tufts of hair that finished them off, were a third longer than those of their Eastern brothers.

—M. Dartt, *On the Plains and Among the Peaks, or How Mrs. Maxwell Made Her Natural History Collection,* 1879

I live in the middle of an almost two-million-acre ponderosa pine forest—the largest in the world. In moments I can leave my home and be in the habitat of the tassel-eared squirrel, which I have studied for more than twenty-five years. From my dining table I can watch these tassel-eared rascals climb along a branch of a ponderosa pine, clip terminal pine shoots for inner bark, gather pollen cones for their rich golden pine pollen, and consume the seeds from developing ovulate cones. Any of us in Flagstaff, Arizona, or Boulder, Colorado, or Santa Fe, New Mexico, who live in houses placed in the habitat of these squirrels have the opportunity to see these animals whose relationship with the ponderosa pine forest is so unique, since with rare exception these animals live only in ponderosa habitat. Tassel-eared squirrels can bring both endless entertainment and numerous frustrations to homeowners. Some encourage them by placing foods out for them to eat, and others desperately try to keep these one and one-half–pound acrobats from raiding their bird feeders.

I receive phone calls from concerned homeowners because a tassel-eared squirrel has decided to use their ponderosa pine trees for feeding:

clipping the upper terminal branches, stripping the needles, and creating piles of cone scales below. I assure these worried folks that the tree will not be killed though it will be pruned to some extent, and I urge them to feel fortunate that their trees were selected by the squirrel, because this activity so perfectly demonstrates the unique relationship between the tassel-eared squirrel and the ponderosa pine.

These little tassel-eared creatures are so charismatic that anyone seeing them for the first time must smile with surprise. Photographers and artists wish to capture their essence. Backyard naturalists are able to see a special ecological relationship. Scientists now recognize the tassel-eared squirrels as critical indicators of the health of the forest. This natural history book on tassel-eared squirrels started in the summer of 1985 when I began my doctoral research at Northern Arizona University on tassel-eared squirrel herbivory and ecology with Dr. William Gaud, in a ponderosa pine forest located at Lowell Observatory. Other members of my doctoral committee were Dr. Jack States, a mycologist with an interest in squirrel mycophagy; Dr. Gilbert Pogany, an embryologist; and Dr. David Patton, a forest wildlife ecologist. Four and a half years later with PhD finished and a faculty position with the Department of Biological Sciences at Northern Arizona University, I continued the ecological research, expanding my studies into tassel-eared squirrel reproductive biology and embryology, home range studies, and studies of parasites of these squirrels. I attended numerous scientific meetings and met other scientists whom I had known only by their publications on squirrels. I first met Dr. Joe Hall, noted Kaibab squirrel researcher, at a mammalogy meeting in Albuquerque, New Mexico. I met Dr. Jim Keith, author of the first and often cited ecology paper on Abert's squirrels, when he was traveling through Flagstaff.

Melissa Lema, Debra Guzman, Anne Minard, and Mike Rose conducted graduate research on Abert's squirrels with me. Numerous undergraduates have participated with me in various tassel-eared squirrel research projects.

Through the years I have given presentations about tassel-eared squirrels to numerous groups including those at the Grand Canyon National Park, the Museum of Northern Arizona, the U.S. Forest Service, the Flagstaff Festival of Science, and several Audubon chapters. At one of the Audubon chapter meetings in Prescott, I met wildlife illustrator Diane Iverson. We immediately began discussions on a children's book about tassel-eared squirrels, and in 2007 the Grand Canyon

Association published *Rascal, the Tassel-Eared Squirrel*, a richly illustrated, full-color book that describes the first year of life of a tassel-eared squirrel living in the pine forest at the Grand Canyon.

Jim Keith, Joe Hall, and I discussed collaborating on a natural history book on tassel-eared squirrels, but since Jim and Joe are now deceased, the writing of this book has been left for me to do.

Introduction

The Abert squirrel (*Sciurus aberti aberti*) is often described as one of the most beautiful squirrels in North America. Since the animal was first described by Woodhouse in 1853 it has held the fascination of the zoologist, the naturalist, and the tourist.

—J. O. Keith, "The Abert Squirrel (*Sciurus aberti aberti*) and Its Relation to the Forests of Arizona," 1956

Tassel-eared squirrels were first described and collected near the San Francisco Peaks in northern Arizona by Dr. Samuel W. Woodhouse, a physician and naturalist with Captain Lorenzo Sitgreaves' expedition in 1851. "Ears large and broad, tufted with long black gray hairs" began Woodhouse's description of the squirrels he found in abundance during the month of October (ref. 1).

With the conspicuous long, soft, blackish tufts of hair (tassels) extending from the tips of their ears accounting for the unique appearance of these squirrels, naturalists referred to them as tufted-eared squirrels, big-eared pine squirrels, mule-eared or donkey-eared squirrels, long-eared squirrels, saddle-backed gray squirrels, white-tailed squirrels, silver-tail squirrels, tassle-eared squirrels, and tassel-eared squirrels (ref. 1, 2, 3, 4, 5, 6). "Tassel-eared squirrel" is now the commonly used name.

Woodhouse assigned the scientific name *Sciurus dorsalis* in 1853 to the specimens he had collected. However, the species name *dorsalis* had already been designated to another squirrel species, requiring Woodhouse to rename his specimen *S. abertii* in honor of Colonel John James Abert, chief of the Corps of Topological Engineers (later the U.S. Army Corps of Engineers), "to whose exertions science is so much indebted" (ref. 7). Later the second *i* was dropped for the more correct

FIGURE 1.1 First engraved image of *Sciurus aberti* by R. H. Kern. Taken from the Report of an Expedition down the Zuni and Colorado Rivers by Captain L. Sitgreaves. Senate Executive Document 59, 32nd Cong., 2nd sess., p. 53. Washington, DC, 1853.

Latin usage, *aberti*. Tassel-eared squirrels are now all referred to as Abert's squirrels with one exception: the Kaibab squirrel.

Squirrels on the north side of the Colorado River on the Kaibab Plateau have been known as Kaibab squirrels since 1904 when that squirrel was identified and named as a separate species from the Abert's squirrel living on the south side of the Colorado River (ref. 8). Geographical isolation of species can lead to allopatric speciation, a type of speciation that can occur if a barrier is present. Though the Grand Canyon and the Colorado River are such barriers, at present there is no strong evidence that a speciation event has occurred. The distinct species recognition of the Kaibab squirrel was later reexamined, resulting in both the Kaibab and the Abert's squirrels being regarded as subspecies (ref. 9). A subspecies is defined as "a taxonomic category used by some systematists to designate a genetically distinct set of populations of a species that have a discrete range" (ref. 10).

Taxonomists do not generally give subspecies distinct common names, but these two names have been allowed to stand since they have been widely accepted both in the lay and the scientific literature for well over a century. Appendix 1 gives a brief introduction to the Order Rodentia and the hierarchical system of nomenclature of the tassel-eared squirrels. Over the years there have been as many as nine subspecies and two species of tassel-eared squirrels reported in the literature, but extensive revisions have resulted in a reduction to six subspecies (ref. 9). Appendix 2 provides more detail of their discovery and nomenclature history.

Tassel-eared squirrels are indigenous to and dependent on ponderosa pine (*Pinus ponderosa* var. *scopulorum*) forest habitats that exist in the southwestern United States and Mexico (ref. 11, 12, 13, 14). Some rare exceptions of habitat are discussed in chapters 4 and 5 on food and nests. Within the United States, tassel-eared squirrels are found in Arizona, Colorado, New Mexico, Utah, and Wyoming. Arizona and New Mexico each have three of the subspecies existing within their borders. Two of the six subspecies live in the Sierra Madre Occidental in Mexico.

This book describes every aspect of the tassel-eared squirrel from the DNA analysis of the six subspecies to the histology of its ovaries and testes to its complex ecological relationships within the ponderosa pine forests. Chapter 10 discusses the history of the picturesque and possibly endangered Kaibab squirrel in its sky island habitat. Appendix 3 provides brief biographies of the naturalists who first described the subspecies of these squirrels. Appendix 4 covers fossils and other remains, including a mysterious thousand-year-old artifact of squirrel pelts and macaw feathers found in a Utah cave. Appendix 5 presents a brief evolutionary history of tassel-eared squirrels. Chapter 13 recommends management strategies for the tassel-eared squirrel as a forest management indicator species within the ponderosa pine forests.

Though this book is a comprehensive review of the current state of knowledge, it will be clear to the reader that there are many unanswered questions and contradictory studies providing opportunities for further research of these unique and fascinating animals. Within this book I have identified more than forty research topics for future explorations.

Note to the reader: All measurements given in this book have been converted to metric measurements. All numbers have been rounded for brevity.

References for Chapter One

1. Sitgreaves, L. 1853. Report of an Expedition Down the Zuni and Colorado Rivers. United States Army Corps of Topographical Engineers. Washington, DC: R. Armstrong.
2. Coughlin, L. E. 1938. The case against the tuft-eared squirrel. U.S. Forest Service. *Rocky Mountain Region Bulletin* 21 (4): 10–12.
3. Potter, R. M. 1980. The development of ponderosa pine cone processing ability in young tassel-eared squirrels (*Sciurus aberti*). PhD diss., Miami University.
4. Hoffmeister, D. F. 1971. Mammals of the Grand Canyon. Chicago: University of Illinois Press.
5. Seton, E. T. 1953. Lives of Game Animals. Vol. 4, pt. 1. Boston: Charles T. Branford Co.
6. Findley, J. S. 1987. The Natural History of New Mexican Mammals. Albuquerque: University of New Mexico Press.
7. Woodhouse, S. W. 1853b. Renaming for *S. dorsalis* Woodhouse, 1853. *Proceedings Academy of Natural Science Philadelphia* 6:200.
8. Merriam, C. H. 1904. Two new squirrels of the *aberti* group. *Proceedings of Biological Society of Washington* 17:129–30.
9. Hoffmeister, D. F., and V. Diersing. 1978. Review of the tassel-eared squirrels of the subgenus *Otosciurus*. *Journal of Mammalogy* 59:402–13.
10. Brown, J. H., and A. C. Gibson. 1983. Biogeography. St. Louis: C. V. Mosby Co.
11. Merriam, C. H. 1890. Results of a biological survey of the San Francisco Mountain region and desert of the Little Colorado, Arizona. U.S. Bureau of the Biological Survey. *North American Fauna* 3.
12. Merriam, C. H. 1894. Laws of temperature control of the geographic distribution of terrestrial animals and plants. *National Geographic* 6:229–38.
13. Merriam, C. H. 1898. Life Zones and Crop Zones of the United States. U.S. Department of Agriculture Bulletin no. 10. Washington, DC: U.S. Government Print Office.
14. Keith, J. O. 1965. The Abert squirrel and its dependence on ponderosa pine. *Ecology* 46:150–63.

PHYSICAL
CHARACTERISTICS OF
TASSEL-EARED SQUIRRELS

The most characteristic, as well as the most abundant species of Squirrel, is the Tuft-eared discovered by Dr. Woodhouse in the San Francisco Mountains. It is one of the largest, and certainly the very handsomest of all the North American species. Besides very beautiful and harmonious colors, it rejoices in the possession of long pointed ear-tufts, extending an inch or more from the edge of the conch of the ear, which gives it a peculiarly sprightly and truly elegant appearance.

—E. Coues, "The Quadrupeds of Arizona," 1867

Tassels

Ear tassels have been the identifying characteristic from the very first published account of these squirrels given by Dr. Samuel Woodhouse (ref. 1). Other researchers have either reported tassel measurements or noted their existence and colorations upon collecting the various subspecies (ref. 2, 3, 4, 5, 6). No significant difference is found in the tassel lengths of females and males during the year (ref. 7). Black coloration of the tassels is consistent across all reports. Tassels begin growing from the tips of the squirrel's ears beginning in the early fall. By January the tassels are at their maximum length of about 4 cm, sometimes drooping at the tips (ref. 7, 8, 9, 10). Researchers speculate that tassels may offer some thermal protection for the ear tips from the winter temperatures since these squirrels do not hibernate but remain active throughout the winter. Thermoregulatory characteristics of squirrels such as increased lengths of guard hairs and darker colored fur in the winter have been reported in some squirrels that do not hibernate (ref. 11).

During the late spring, the black color bleaches to a dark brown or tan color, and as the squirrels gradually shed their tassels by July they are left with very short hairs along the edges of the pinna (ref. 8, 12). Adults of *S. a. kaibabensis* completely lack tassels in the summer (ref. 10, 13).

While *S. a. aberti* and its related subspecies are the only tassel-eared tree squirrels in North America, there are tassel-eared red tree squirrels in Europe (*S. vulgaris*) and Japan (*S. lis*), and in Borneo, the tassel-eared ground squirrel (*Rhithrosciurus macrotis*) (ref. 11, 12, 14, 15). In 1941, Ed McKee cited a personal communication received from Vernon Bailey, author of *Mammals of New Mexico*, regarding a comparison of tassels of the Old World squirrels to tassels of squirrels of North America: "the ear tufts . . . are very different in the two groups and probably do not indicate relationships" (ref. 14).

Physical Characteristics—Pelage and the Colors

Colors of the Type Specimens of *S. a. aberti* and *S. a. kaibabensis* in Arizona

Woodhouse described the dorsal color of the *S. a. aberti* specimen he collected in 1851 as "dark gray" and the ventral surface as white with the tail being gray on top and white underneath (ref. 1). *S. a. aberti* is the type specimen for the subspecies of tassel-eared squirrels. The term "agouti," which means "banded pattern," refers to the combination of white, black, and grayish blends of colors comprising the dorsal pelage of *S. a. aberti*. C. Hart Merriam gave the following description of *S. a. kaibabensis* in 1904: "Similar in size and general characters to *S. aberti*, but underparts mainly black instead of white, and tail mainly white all over instead of under side only" (ref. 5).

Colors of *S. a. ferreus* in Colorado

A study conducted in Rocky Mountain National Park described the three color phases of *S. a. ferreus*: typical *S. a. aberti* pattern, totally black, and dark brown. The latter two did not have any dorsal patches of reddish fur nor the black lateral line that separates the dorsal from the ventral fur on a typical *S. a. aberti* (ref. 16). When I visited the Denver Museum of Nature and Science and examined the collection of specimens of tassel-eared squirrels, the colors of *S. a. ferreus* brought to mind

– TABLE 2.1 –

Descriptive terms applied to the pelages of *S. a. ferreus* in Colorado

Term	Meaning	Researcher, year
melanism	Referring to the pelage's being darker than the typical *S. a. aberti*	Coues and Allen, 1877; Farentinos, 1972c; Ramey and Nash, 1976b
dichromatic	Applied to squirrels that are partially or entirely black	V. Bailey, 1931
light and dark phases	Light if dorsal surface is gray; dark if the dorsal surface is brown or black	Lechleitner, 1969
pelage polymorphisms	Referring to the many different shades of colors of gray, brown, and black	Farentinos, 1972c
agouti and nonagouti	Agouti refers to typical *S. a. aberti* coloration; nonagouti refers to other colors	Ramey, 1973

various shades of coffee—mocha, latte, cocoa—and spices such as cinnamon and nutmeg. The many published reports of tassel-eared squirrels use numerous descriptive terms and colors to portray the subjective descriptions of fur color (tables 2.1 and 2.2).

In 1877, Elliott Coues and Joel A. Allen were the first to report melanism, in their *Monographs of North American Rodentia*, as a common occurrence in *S. a. ferreus*, specifically noting, "Melanism of this species largely predominates over the normal coloration in Colorado" (ref. 17). Brown and black pelages (nonagouti) on *S. a. ferreus* were reported to outnumber the agouti (ref. 18). In reference to the multiple coat colors found in *S. a. ferreus*, Merritt Cary wrote in 1911 that these squirrels offer "one of the most striking examples of extreme melanism among mammals" (ref. 19). The majority of tassel-eared squirrels observed in northern Colorado were dark in color whereas lighter colored squirrels were more common in southern Colorado. Light-colored and brown tassel-eared squirrels were more common in central Colorado (ref. 20, 21, 22, 23). Melanistic coat colors of these squirrels may be advantageous in colder regions of higher latitudes and higher elevations because of heat absorption (ref. 24). However, in other studies with *S. a. ferreus* and *S. carolinensis leucotis* (eastern gray squirrel), no evidence was found to support an advantage of darker coloration (ref. 22, 25). Gray,

– TABLE 2.2 –

Color descriptors used by researchers for pelage areas on tassel-eared squirrels

Area of pelage	Color descriptor	Researcher, year
dorsal fur color	plumberous gray	Mearns, 1907
	grizzled gray	Allen, 1904; Merriam, 1904; McKee, 1941
mid-dorsal patch on back	ferruginous-brown	Woodhouse, 1853a
	ferruginous	Merriam, 1904
	reddish-brown	Mearns, 1907
	chestnut or color of iron	Warren, 1910
	chestnut brown	V. Bailey, 1935
	rusty red	McKee, 1941
	cinnamon rufous	Goldman, 1931; Durrant and Kelson, 1947
	rufous	Findley et al., 1975
	brownish-red	Armstrong, 1987
Tail (undercolor)	solid white (*S. a. aberti*) grizzled gray (*S. a. phaeurus*)[1] white tip, gray base (*S. a. barberi*)	McKee, 1941

1 —*S. a. durangi*—since revision by Hoffmeister and Diersing (1978)

brown, and black colors have all appeared in the same litter of tassel-eared squirrels (ref. 26). A similar observation was made in a study of the eastern gray squirrel, of a litter with one gray, one black, and one albino squirrel (ref. 25).

Colors of *S. a. aberti*, *S. a. chuscensis*, and *S. a. kaibabensis* from Arizona and New Mexico

The agouti form of the Abert's squirrel is the most common across its distribution. Occasionally black-bellied Abert's squirrels have been observed ranging from Fort Verde to Fort Apache, Arizona, 80 km south and 241 km southeast, respectively, of the San Francisco Peaks (ref. 12). A black-bellied form of an *S. a. aberti* squirrel was found as a road-killed specimen from the San Francisco Peaks area near Flagstaff, Arizona. The specimen is in the zoological collection (# Z9.4186) of the Museum of Northern Arizona, Flagstaff (ref. 27). The first and only report of an albino *S. a. aberti* is from northern Arizona (ref. 9). *S. a. kaibabensis* are typically black-bellied; however, white-bellied forms from the North Rim of the Grand Canyon have been observed (ref. 10, 28).

The colors of tassel-eared squirrels in New Mexico vary geographically within the state. Vernon Bailey noted in 1931 that in the Black Range and the San Mateo Mountains of New Mexico, tassel-eared squirrels are "partly or entirely black, a case of dichromatism comparable to that of the gray and black squirrels of the Northeastern States." He also examined tassel-eared squirrel specimens from the Mogollon Peaks, Frisco, and Datil ranges, and the Magdalena Mountains in southwestern New Mexico, and could not distinguish any of the squirrels from the typical *S. a. aberti* of the White Mountains and San Francisco Peaks in Arizona (ref. 29). Tassel-eared squirrels from the Jemez, San Juan, and Sangre de Cristo mountain ranges had reduced rufous dorsal patches, with some specimens having no dorsal patch; however, all had white bellies. Squirrels from the mountain ranges of the Sandias, Mt. Taylor, and ranges southward had broader dorsal patches, with many individuals in certain ranges having black bellies (ref. 30).

In 1931, E. A. Goldman described *S. a. chuscensis* from the Chuska Mountains of Arizona and New Mexico as being "[v]ery similar in general to *S. a. aberti*, but still lighter gray" (ref. 31).

Colors of Tassel-Eared Squirrels from Mexico

One study described *S. a. durangi* as being similar to *S. a. aberti* but with "less reddish chestnut" on its dorsal patch (ref. 14). A different study reported the color descriptions of *S. a. barberi* and *S. a. durangi* to be similar to that of *S. a. aberti* (ref. 32).

Genetics of Pelage Colors

Polymorphisms in coat color in tassel-eared squirrels are thought to be the results of mutations involving at least two gene loci (ref. 23). It has been hypothesized that the difference in body coat color of Abert's and Kaibab squirrels is due to a single gene mutation (ref. 33). Several researchers have speculated on the genetic basis of the white-bellied form of the Kaibab squirrels and the black-bellied form of the Abert's squirrel (ref. 10, 14, 33, 34).

− TABLE 2.3 −

Dorsal guard hair and underfur measurements of *S. a. ferreus*

Type of guard hair	$\bar{X}$ Dorsal guard hair length (mm)	$\bar{X}$ Underfur (mm)	Diameter (µ)
Unbanded	24.3	NG	83
Triple banded	22.8	NG	80
Pelage color			
Agouti colored	20.9	13	NG
Nonagouti colored	23.5	15	NG

NG—not given

Guard Hair

Microscopic measurements and descriptions of the dorsal guard hairs (outside fur) and the underfur of *S. a. ferreus* living in Wyoming were made to determine if any differences were present in the guard hairs and to determine if a relationship existed between coat color (agouti and nonagouti) and guard hair length. No significant differences were determined when all data were compared statistically (table 2.3) (ref. 35).

Dorsal Patch

Along the mid dorsal section of many tassel-eared squirrels, a deep reddish or rust-colored patch of fur extends from their shoulders to near the base of their tails. Table 2.2 gives other descriptors of the color of the dorsal patch. The color of the patch is similar to the red-brown-orange bark exhibited by mature ponderosa pines.

Lateral Stripe

The dorsal pelage of the Abert's squirrels in New Mexico and Arizona is separated from the ventral white fur by a thin, well-defined black lateral stripe (ref. 14, 26, 36).

Tail Colors

Kaibab squirrels have amazing snowy white tails that are very noticeable when the squirrels are on branches within the forest (ref. 10, 13). The solid white tails of the Kaibab squirrels are in stark contrast to the grayish-white tails of Abert's squirrels, which do have white-colored fur on the underside. Vernon Bailey reported some Kaibab tails were tipped with black (ref. 37). I examined *S. a. ferreus* specimens at the Denver Museum of Nature and Science and found a wide variation in tail colors, ranging from the typical grayish-white of *S. a. aberti* to solid black.

Tail Lengths

Adult Abert's females were reported to have longer tails than adult males in one study; however, this was not the case reported in another study that found no differences in tail lengths between the two sexes (ref. 7, 9).

Faces

Each eye is surrounded with a small white ring. Vibrissae, or whiskers, serve as tactile structures on mammal faces. Tassel-eared squirrels' cheek vibrissae are black and less stiff than domestic cat whiskers (ref. 36).

Molting

Tassel-eared squirrels go through seasonal molting twice per year during the late spring to midsummer (May–July) and early fall (October). The fall molt is more rapid than the spring molt as winter is approaching. *S. a. aberti* have brighter fur with more whitish hairs after their spring molt than after their fall molt (ref. 9, 38). Complete descriptions and diagrams of the process of squirrel molting have been published by John Gurnell and Jim Keith (ref. 11, 38). Figure 2.1 (on the following page) shows a diagram of the progress of the spring molt for *S. a. aberti*.

Physical Characteristics—Body Measurements

Size

Adult female tassel-eared squirrels weigh between 525 and 745 g, and adult males weigh between 551 and 731 g (table 2.4; appendix 6). Adult females have body lengths ranging from 47.7 to 63.5 cm, and adult males range from 47.8 to 56.0 (table 2.5). Adult tassel-eared squirrels have a height range of 10–11.5 cm at the shoulders (ref. 34). Tail lengths, hind foot lengths, and ear lengths are listed in tables 2.6, 2.7, and 2.8, and in appendix 6.

Body weights of tassel-eared squirrels in northern Arizona were recorded in a three-year study. The averaged squirrel weights declined in the summer and increased throughout the fall, decreased again in the

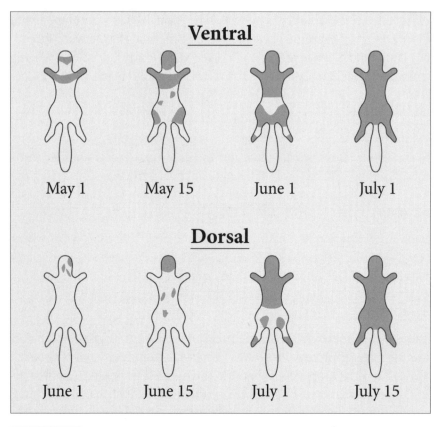

Ventral

May 1   May 15   June 1   July 1

Dorsal

June 1   June 15   July 1   July 15

FIGURE 2.1 Molting pattern of an Abert's squirrel. Redrawn from J. O. Keith, 1956. Used with permission from Bernice Keith.

winter, and began to show increases in the spring. One male began the summer below 700 g, gained 100 g by late fall, and lost 140 g during the winter. A female weighed around 680 g in the summer, gained 100 g by late fall, then lost 110 g in the winter (ref. 39). This pattern of seasonal gain and loss of weight has also been reported for fox and gray squirrels (ref. 40).

Feet and Claws

Tassel-eared squirrels are extremely well adapted to living in trees. Their re-curved claws permit the squirrels to have tenacious grips on branches and trunks of trees. Squirrels are able to move quickly in all directions on the trunk of a tree. Often tassel-eared squirrels can be seen literally hanging upside down from the trunk or branch of a tree.

Weights of female and male tassel-eared squirrels

Female weight (g)	n	Male weight (g)	n	Subspecies	Researcher, year
585–640	NG	572–665	NG	S. a. mimus[1]	Hill, 1942
602	13	589	27	S. a. aberti	Keith, 1965
588	15	626	11	S. a. kaibabensis	Patton et al., 1976
525–682	41	602–702	64	S. a. navajo[2]	Pederson et al., 1976
580.0 ± 50.16	2	569.57 ± 26.81	7	S. a. ferreus	Ramey and Nash, 1976a
657.35 ± 14.79	23	634.17 ±11.82	36	S. a. aberti	
742	17	651	15	S. a. kaibabensis	J. G. Hall, 1981
953 road-killed lactating	1	——	——	S. a. kaibabensis	J. G. Hall, 1981
586–743	103	566–702	134	S. a. aberti	Allred, unpublished data
——	——	905	1	S. a. aberti	Allred, unpublished data
549–700	7	582–605	2	S. a. durangi	Baker and Greer, 1962
387–745[3]	26	551–731[3]	11	S. a. ferreus	Littlefield, 1984

1 —*S. a. aberti* since revision by Hoffmeister and Diersing (1978)
2 —*S. a. aberti* since revision by Hoffmeister and Diersing (1978)
3 —no distinction made between juveniles and adults
NG—not given

Their ability to rotate their feet 180 degrees is an interesting phenomenon to observe. When moving on any surface, squirrels have all four feet planted, a condition known as *plantigrade*. The hind feet have five digits, while their forefeet have four, all equipped with sharp curved black claws.

— TABLE 2.5 —

Average body lengths of female and male tassel-eared squirrels

Female length (cm)	n	Male length (cm)	n	Subspecies	Researcher, year
47.7–49.0	NG	47.8–48.7	NG	*S. a. aberti*	Keith, 1965
51.4–63.5	19	48.0–56.0	25	*S. a. navajo*[1]	Pederson et al., 1976
49.6	20	49.0	14	*S. a. kaibabensis*	J. G. Hall, 1981
51.8–56.4	91	53.4–53.8	128	*S. a. aberti*	Allred, unpublished data
38.7–43.3[2]	26	31.3–36.72	11	*S. a. ferreus*	Littlefield, 1984

1 —*S. a. aberti* since revision by Hoffmeister and Diersing (1978)
2 —no distinction made between juveniles and adults
NG—not given

— TABLE 2.6 —

Average tail lengths of female and male tassel-eared squirrels

Female tail length (cm)	n	Male tail length (cm)	n	Subspecies	Researcher, year
21.6–22.6	NG	20.4–21.2	NG	*S. a. aberti*	Keith, 1965
23.2–26.0	19	20.0–27.0	25	*S. a. navajo*[1]	Pederson et al., 1976
22.4	19	21.9	14	*S. a. kaibabensis*	J. G. Hall, 1981
24.9–29.6	97	25.0–29.6	129	*S. a. aberti*	Allred, unpublished data

1 —*S. a. aberti* since revision by Hoffmeister and Diersing (1978)
NG—not given

Teeth

Twenty-two teeth are present in adult tassel-eared squirrels. Members of the Order Rodentia have incisors that continue to grow throughout their lives. The frontal surfaces of the incisors are covered with enamel, which reduces the wear in that area. The lingual side of the incisors is not covered with enamel and wears down into a bevel or chisel-shaped

Average lengths of the hind foot of female and male tassel-eared squirrels

Female hindfoot length (cm)	n	Male hindfoot length (cm)	n	Subspecies	Researcher, year
69–71	NG	68–70	NG	*S. a. aberti*	Keith, 1965
68–73	19	69–77	25	*S. a. navajo*[1]	Pederson et al., 1976
69–75	99	69–75	130	*S. a. aberti*	Allred, unpublished data

1 —*S. a. aberti* since revision by Hoffmeister and Diersing (1978)
NG—not given

Average lengths of the ear from the ear notch of female and male tassel-eared squirrels

Female length of ear from notch (mm)	n	Male length of ear from notch (mm)	n	Subspecies	Researcher, year
39–43	NG	39–43	NG	*S. a. aberti*	Keith, 1965
37–52	19	36–40	25	*S. a. navajo*[1]	Pederson et al., 1976
44–51	94	44–51	126	*S. a. aberti*	Allred, unpublished data

1 —*S. a. aberti* since revision by Hoffmeister and Diersing (1978)
NG—not given

pattern toward the tongue. The dental formula (incisors, canines, premolars, molars) x 2 is the method used by biologists to describe the arrangement of teeth in the jaw of a mammal (ref. 41). The dental formula for tassel-eared squirrels is (1/1, 0/0, 2/1, 3/3) x 2 = 22 (ref. 42, 43). Rodents lack canines in their dental formula, thus the 0/0. The third premolar (Pm3) has been used as an aging technique for tassel-eared

— TABLE 2.9 —

Averaged measurements of the cranium of three female tassel-eared squirrels
(*S. a. ferreus*, modified from Armstrong, 1972)

Area of cranium measurement	mm
Greatest length of skull	59.5
Condylobasal length	54.7
Zygomatic breadth	35.4
Interorbital breadth	19.3
Postorbital breadth	18.2
Length of nasals	18.6
Mastoid breadth	25.2

squirrels. If the Pm3 are fully erupted and in their occluding position, then the animal is considered an adult (ref. 43). The lower molars have four roots and the upper molars have three (ref. 12).

Cranium Measurements

Several researchers have conducted measurements of the crania of the subspecies of tassel-eared squirrels (ref. 14, 20, 43). Measurements of the crania of three female *S. a. ferreus* in Colorado are given in table 2.9 (ref. 20).

Determining the Differences between Juveniles and Adults by Physical Characteristics

For age determination in females, Jim Keith proposed using nipple descriptors. Adults have dark pigmentation and enlargement of the nipples whereas the nipples of juveniles and subadult females lack these conditions. He suggested that tassel lengths might also be incorporated in age determination. Young squirrels' tassels are "short thick tufts during September," whereas adult squirrels lose their tassels in June and regrow them in early fall. Keith also suggested that dead animals could be aged by examination of the scrotums and uteri (ref. 9). Characteristics such as visible scrotum (descended versus abdominal testes) and penis size of live-trapped males have been used for age determination (ref. 44). The closure of the epiphyseal cartilages, lens weights, and tooth wear, as well as body weights and measurements, have been used for deciding whether a squirrel was a juvenile or an adult (ref. 45).

Do Tassel-Eared Squirrels Conform to Allen's and Bergmann's Rules?

Joel A. Allen in 1877 stated that mammals and birds that live in colder climates tend to have shorter appendages than their counterparts in warmer climates. Carl Bergmann in 1847 predicted that animal species living in higher latitudes and colder climates would have higher body masses than the same species living in lower latitudes.

A study of five subspecies (*S. a. aberti, S. a. phaeurus, S. a. barberi, S. a. ferreus, S. a. mimus*) and two species (*S. durangi* and *S. kaibabensis*) of tassel-eared squirrels, looking for coat color and body size differences across latitudes and elevations, found "no transition from north to south, or along other lines of differentiation can be noted either in size or color . . . some of the smallest forms are in the north and others in the south; some of the darkest at one extreme, some at the other" (ref. 14). Another study explored geographical differences in three of the subspecies (*S. a. aberti, S. a. mimus,* and *S. a. ferreus*) of tassel-eared squirrels and could not find any evidence for support of either Allen's or Bergmann's Rules (ref. 46).

Temperatures of Tassel-Eared Squirrels

David Patton, a wildlife biologist, forester, and prominent tassel-eared squirrel researcher, found that the range of rectal temperatures of fifty-one tassel-eared squirrels (Abert's and Kaibab) in Arizona was 38.5°–42.7° C, with an average of 40.7° C. He hypothesized that this temperature range could indicate that tassel-eared squirrels might be heterothermic animals, but stated more research should be conducted to establish if this temperature range is related to their food and cover availability (ref. 47). In another temperature study, seven Abert's squirrels in Arizona were monitored with implanted temperature-sensitive radio transmitters. The range was 35.2°–41.1° C, with a mean of 39.0° C. These researchers reported hyperthermic conditions in these squirrels during periods of intense activity, in both summer and winter. Squirrels were observed seeking shade after activities leading to hyperthermia. Hypothermia was also related to the level of activity. Hypothermic temperatures were recorded while squirrels were in their nests during both day and night. They were observed basking in the sun on limbs during winter afternoons and upon morning emergence from nests throughout the year. Tail position during basking affected the body temperature, as did rain and wind (ref. 24).

Future Research

There have been limited studies on the body temperatures of tassel-eared squirrels. Four (*aberti*, *chuscensis*, *ferreus*, and *kaibabensis*) of the six subspecies live in snowy conditions for several months of the year. (1) Do they differ in their body temperatures during the winter months? summer months? We know nothing about the body temperatures of the two subspecies (*barberi and durangi*) living in Mexico. (2) Could there be a noticeable variation in the four northern subspecies when compared with the two southern subspecies?

References for Chapter Two

1. Woodhouse, S. W. 1853a. Description of a new species of *Sciurus*. *Proceedings Academy of Natural Sciences Philadelphia* 6:110.
2. Baird, S. F. 1855. Characteristics of some new species of mammalia, collected by the U.S. and Mexican Boundary Survey, Major W. H. Emery, U.S.A. Commissioner. *Proceedings Academy of Natural Sciences Philadelphia* 7:331–36.
3. Coues, E. 1867. The quadrupeds of Arizona. *American Naturalist* 1:281–92, 351–63, 393–400, 531–41.
4. Allen, J. A. 1904. Further notes on the mammals from Northwestern Durango. *Bulletin of the American Museum Natural History* 20:205–10.
5. Merriam, C. H. 1904. Two new squirrels of the *aberti* group. *Proceedings of Biological Society of Washington* 17: 129–30.
6. Durrant, S. D., and K. R. Kelson. 1947. A new Abert squirrel from Utah. *Proceedings of Biological Society of Washington* 60:79–82.
7. Minard, A. 2000. Morphological and genetic investigations of Abert squirrels (*Sciurus aberti aberti*). MS thesis, Northern Arizona University.
8. Seton, E. T. 1953. Lives of Game Animals. Vol. 4, pt. 1. Boston: Charles T. Branford Co.
9. Keith, J. O. 1965. The Abert squirrel and its dependence on ponderosa pine. *Ecology* 46:150–63.
10. Hall, J. G. 1981. A field study of the Kaibab squirrel in Grand Canyon National Park. *Wildlife Monographs* 75.
11. Gurnell, J. 1987. The Natural History of Squirrels. New York: Facts on File.

12. Mearns, E. A. 1907. Mammals of the Mexican Boundary of the United States. Part 1. U.S. National Museum Bulletin 56. Washington, DC: Smithsonian Institution.

13. Goldman, E. A. 1928. The Kaibab or white-tailed squirrel. *Journal of Mammalogy* 9:127–29.

14. McKee, E. D. 1941. Distribution of the tassel-eared squirrels. *Plateau* 14:12–20.

15. Moore, J. C. 1959. Relationships among the living squirrels of the Sciurinae. *Bulletin of the American Museum of Natural History* 118 (4): 153–206.

16. Armstrong, D. M. 1987. Rocky Mountain Mammals. Boulder: Colorado Associated University Press.

17. Coues, E., and J. A. Allen. 1877. Monographs of North American Rodentia. Department of the Interior, Report of the U.S. Biological Survey of the Territories, F. V. Hayden, U.S. Geologist in charge. Vol. 11. Washington, DC: U.S. Government Printing Office.

18. Warren, E. R. 1910. The Mammals of Colorado. New York: G. P. Putnam's Sons.

19. Cary, M. 1911. *North American Fauna*. No. 33. U.S. Department of Agriculture, Bureau of Biological Survey. Washington, DC: U.S. Government Printing Office.

20. Armstrong, D. M. 1972. *Distribution of Mammals in Colorado*. Monograph no. 3 of the Museum of Natural History. Lawrence: University of Kansas.

21. Lechleitner, R. R. 1969. Wild Mammals of Colorado—Their Appearance, Habits, Distribution, and Abundance. Boulder, CO: Pruett Publishing Co.

22. Ramey, C. A., and D. J. Nash. 1976b. Coat color polymorphism of Abert's squirrel, *Sciurus aberti*, in Colorado. *Southwestern Naturalist* 21 (2): 209–17.

23. Hancock, D. C., Jr., and D. J. Nash. 1982. Dorsal hair length and coat color in Abert's squirrel (*Sciurus aberti*). *Great Basin Naturalist* 42:597–98.

24. Golightly, R. T., and R. D. Ohmart. 1978. Heterothermy in free-ranging Abert's squirrels (*Sciurus aberti*). *Ecology* 59:897–909.

25. Creed, W. A., and W. M. Sharp. 1958. Melanistic gray squirrels in Cameron County, Pennsylvania. *Journal of Mammalogy* 39 (4): 532–37.

26. Keith, J. O. 2003. The Abert's Squirrel (*Sciurus aberti*): A Technical Conservation Assessment. Golden, CO: USDA Forest Service, Rocky Mountain Region.

27. Allred, W. S. 1995. Black-bellied form of an Abert squirrel (*Sciurus aberti aberti*) from the San Francisco Peaks area, Arizona. *Southwestern Naturalist* 40:420.

28. Allred, W. S. Unpublished observation.

29. Bailey, V. 1931. Mammals of New Mexico. North American Fauna no. 53. Washington, DC: USDA, Bureau of Biological Survey.

30. Findley, J. S., A. H. Harris, D. E. Wilson, and C. Jones. 1975. Mammals of New Mexico. Albuquerque: University of New Mexico Press.

31. Goldman, E. A. 1931. Three new rodents from Arizona and New Mexico. *Proceedings of Biological Society of Washington* 44:133–36.

32. Hoffmeister, D. F., and V. Diersing. 1978. Review of the tassel-eared squirrels of the subgenus *Otosciurus*. *Journal of Mammalogy* 59:402–13.

33. Wettstein, P. J., and J. States. 1986b. The major histocompatibility complex of tassel-eared squirrels. II. Genetic diversity associated with Abert squirrels. *Immunogenetics* 24:242–50.

34. Cahalane, V. H. 1947. Mammals of North America. New York: Mac-Millan Co.

35. Moore, T. D., L. E. Spense, and C. E. Dugnolle. 1974. Identification of Dorsal Guard Hairs of Some Mammals of Wyoming. Laramie: Wyoming Game and Fish Department.

36. Brown, D. E. 1986. Arizona's Tree Squirrels. Phoenix: Arizona Game and Fish Department.

37. Bailey, V. 1935. Mammals of the Grand Canyon Region. Natural History Bulletin no. 1. Grand Canyon, AZ: Grand Canyon Natural History Association.

38. Keith, J. O. 1956. The Abert squirrel (*Sciurus aberti aberti*) and its relation to the forests of Arizona. MS thesis, University of Arizona.

39. Austin, W. J. 1990. The foraging ecology of Abert squirrels. PhD diss., Northern Arizona University.

40. Short, H. L., and W. B. Duke. 1971. Seasonal food consumption and body weights of captive tree squirrels. *Journal of Wildlife Management* 35:425–39.

41. Feldhamer, G. A., L. C. Drickamer, S. H. Vessey, and J. F. Merritt. 2004. Mammalogy. 2nd ed. Dubuque, IA: McGraw-Hill.

42. Booth, E. S. 1982. How to Know the Mammals. 4th ed. Dubuque, IA: William. C. Brown Co.

43. Hoffmeister, D. F. 1986. Mammals of Arizona. Tucson: University of Arizona Press.

44. Farentinos, R. C. 1972c. Observations on the ecology of the tassel-eared squirrel. *Journal of Wildlife Management* 36 (4): 1234–39.

45. Stephenson, R. L. 1975. Reproductive biology and food habits of Abert's squirrels in central Arizona. MS thesis, Arizona State University.

46. Ramey, C. A., and D. J. Nash. 1976a. Geographic variation in Abert's squirrel (*Sciurus aberti*). *Southwestern Naturalist* 21 (2): 135–39.

47. Patton, D. R., T. D. Ratcliff, and K. J. Rogers. 1976. Weights and temperatures of the Abert and Kaibab squirrels. *Southwestern Naturalist* 21:236–38.

Habitat, Home Range, and Distribution

3

Few animals are as closely associated with a single habitat type as these squirrels, they are found only in the dry ponderosa pine forests of the interior Southwest. Even here they are not universal and are restricted to forests where winter snows are moderate and continuous snow cover generally lasts less than three months.

—D. E. Brown, *Arizona's Tree Squirrels*, 1986

Introduction

The natural habitat of the tassel-eared squirrels is characterized by ponderosa pines. The home range is the area that includes all the travels of an individual squirrel daily and throughout the year. The geographical distribution of these squirrels is that of specific stands of ponderosa pine forests found in the southwestern United States and in Mexico.

In 1853, Woodhouse described the area where tassel-eared squirrels were first located and identified: "This truly elegant squirrel I procured in the San Francisco Mountain, during the month of October, where I found it quite abundant, and after leaving which place I did not see it again. I have been informed lately . . . that they are quite numerous near Fort Defiance, in the Navajoe country" (ref. 1). Indeed, the Sitgreaves expedition never again passed through the ponderosa pine habitat of the squirrels.

Habitat

Habitat includes the resources required by a species for survival and reproduction. Ponderosa pine forest cover for Abert's squirrels is described as the vegetative shelter including the nest, the nest tree, and the vegetation surrounding the nest tree (ref. 2).

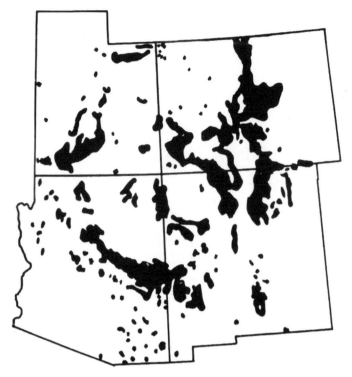

FIGURE 3.1 Distribution of ponderosa pine forests in the southwestern United States and Mexico. Used with permission from David Patton.

A live-trapping study with *S. a. ferreus* in Colorado examined five habitat types and found 92% of the squirrels in the ponderosa pine forest, 7% between grassland and ponderosa pine forest, and 1% in ponderosa pine–Douglas fir. No squirrels were trapped in the grassland or deciduous habitats (ref. 3).

Good squirrel habitat can provide sources of squirrels that move into poor habitats or "sinks," which are characterized by low survival rates. "Source areas" for tassel-eared squirrels are characterized by high basal areas, high level of interlocking canopies, large trees, and stable populations of squirrels. Characteristics of sink habitats are opposite of those of source areas, with low basal areas, low level of interlocking canopies, small trees, and fluctuating squirrel populations (ref. 4).

Basal areas of ponderosa pine forests and tassel-eared squirrel population densities have been shown by numerous researchers to be linked (ref. 4, 5, 6, 7, 8). The basal area of a stand of trees is the cross-sectional area of all trees within the stand and is expressed as m²/hectare (ha). Higher basal areas have better recruitment of squirrels. Norris Dodd, a research

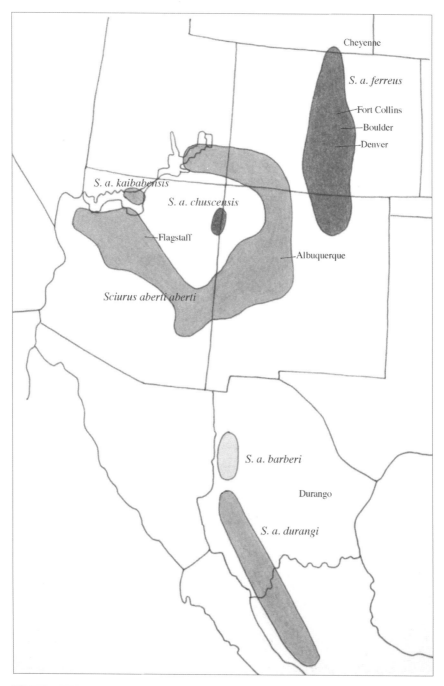

Cheyenne

S. a. ferreus

Fort Collins
Boulder
Denver

S. a. kaibabensis

S. a. chuscensis

Flagstaff

Albuquerque

Sciurus aberti aberti

S. a. barberi

Durango

S. a. durangi

FIGURE 3.2 Distribution of the six subspecies of tassel-eared squirrels in the southwestern United States and Mexico. Redrawn by Diane Iverson from Hoffmeister and Diersing, 1978.

Habitat, Home Range, and Distribution   23

biologist with the Arizona Game and Fish Department (AZGFD), compared squirrel habitats across nine landscape-sized (280 ha) ponderosa pine forested areas and found that a basal area > 35 m²/ha qualified as optimum squirrel habitat (ref. 9). Examinations of squirrel diets with respect to mycophagy was found to have significant relationships with basal area, denser canopy cover, and fungal biomass (ref. 10, 11).

A habitat quality study on *S. a. kaibabensis* in a virgin ponderosa pine stand of the Kaibab National Forest found an association between the number of Kaibab squirrels and the number of nests, concluding that the number of nests was a good indicator of habitat quality (ref. 5).

A "status of knowledge" paper on ponderosa pines compiled by Gilbert Schubert of the U.S. Forest Service in 1974 estimated that ponderosa pine forests in Arizona, Colorado, New Mexico, and Utah cover approximately four and one-half million hectares. New Mexico has the most hectares and Utah the fewest (ref. 12). Assessments of the pre-settlement conditions around 1870 that existed in the ponderosa pine forests of northern Arizona found that forests had stands of older trees with open areas separating those stands, in contrast to the current conditions of forests consisting of dense young trees (ref. 9).

The amount of ponderosa pine forest habitat of the southwestern United States available to tassel-eared squirrels was calculated in 1995 (table 3.1) (ref. 13). Table 3.2 lists the subspecies of squirrels that inhabit the ponderosa pine forests in the southwestern United States. A few researchers have noted that tassel-eared squirrels inhabit other forest types in addition to ponderosa pine forests (table 3.3).

In 1977, Patton evaluated squirrel habitats ranging from poor quality to optimum quality. Parameters used in this study included tree arrangement within the stand, basal area of the stand, stand diameter at breast height (dbh), levels of canopies, dbh of nest and feed trees, and trees/ha.

— TABLE 3.1 —

Total habitat size of the four southwestern United States tassel-eared squirrels

(from Wettstein et al., 1995)

Subspecies	Size of habitat (ha)
S. a. aberti	1,308,000
S. a ferreus	650,000
S. a. kaibabensis	177,000
S. a. chuscensis	142,000

Optimum habitat had specific characteristics that provided the best cover conditions for the squirrels. These included uneven-aged ponderosa pine stands with trees spaced in small even-aged groups within the stand, average tree diameter between 28 and 33 cm dbh, and basal area of trees between 35 and 47 m²/ha (ref. 14). In another study, which measured more than seven thousand trees, Patton concluded that a basal area from 9 m²/ha to 23 m²/ha accounted for 84% of nest sites within the forest and found no nests within stands with basal areas less than 5 m²/ha (ref. 6).

In a review of sixteen previous squirrel habitat studies, Patton selected habitat characteristics to develop a habitat model for Abert's squirrels. His model included tree size, tree density, and tree dispersion patterns. He and coworkers then conducted eight years of trapping studies using this model to define the capability of habitat to maintain squirrel populations. His model predicted that in optimum quality habitat the habitat capability was 2.4 squirrels/ha and in poor quality habitat the habitat capability was 0.05 squirrels/ha. Patton used John Vandermeer's "common sense phenomenon" (1981) to explain poor quality habitat by stating, "Squirrels need trees; a lack of trees indicates a lack of squirrels and this is indicative of the poor quality class" (ref. 7).

Dodd evaluated optimum squirrel habitat using a method of comparison of sections of habitats of tassel-eared squirrels. The Ratio of Optimum to Marginal Patch Area (ROMPA) compares two classes of habitat: optimum and marginal. A ROMPA of 40%, for example, defines

— TABLE 3.2 —

Geographical areas of the six subspecies of tassel-eared squirrels[1,5]

Location	Subspecies
Arizona	*S. a. aberti, S. a. chuscensis, S. a. kaibabensis*
Colorado	*S. a. aberti, S. a. ferreus*
New Mexico	*S. a. aberti, S. a. chuscensis, S. a. ferreus*
Wyoming[1,2,3,4]	*S. a. ferreus*
Utah	*S. a. aberti*
Mexico	*S. a. barberi, S. a. durangi*[5]

1 —Hoffmeister and Diersing (1978)

2 —L. N. Brown (1965) described two melanistic (black) *S. a. [ferreus]* and two that "exhibited . . . gray and white pelage" in southern Wyoming.

3 —Clark and Stromberg (1987): *S. a. ferreus* "occurs only in the rocky ponderosa pine grassland community of Harriman [Wyoming]."

4 —Northernmost geographical reach of this subspecies (Armstrong, 1972).

5 —Baker and Greer (1962) reported the southernmost limit of *S. a. durangi* in the pine-oak forests of the Sierra Madre Occidental in western Durango, Mexico.

— TABLE 3.3 —

Tassel-eared squirrel habitat characteristics—trees—forest types

Researcher / location/year	% PP[1]	% GO[2]	% PPA[3]	% PPPJS[4]	% PPDF[5]	Other[6]	# of squirrels
Pederson et al./ Utah/1976	91	2	5	2			183
Hall/Arizona/ 1981	X						X
Littlefield/ Colorado/ 1984	76				24		37
Ratcliff et al./ Arizona/1975; Stephenson/ Arizona/1975; Findley et al./ New Mexico/ 1975; Hutton et al./Arizona/ 2003	X	X		X		X	X

1 —ponderosa pine
2 —Gambel's oak
3 —ponderosa pine/aspen
4 —ponderosa pine/pinyon/juniper/spruce

5 —ponderosa pine/Douglas fir
6 —includes Apache pine (*P. englemannii*), Chihuahua pine (*P. leiophylla*)
X—squirrels present but no % or # of squirrels given

40% of the area as optimum habitat and the remaining 60% as marginal. Across the nine sites in his study, ROMPA ranged from almost 5% to 99% optimum habitat. He concluded that optimum squirrel habitat:

1. exhibited multiple age classes
2. had a large tree component defined as > 50 trees/ha with 45+ cm dbh
3. had a basal area > 35 m2/ha
4. had > 50% canopy closure with interlocking canopies.

The reason the intermediate ROMPA sites had higher squirrel densities was because of the "habitat mosaic and . . . edge effect." Mean squirrel densities were more that 2.5 times greater on the optimum sites than on the marginal areas (ref. 9).

Another investigation using ROMPA found that optimal habitat had dense stands of ponderosa pines > 29.4 cm dbh with many interlocking canopies, while marginal habitat had trees between 2.5 and 30.3 cm dbh with little canopy overlap (ref. 15).

Tree characteristics of significance to tassel-eared squirrels

Researcher / location/date	*FT dbh range (cm)	Density[1]	Live Crowns[2]
Patton and Green Arizona/1970	25.5–71.6	NG	NG
Hall[3]/Arizona/1981	NG	X	X
Ffolliott/Arizona/1990	20.0–85.0		
Allred and Gaud/ Arizona/1994a	30.98 ± 12.7	NG	NG

1 —density of ponderosa pines > 17 cm dbh
2 —ponderosa pines with 65% live crowns
3 —"quality of [squirrel] habitat is . . . reflected in a number of variables [including] density of larger trees, trunk diameter, crown density and height, and foliage weight."

*FT—feed tree
X—greater than 0.500 Correlation Coefficient Relationship
NG—not given

In addition to providing escape routes and travel corridors, inter-locking canopies also provide a better environment for the growth of hypogeous fungi. There is a strong association between hypogeous fungi production and canopy closure of ponderosa pine forests and squirrel abundance (ref. 10, 16). Hypogeous fungi are a crucial dietary component of tassel-eared squirrels (ref. 11, 16, 17, 18).

Dodd and his colleagues assessed four characteristics of habitats of Abert's squirrels in eight different areas in north-central Arizona:

1. basal area by tree species
2. quadratic mean diameter by tree species
3. stand density index
4. tree density corresponding to vegetation structural stage classes.

The conclusion drawn from this research confirmed earlier research conducted by Patton that interlocking canopies of ponderosa pines were strongly correlated with squirrel densities and recruitment (ref. 4, 14). Table 3.4 presents the work of several other researchers who have reported feed tree dbh, density of trees, and live crowns of trees as contributing to overall habitat quality.

Home Range

Home range is an area that includes "the daily, seasonal, and annual travels of an individual animal" (ref. 19) and the "normal activities of food gathering, mating, and caring for young" (ref. 20). Factors that influence home range sizes of different animals include densities of the populations, seasons of the year, sex of the individuals, age of the individuals (juvenile vs. adult), and food resources available within the area (ref. 21). Methods that have been used to elucidate the home range of tassel-eared squirrels are direct observations (ref. 22, 23), trapping for tagging or marking (ref. 24), and telemetry (ref. 22, 24, 25, 26).

Another study reported that ROMPA of 45–65% reduced squirrel home range size, thus reducing travel while offering adequate resources for Abert's squirrels. There was higher mortality of juvenile squirrels in the areas of higher ROMPA due to predation by goshawks, which select high ROMPA sites for foraging and building nests. The same was not true for adult squirrels, most likely because of their experience in avoiding goshawks (ref. 15).

Tassel-eared squirrels can move many hectares in short periods of time. For example, a *S. a. kaibabensis* traversed 8.8 ha in seven days (ref. 27) and a *S. a. aberti* in Utah covered 45 ha in forty days (ref. 22). Numerous researchers have described home range sizes for tassel-eared squirrels; these range from 4 to 34 ha (table 3.5). The large variation in size can be attributed to several factors: (1) length of study, (2) sex of the individual squirrel, (3) time of the year, and (4) the specific habitat where the squirrel was tracked. Home range sizes are expected to be larger in poor quality and smaller in better quality areas. In one study a squirrel had a 98% overlap of space with twelve other squirrels in the study area (table 3.5) (ref. 21). Margaret Halloran, in a squirrel study in Utah, stated, "If Abert squirrels decrease their home ranges when population densities are high because of social pressures, then they must avoid each other temporally, rather than spatially, since their home ranges overlap so extensively" (ref. 21).

Home range size for male tassel-eared squirrels increases significantly during the breeding season. This increase in home range size is attributed to males searching widely for females in estrus. Females do not have a larger home range during breeding season (ref. 21, 28). In one study, during the nonbreeding season the home range size of males averaged 7 ha and of females averaged 6 ha. The winter home range for males averaged 5.3 ha and the summer home range averaged 2.6 ha, while females averaged 4.9 ha during the winter and 1.3 ha during the summer (ref. 28). Melissa Lema, in a study near Flagstaff in 2001, combined data for both females and males from two different study sites with radically different forest management treatments in northern Arizona (table 3.5) and found

— TABLE 3.5 —

Home range (HR) size of tassel-eared squirrels

Researcher / location/date	Subspecies	Calculated average HR (ha)	# of squirrels	Sex of squirrels
Patton/Arizona/ 1975a	*aberti*	4 12, 34	1 2	female male
Pederson et al./ Utah/1976	*aberti*	2.5*/12.9**	14	not given
Farentinos/ Colorado/1979	*ferreus*	9 18	8 8	female male
Hall/Arizona/ 1981	*kaibabensis*	14	1	female
Halloran/ Colorado/1993	*ferreus*	17 21	7 6	female male
Lema/Arizona/ 2001	*aberti*	19[1] 24[2]	all squirrels over two-years/ averaged	NA

1 —Marshall Site—72 ha—53% canopy closure— basal area 32 m²/ha

2 —Tuthill Site—6² ha—32% canopy closure— basal area 16 m2/ha

*—precut

**—postcut treatment

the poor site home range averaged 24 ha while the better site home range averaged 19 ha (ref. 26).

Seasonal variation (i.e., expansions or contractions) in home range size can be attributed to food quality and quantity. Seeds from ovulate cones in years of good cone crops promote smaller home ranges for squirrels. In years of poor or no cones, squirrels are forced to consume more inner bark from feed trees that are spread throughout the forest and to extend their hunting forays for hypogeous fungi. Proximity to water sources also contributes to variations in home range size (ref. 21, 28).

In Utah, a study was conducted to evaluate the effects of logging on the home range size of squirrels, comparing precut data with postcut data. Home range size of males was 6 ha and of females was 0.9 ha precut. The average home range size of males and females increased to 17 ha and 4 ha, respectively, postcut. This tremendous increase in home range size was attributed to the decrease in habitat quality. Three patterns of movement by the squirrels during the logging activities were observed: (1) squirrels moved directly away from the logging activity, (2) later in the logging activity squirrels moved even farther away, and (3) some squirrels moved back to the area after logging ceased. One squirrel in this study increased its home range to 31 ha postcut. This study reported no change in home range size in the control group of squirrels living in an area that was not logged (ref. 22).

Another study in Arizona found that the average home range of squirrels differed by 5 ha when comparing an unthinned area to an area that had been thinned to one-half the basal area of the unthinned site (table 3.5) (ref. 26). This finding strongly suggests that home range size of squirrels will increase in forest stands with low basal area and canopy closures because there are fewer escape routes and fewer available resources such as food, cover, and nesting sites when compared with forest stands with higher basal areas and canopy closures that offer a higher quality area.

When home range sizes of transplanted *S. a. aberti* in a mixed conifer forest in southern Arizona where they compete with red squirrels were studied, the researchers found no differences in female home range size between breeding and nonbreeding seasons. Of interest, females reduced the distances traveled within their home ranges during the breeding season. Male squirrels were exactly opposite in their home range behavior during breeding season. Their home range size increased as did overlaps with female home ranges, and the distances traveled increased within their home range. Tassel-eared squirrels had smaller home ranges during the nonbreeding season in the mixed conifer forests when compared with tassel-eared squirrel home range sizes during nonbreeding season in ponderosa pine forests. Several possible explanations were proposed: (1) better resources in the mixed conifer forests, (2) competition with the red squirrels that are indigenous to the mixed conifer forests, and (3) severe winter environmental conditions of that location (ref. 29).

Geographical Distribution of Tassel-Eared Squirrels

The first map showing the distributions of the tassel-eared squirrels in the southwestern United States and Mexico was published in 1941. It showed that tassel-eared squirrels were strongly coupled to the "cool, relatively dry interior areas where western yellow pines exist in the Transition Zone. . . . Tassel-eared squirrels are confined in the southern Rocky Mountains and the Colorado Plateau in the United States, and to the Sierra Madre Mountains of Chihuahua and Durango, Mexico." The range of elevations given for tassel-eared squirrel distributions was from 1,676 m in Colorado to 2,591 m in Mexico (ref. 30).

Post-Pleistocene immigrations and extinctions have been proposed as a possible explanation for the montane mammal communities and their distributions in the southwestern United States. *S. aberti* is one of the twenty-six species listed that inhabit nine of the twenty-seven sky islands that were considered in the montane areas of the Southwest (ref. 31).

The present-day distribution of tassel-eared squirrels may have resulted from the climatic changes affecting ponderosa pines at lower elevations. As the pine forests retreated to more elevated areas, so did the squirrels, which effectively isolated them "where they have remained for thousands of years" (ref. 30). James Findley and Sydney Anderson, in a paper published in 1956, described the zoogeography of the montane mammals of Colorado, hypothesizing that the Wyoming Basin and the Green River were natural barriers to *S. a. ferreus* in Colorado, preventing their westward expansion (ref. 32). The amount of snowfall and subsequent greater snow depth could offer a "plausible explanation" as to why tassel-eared squirrels are not found in other ponderosa pine forests, e.g., the Sierra Nevada Range and the northern Rocky Mountain Range (ref. 33).

The present distribution of tassel-eared squirrels north of the 36th parallel could be explained by a post-Pleistocene dispersal. Any dispersal of tassel-eared squirrels would have required the squirrels to traverse non–ponderosa pine habitat to reach suitable habitat because of the fragmentation of the conifer forests in the northern mountains. Successful transplants of tassel-eared squirrels have provided evidence of their ability to accomplish such dispersals through unsuitable habitats (ref. 34). The absence of tassel-eared squirrels north of the 41st parallel could be explained by the climate conditions that might not be conducive for the growth of hypogeous fungi, a crucial dietary component of tassel-eared squirrels (ref. 16).

Natural Range Expansions of Tassel-Eared Squirrels

A range expansion of *S. a. ferreus*, by 58 km east and 33 km west, of a previously mapped distribution in Colorado was reported in 1971 (ref. 35, 36). A fauna survey in southern Colorado reported six *S. a. aberti* in the Culebra Range, which was an extension of their range by 72 km southeast from that previously reported (ref. 37, 38). Another study reported a range expansion of *S. aberti* into eleven counties of Colorado not previously reported (ref. 39, 40). A first report of a tassel-eared squirrel at 3,850 m elevation on the tundra area of Mt. Humphreys, in the San Francisco Peaks in northern Arizona, was submitted in 1987 (ref. 41). Several *S. a. aberti* populations expanded their range by crossing into areas without ponderosa pine trees to establish new populations, thus giving more credence to other research that reported that tassel-eared squirrels can be successful in coniferous forests other than ponderosa pine (ref. 29, 34).

Transplants of Tassel-Eared Squirrels

Abert's squirrels have been transplanted several times by the AZGFD and the U.S. Fish and Wildlife Service (ref. 34, 42, 43, 44). In the fall of 1941, eighty-eight female and one hundred male Abert's squirrels were captured and released in the Pinal Mountain, Horsethief Recreational Area, Santa Catalina Mountains, Hualapai Mountains, and Mt. Graham in the Pinaleño Mountains. The transplants of squirrels were done to introduce more game animals into areas that were considered previously occupied by these squirrels in the past, though Donald Hoffmeister, author of numerous scientific papers and books on mammals, wrote, "Abert squirrels did not occur in the Grahams before this transplant" (ref. 45). The success of the Abert's squirrels at one of the Mt. Graham areas was reported in 1953 by Steve Galliziolli with the AZGFD. He wrote, "This is one species which has evidently found the Grahams to its liking . . . this species has multiplied and spread to the point where it is almost impossible to walk anywhere in the coniferous areas without finding either squirrels or evidence of their presence" (ref. 46).

Again in the late winter of 1941 another group of Abert's squirrels—forty-three females and forty-two males—were captured at the Fort Valley Experimental Station near Flagstaff, Arizona, and released in the Pinal Mountain, Bradshaw Mountains, Granite Basin Recreational Area, Horsethief Recreational Area, and Catalina Mountains in Arizona. A few squirrels of the 1941 winter capture were shipped to Idaho and West Virginia, for "captive studies or exhibits and not for introduction." All introductions were successful and some of the transplanted squirrels dispersed to the Superstition, Rincon, and Mazatzal Mountains (ref. 44). It was proposed that tassel-eared squirrels were not present in any of these areas prior to the transplants because either the squirrels experienced a local extinction event or they were never in the areas because no adequate corridors for dispersal existed from other ponderosa pine forests that could have served as a source of squirrels (ref. 34, 44).

"In view of the unique contribution of the Kaibab squirrel to the observable wildlife of the Grand Canyon National Game Preserve its transportation to other regions for stocking purposes is not favored," W. P. Taylor reported to the Bureau of Biological Survey in 1926 (ref. 47). "Thirty or forty years ago, . . . there were several tame Kaibab squirrels released on the Yarkagunt Plateau by the Thorley brothers of Cedar City; the descendants of those unwilling migrants have since been seen at rare intervals by persons motoring over the plateau to Cedar Breaks, but none have been reported within the monument," according to a 1938 Zion-Bryce bulletin (ref. 48). Twenty-one Kaibab squirrels were successfully relocated from the Kaibab Plateau to Mt. Logan between 1971 and 1977, and Kaibab squirrels continue to inhabit the ponderosa pine forests of the Sawmill Mountains, Mt. Emma, and Mt. Trumbull (ref. 44).

"The distribution of tassel-eared squirrels in Arizona is now greater than at any historic time," David Brown wrote in *Arizona's Tree Squirrels*. Tassel-eared squirrels are not in the ponderosa pine forests of the Pine Mountain Wilderness Area, Santa Rita, Huachuca, and Chiricahua Mountains, nor on the Four Peaks in the Mazatzal Mountains (ref. 44).

Abert's squirrel introductions into the Sandia Mountains in 1940, the Manzano Mountains in 1929 and 1940, and the Sacramento Mountains during 1955 and 1969 in New Mexico and into the Dixie National Forest in Utah from 1898 to 1908 were documented in several research projects (ref. 34, 44, 49). None has been transplanted into Colorado or Wyoming. After the 1940s introductions of Abert's squirrels, further transplants were stopped because of concerns for the endemic squirrels that were in the particular areas where the transplants had occurred (ref. 44).

In a 1989 study in the southwestern United States that examined island biogeography of montane forest mammals, Mark Lomolino and colleagues noted that after tassel-eared squirrels were successfully transplanted they were able to successfully colonize "at least six nearby montane forests." They reported that the time from transplantation of tassel-eared squirrels to their colonization of new areas increased with the distance from their original release, "8–12 km in 10 yr, 23 km in 20 yr, 29 km in 30 yr, and 35 km in 40 yr" (ref. 31).

Summary

Tassel-eared squirrels are, for the most part, obligate herbivores living in ponderosa pine forests. It is known that tassel-eared squirrels are capable of sustained existence in other coniferous forests. Their current distribution is the result of isolation within forests that are surrounded by desertlike habitats that reduce or eliminate their range expansion. Some research has shown that tassel-eared squirrels that have been transplanted have been able to colonize other areas by passing through marginal habitats, though these are the exception rather than the rule. Home range sizes vary by sex, season, density of squirrels, and habitat conditions such as food resources, tree size, tree density, and amount of interlocking canopies. Current conditions of forests with younger trees in greater densities have increased the potential for greater habitat for squirrels since interlocking canopies provide more cover, escape routes, and hypogeous fungi. Although no records exist about squirrel populations during presettlement times, it has been well established that greater tree densities correlate with optimum squirrel habitat.

Future Research

Habitat and home range studies of three subspecies—*S. a barberi* and *S. a. durangi* in Mexico and *S. a. chuscensis* in Arizona and New Mexico—are lacking, presenting interesting topics for future research. Anthropological studies of faunal remains found in southwestern ruins could further expand our knowledge of past distributions (appendix 4).

References for Chapter Three

1. Woodhouse, S. W. 1853a. Description of a new species of *Sciurus*. *Proceedings Academy of Natural Sciences Philadelphia* 6:110.
2. Patton, D. R. 1974b. Characteristics of ponderosa pine stands selected by Abert's squirrels for cover. PhD diss., University of Arizona.
3. Littlefield, V. M. 1984. Habitat interrelationships of Abert squirrels (*Sciurus aberti*) and fox squirrels (*Sciurus niger*) in Boulder County, Colorado. PhD diss., Miami University.
4. Dodd, N. L., S. S. Rosenstock, C. R. Miller, and R. E. Schweinsburg. 1998. Tassel-eared squirrel population dynamics in Arizona: Index techniques and relationships to habitat conditions. Research Branch Technical Report no. 27. Phoenix: Arizona Game and Fish Department.

5. Ratcliff, T. D., D. R. Patton, and P. F. Ffolliott. 1975. Ponderosa pine basal area and the Kaibab squirrel. *Journal of Forestry* 75:284–86.

6. Patton, D. R. 1977. Managing southwestern ponderosa pine for the Abert squirrel. *Journal of Forestry* 75:264–67.

7. Patton, D. R. 1984. A model to evaluate Abert squirrel habitat in uneven-aged ponderosa pine. *Wildlife Society Bulletin* 12:408–14.

8. Ffolliott, P. F., and D. R. Patton. 1978. Abert squirrel use of ponderosa pine as feed trees. Research Note RM-362. Fort Collins, CO: USDA Forest Service.

9. Dodd, N. L. 2003b. Landscape-scale habitat relationships to tassel-eared squirrel population dynamics in north-central Arizona. Technical Guidance Bulletin 6. Phoenix: Arizona Game and Fish Department.

10. States, J., and W. S. Gaud. 1997. Ecology of hypogeous fungi associated with ponderosa pine. I. Patterns of distribution and sporocarp production in some Arizona forests. *Mycologia* 89:712–21.

11. Dodd, N. L., J. S. States, and S. S. Rosenstock. 2003. Tassel-eared squirrel population, habitat condition, and dietary relationships in north-central Arizona. *Journal of Wildlife Management* 67 (3): 622–33.

12. Schubert, G. H. 1974. Silviculture of the southwestern ponderosa pine: The status of our knowledge. Research Paper RM-123. Fort Collins, CO: USDA Forest Service.

13. Wettstein, P. J., M. Strausbauch, T. Lamb, J. States, R. Chakraborty, L. Jin, and R. Riblet. 1995. Phylogeny of six *Sciurus aberti* subspecies based on nucleotide sequences of cytochrome b. *Molecular Phylogenetics and Evolution* 4 (2): 150–62.

14. Patton, D. R. 1975b. Abert squirrel cover requirements in southwestern ponderosa pine. Research Paper RM-145. Fort Collins, CO: USDA Forest Service, Rocky Mountain Forest and Range Experiment Station.

15. Sieg, M. J. 2002. Landscape composition and Abert squirrel survivorship, predator-based mortality, home range size and movement. MS thesis, Northern Arizona University.

16. States, J. S., and P. J. Wettstein. 1998. Food habits and evolutionary relationships of the tassel-eared squirrel (*Sciurus aberti*). *In* Ecology and Evolutionary Biology of Tree Squirrels, ed. M. A. Steele, J. F. Merritt, and D. A. Zegers, 185–94. Special Publications 6. Martinsville: Virginia Museum of Natural History.

17. Stephenson, R. L. 1975. Reproductive biology and food habits of Abert's squirrels in central Arizona. MS thesis, Arizona State University.

18. Maser, C., J. M. Trappe, and R. A. Nussbaum. 1978. Fungal–small mammal interrelationships with emphasis on Oregon coniferous forests. *Ecology* 59 (4): 799–809.

19. Bolen, E. G., and W. L. Robinson. 2002. Wildlife Ecology and Management. 5th ed. Upper Saddle River, NJ: Prentice Hall.

20. Burt, W. H. 1940. Territorial behavior and population of small mammals in southern Michigan. *Miscellaneous Publication of the Museum of Zoology, University of Michigan* 45:1–58.

21. Halloran, M. E. 1993. Social behavior and ecology of Abert squirrels (*Sciurus aberti*). PhD diss., University of Colorado.

22. Pederson, J. C., R. N. Hasenyager, and A. W. Heggen. 1976. Habitat Requirements of the Abert Squirrel (*Sciurus aberti navajo*) on the Monticello District, Manti-LaSal National Forest. Publication 76–9. Salt Lake City: Utah State Division of Wildlife.

23. Hall, J. G. 1981. A field study of the Kaibab squirrel in Grand Canyon National Park. *Wildlife Monographs* 75.

24. Austin, W. J. 1990. The foraging ecology of Abert squirrels. PhD diss., Northern Arizona University.

25. Patton, D. R. 1975a. Nest use and home range of three Abert squirrels as determined by radio tracking. Research Note RM-281. Fort Collins, CO: USDA Forest Service, Rocky Mountain Forest and Range Experiment Station.

26. Lema, M. F. 2001. Dynamics of Abert squirrel populations: Home range, seasonal movements, survivorship, habitat use and sociality. MS thesis, Northern Arizona University.

27. Hall, J. G. 1967b. The Kaibab squirrel in Grand Canyon National Park—a seven seasons summary—1960–1967. Grand Canyon, AZ: Grand Canyon National Park.

28. Farentinos, R. C. 1979. Seasonal changes in home range size of tassel-eared squirrels (*Sciurus aberti*). *Southwestern Naturalist* 24:49–62.

29. Edelman, A. J., and J. L. Koprowski. 2006b. Seasonal changes in home range of Abert's squirrels: Impact of mating season. *Canadian Journal of Zoology* 84:404–11.

30. McKee, E. D. 1941. Distribution of the tassel-eared squirrels. *Plateau* 14:12–20.

31. Lomolino, M. V., J. H. Brown, and R. Davis. 1989. Island biogeography of montane forest mammals in the American Southwest. *Ecology* 70 (1): 180–94.

32. Findley, J. S., and S. Anderson. 1956. Zoogeography of the montane mammals of Colorado. *Journal of Mammalogy* 37 (1): 80–82.

33. Stephenson, R. L., and D. E. Brown. 1980. Snow cover as a factor influencing mortality of Abert's squirrels. *Journal of Wildlife Management* 44 (4): 951–55.

34. Davis, R., and D. E. Brown. 1989. Role of post-Pleistocene dispersal in determining the modern distribution of Abert's squirrel. *Great Basin Naturalist* 49 (3): 425–34.

35. Ramey, C. A., and D. J. Nash. 1971. Abert's squirrel in Colorado. *Southwestern Naturalist* 16:125–26.

36. Hall, E. R., and K. R. Kelson. 1959. The Mammals of North America. 2 vols. New York: Ronald Press.

37. Mellott, R. S., and J. R. Choate. 1984. *Sciurus aberti* and *Microtus montanus* on foothills of the Culebra Range in southern Colorado. *Southwestern Naturalist* 29:135–37.

38. Ramey, C. A. 1973. The movement patterns and coat color polymorphism of Abert's squirrel, *Sciurus aberti ferreus*. PhD diss., Colorado State University.

39. Davis, R., and S. J. Bissell. 1989. Distribution of Abert's squirrel (*Sciurus aberti*) in Colorado: Evidence for a recent expansion of range. *Southwestern Naturalist* 34 (2): 306–9.

40. Armstrong, D. M. 1972. Distribution of Mammals in Colorado. Monograph no. 3 of the Museum of Natural History. Lawrence: University of Kansas.

41. Cooper, D. J. 1987. Abert's squirrel above treeline on the San Francisco Peaks, Arizona. *Southwestern Naturalist* 32 (4): 507.

42. Trowbridge, A. H., and L. L. Larson. 1942. Abert squirrel–ponderosa pine relationships at the Fort Valley Experimental Forest, Flagstaff, Arizona (copy in author's files).

43. Keith, J. O. 1956. The Abert squirrel (*Sciurus aberti aberti*) and its relation to the forests of Arizona. MS thesis, University of Arizona.

44. Brown, D. E. 1986. Arizona's Tree Squirrels. Phoenix: Arizona Game and Fish Department.

45. Hoffmeister, D. F. 1956. Mammals of the Graham (Pinaleño) Mountains, Arizona. *American Midland Naturalist* 55 (2): 257–88.

46. Galliziolli, S. 1953. Investigation of the Mt. Graham area. Completion Report. Project W-53-R-3, work plan 5, job 1. Phoenix: Arizona Game and Fish Commission.

47. Taylor, W. P. 1926a. Narrative report, Tucson Office, Division of Biological Investigations, Bureau of Biological Survey, U.S. Department of Agriculture. Smithsonian Institution Archives, record unit 7176, box 29, folder 22.

48. Presnall, C. C. 1938. Mammals of Zion, Bryce and Cedar Breaks. Zion-Bryce Bulletin no. 2. N.p.: Zion-Bryce Natural History Association.

49. Raught, R. W. 1967. Tree squirrels. *In* New Mexico Wildlife Management, 95–100. Santa Fe: New Mexico Game and Fish Department.

FOUR AND FEEDING ACTIVITIES

4

Although I hunted persistently for squirrels . . . I saw nothing more
than their signs, in the form of cutoff yellow pine cones, ground to
pieces for the seeds, together with freshly cut green ends of pine
branches.

—W. P. Taylor, "Field Notes: Arizona—
Jerome and Mingus Mountain," 1916

Introduction

Feeding almost exclusively on various parts of ponderosa pine
trees, Abert's squirrels' diets include inner bark or phloem of terminal shoots, seeds of ovulate cones, pollen of staminate cones,
and new apical buds (ref. 1). Two other items fed upon by squirrels,
associated with ponderosa pines, are dwarf mistletoe and the fruiting bodies (sporocarps) of the hypogeous fungi. Sporocarps are also
called "false truffles." Tassel-eared squirrels have been described as an
oligophagous species, literally one that "eats only a few types of foods"
(ref. 2). Others have described these squirrels as obligate herbivores on
ponderosa pines. Information on the seasonal food categories of the
squirrels is presented in table 4.1. As more data has been collected, it
has now been established that tassel-eared squirrels will eat other plants
given the opportunity. Tassel-eared squirrels have been successfully
introduced into other conifer forests, providing evidence they are not
exclusively dependent on ponderosa pine forests (ref. 3).

Stomach contents of *S. a. aberti*, *S. a. chuscensis*, *S. a. ferreus*, and
S. a. kaibabensis were analyzed during autumn, the season when the
greatest diversity of food items are present, to determine the squirrels'
diets. Pine seeds ranged from 29 to 40%, inner bark 6 to 12%, all species

— TABLE 4.1 —

Seasonal food categories[1]

Food item	Month											
	Jan	Feb	Mar	Apr	May	Jun	Jul	Aug	Sep	Oct	Nov	Dec
Inner bark	x	x	x	x	x	x	x	x	x	x	x	x
Pine seed					x	x	x	x	x	x	x	
Fungi [2] (hypogeous and epigeous)	x	x	x	x	x	x	x	x	x	x	x	x
Mistletoe	x		x				x	x	x			
Pine buds	x	x	x	x	x	x				x	x	x
Acorns			x	x			x	x	x	x	x	
Staminate cones					x	x						

1 —modified from Keith, 1965; Stephenson, 1975; Sanford, 1986; States et al., 1988; Austin, 1990; Allred et al., 1994; Allred and Gaud, 1994a; States and Wettstein, 1998
2 —either gathered fresh or cached

of fungi 57 to 64%, other plant matter 0.5 to 2%. The importance of false truffles in tassel-eared squirrels' diets was more distinct than for any other sciurid within the ranges of the four subspecies examined (ref. 4).

Inner Bark of Ponderosa Pine Terminal Shoots

Since ponderosa pine trees are evergreen and thus can photosynthesize year around, squirrels can always obtain some nutrition from the inner bark, which conducts glucose from needles to roots, cones, and seeds (table 4.1). The upper portions as well as the branch extremities of the ponderosa pine trees receive the most sunlight and thus produce the most glucose. Squirrels focus their inner bark herbivory in these areas (ref. 1, 5).

Inner bark is probably the most common food resource during most years. Keith found that during the winter season squirrels consumed the inner bark from an average of fifty terminal shoots/day with some variation depending on other foods consumed. He observed a single squirrel that consumed the inner bark from ninety-five terminal shoots in a single day during the winter (ref. 1).

In 1938, a forester observing *S. a. mimus* [*aberti*] feeding on inner bark wrote the following account: "As the season progresses, the terminal

— TABLE 4.2 —

Food item analysis of tassel-eared squirrels[1]

Food Item	Calories /g	% Protein	% Fats /Oils	% Carb.	Elements[1]	Researcher, year
Inner bark	NG	5.0	NG	NG	N, Ca, K, Mg, Na, S, Mn, Zn, Fe, B, Cu	Patton, 1974a
Inner bark	NG	2.4 ± 0.2	NG	NG	NG	Pederson and Welsh, 1985
Inner bark	4,498	1.6–4.6	3.4	NG	NG	Pederson et al., 1987
Acorns	NG	NG	NG	Highest[2]	NG	Sanford, 1986
Pine seeds	5,479	6.4–9.5	5.5–11.9	NG	NG	Pederson et al., 1987
Pollen cones	NG	4.5	4.8	NG	NG	Pederson et al., 1987
Pine buds	> 5,000	NG	NG	NG	NG	Austin, 1990
Mistletoe	4,999	5.2–7.2	1.2–2.4	NG	NG	Pederson et al., 1987
Various fungi	NG	13.8–25.1	1.7–6.7	NG	NG	Pederson et al., 1987

1 —descending order
2 —of all foods items analyzed
NG—not given

ends become more numerous, with evidence of greatly increased activity during the early snows in December" (ref. 6). Through the years other squirrel researchers have reported more than 1,000 pine needle clusters beneath single trees as squirrels fed on inner bark, especially during the winter (ref. 1, 7, 8).

When feeding on inner bark, squirrels gnaw through the pine shoot several inches behind the green needle cluster with their four sharp incisors and discard the intact cluster, dropping it to the forest floor. Squirrels swivel the remaining pine twig with their forepaws, similar to a human eating corn on the cob, and gnaw away the coarse outer bark. They scrape the extremely thin layer of inner bark from the twig and quickly eat it. They then drop the remaining woody stem to the forest floor. The entire process from clipping the terminal shoot to dropping the peeled woody stem averages three minutes (ref. 1, 9). J. G. Hall observed a Kaibab squirrel clipping twenty-eight terminal shoots from one ponderosa pine in seventy-five minutes. It took the squirrel less than two minutes to complete the process of clipping the terminal shoot

— TABLE 4.3 —

Elements within various food items

(no order implied—from Austin, 1990)

Food item	Elements
Inner bark	Ca,[1] Co, Cu, Mn, Zn
Pine seeds	Mg, Mn, P
Pine buds	Fe
Mistletoe	Zn
Fungi	Fe, K, Na, Zns

1 —four times higher than all other food resources analyzed

from the branch, peeling the outer bark, removing and eating the inner bark, and then discarding the remaining stripped stick (ref. 10).

Stored nutrients contained in the green needles are lost from the tree (ref. 1, 11, 12). Chapter 11 covers the effects of losses of green needles and reproductive effort caused by squirrel herbivory to ponderosa pine trees as well as nutrient cycling resulting from those losses.

Inner bark and other food items have been analyzed for calories, chemical elements, and percentages of protein, fat, carbohydrate, and water (tables 4.2 and 4.3). Inner bark calories vary. During winter, the most stressful season, if squirrels depend entirely on inner bark for winter survival, Patton concluded, "a continuous diet of twigs, without supplemental foods, would put a squirrel in a weak condition susceptible to death from weather extremes" (ref. 13). Even in years when there is an abundant cone crop, with plenty of pine seeds, squirrels do not entirely stop their consumption of inner bark (ref. 4, 7, 8). This behavior certainly suggests the possibility that the phloem provides some essential nutrients not obtained elsewhere (tables 4.2 and 4.3). Inner bark usage increases during the winter when snow depth increases, possibly because squirrels have difficulty recovering buried cones and digging for false truffles (ref. 14).

In years when ovulate cone production is low or nonexistent, tassel-eared squirrels must concentrate almost exclusively on inner bark intake in spite of its relatively poor supply of nutrients, though squirrels may use the inner bark as a certain year-round water source (ref. 14, 15, 16).

Tassel-eared squirrels have gastrointestinal (GI) tracts well adapted to digest the high fiber present in the inner bark and other diet items. The average length of the GI tract of eleven *S. a. aberti* in one study was

284.5 cm (ref. 17). A comparative study of the GI tracts of two squirrel species, *S. a. ferreus* (n = 7), considered a food specialist herbivore, and *S. niger* (n = 8), considered a food generalist herbivore, was conducted in Colorado. The mean length of the GI tract of *S. a. ferreus* was 272 cm with a mean surface area of 640 cm². *S. niger* had a mean GI tract length of 213 cm and a mean surface area of 396 cm². High-fiber foods are digested in the cecum, which is approximately 58% longer in *S. a. ferreus* than the cecum of *S. niger*. The conclusion reached was that the feeding strategies of tassel-eared squirrels of maximizing food intake and retaining their food as long as possible for digestion, coupled with the structure of the GI tract, are evolutionary adaptations allowing the squirrels to exist on the low-quality diet of inner bark of their ponderosa pine habitats (ref. 18).

Selection of Feeding Trees

A number of studies have been conducted to determine how and why squirrels select feed trees (FTs) and reject non-feed trees (NFTs) (ref. 19, 20, 21, 22). Feed trees have been defined by the number of terminal shoots found beneath a single tree or by averaging the number of terminal shoots between trees and using that number to define a feed tree (table 4.4). Though FT status is used in management, there is unfortunately no agreement on a definition of a FT with respect to the number of terminal shoots removed. Research seeking answers to squirrel

— TABLE 4.4 —

Feed tree designations by terminal shoots removed

Researcher, year	Number of terminal shoots selected for defining feed tree
Keith, 1965	50
Ffolliott and Patton, 1978	light < 10; heavy > 50
Soderquist, 1987	> 22
States et al., 1988	> 1
Allred, 1989	> 39
Gaud et al., 1991	< 10
Allred and Gaud, 1994a	> 39
Elson, 1999	> 10

selection of FTs falls into four areas of questioning: (1) Is it the tree chemistry? (2) Is it a physical characteristic? (3) Do squirrels rotate the use of feed trees? and (4) Do feed trees and non-feed trees have different growth rates?

Is It the Tree Chemistry?

Ponderosa pine trees produce different types and varying levels of secondary compounds; some are used for defense against herbivory. Secondary compounds are any chemicals, e.g., terpenes, produced by pathways other than the photosynthetic pathway, which produces glucose. Phloem tissue transports glucose and secondary compounds. Squirrels feed on the phloem. Terpenes in the bark and phloem of some trees have been found that offer protection from squirrel herbivory (table 4.5). Thus, depending on the antiherbivory compounds present in the phloem, squirrels may sample a tree and select it as a FT while rejecting another one. Captive feeding experiments conducted with eleven tassel-eared squirrels demonstrated that squirrels can distinguish between pine shoots from known FTs and those from NFTs (ref. 20). Two hypotheses regarding squirrels and their selection of FTs were proposed in 1991 by Gaud et al.: (1) If squirrels increase their inner bark consumption in some years, perhaps squirrels have an increased tolerance of the chemicals used to defend the tree. (2) Perhaps the increase in clipping of the pine twigs has contributed to a decrease in the concentrations of the chemicals (ref. 8).

Is It a Physical Characteristic?

Ponderosa pine trees have been examined for physical characteristics that would distinguish FTs used by squirrels from NFTs. Jim Keith, who began his research on tassel-eared squirrels near Flagstaff, Arizona, in the 1950s, did not find any preference by squirrels for any particular size of tree nor any observable physical traits to identify FTs from NFTs (ref. 1, 9). A later study examined 668 FTs in another attempt to quantify physical characteristics that might be used to predict FTs. That study measured seven characteristics: (1) dbh, (2) presence of forked bole, (3) pine resin flow on bark, (4) twisted bole, (5) dead top, (6) mistletoe infection, and (7) bark grazing (removal of pine bark from the surface of large limbs infected with mistletoe by squirrels). That study supported several previous studies that found squirrels appear to select trees based on dbh (table 4.6)

– TABLE 4.5 –

Feed tree and non-feed tree differences

Category	Researcher, year
Carbohydrate	
FTs had significantly larger ratios of sugars (particularly fructose) than the non-carbohydrate chemicals	Thomas, 1979[1]
FTs and NFTs showed no difference in the carbohydrate content	Capretta and Farentinos, 1979[2]
FT phloem showed higher concentrations of nonstructural carbohydrates	Snyder, 1992[2]
Nitrogen	
FTs showed higher protein nitrogen content	Capretta and Farentinos, 1979[2]
Terpene Level	
FT phloem lower in the amounts of terpenes	Capretta and Farentinos, 1979[2]; Farentinos et al., 1981[2]
FTs had lower α-terpene level	Farentinos et al., 1981[2]
FTs & NFTs showed no differences in terpene levels	Pederson and Welch, 1985[3]
FTs had lower levels of myrcene & terpinolene terpenes & missing sabinene, tricyclene, 1-borneol, & longifolene from FTs examined	Zhang and States, 1991[1]
FTs have lower β-pinene and β-phellandrene	Snyder, 1992[2]
Other Elements	
FTs higher concentrations of Ca & Co; lower Mg concentration	Austin, 1990[1]
FTs higher concentration of Na & lower concentrations of Fe & Hg	Snyder, 1992[2]
Ease of Bark Removal	
FTs outer and inner bark easier to remove when compared with NFTs	Pederson and Welch, 1985[3]

1 —Arizona   FT—feed tree
2 —Colorado   NFT—non-feed tree
3 —Utah

(ref. 22). Though Keith noted bark grazing by squirrels on mistletoe-infected pine branches as an association in his study, another study found a 100% correlation of mistletoe infection of pine branches with bark grazing by squirrels (ref. 1, 22). Ease of peeling outer and inner bark may be another reason for FT selection (ref. 21).

— TABLE 4.6 —

Dbh range of feed trees by various researchers

dbh (cm)	Researcher, year
38.1–76.2	Keith, 1965[3]
35.6–55.5[1]	Ffolliott and Patton, 1975[3], 1978[3]
28.0–76.0	Capretta and Farentinos, 1979[4]
> 22.0	Soderquist, 1987[3]
30.9 ± 12.7[2]	Allred and Gaud, 1994a[3]
16.1–114.3	Elson, 1999[3]

1 —rarely used trees greater than 76.2 cm   3 —Arizona
2 —no squirrel feeding on trees less than 11.2 cm   4 —Colorado

— TABLE 4.7 —

Use of trees by tassel-eared squirrels as feed trees over a four-year study
(Ffolliott and Patton, 1978)

Percent of trees used (n = 1,830)	Year number
56	1
29	2
13	3
2	4

Do Squirrels Rotate the Use of Feed Trees?

One ponderosa pine tree was observed from which squirrels had removed > 1,200 terminal shoots in their feeding activities during one winter and only thirteen the next winter. The exact opposite observation was made on another tree: little inner bark feeding in the first winter, with an increase to > 1,200 terminal shoots the following winter, suggesting a rotation of use of FTs (ref. 1). A study involving more than 1,300 trees (table 4.7), provides evidence that squirrels allow two to three years to lapse before returning to a tree that has been used for inner bark (ref. 19). Other investigations have not confirmed the rotation of use of FTs; instead, squirrels returned year after year to the same trees (ref. 11, 23). Yet in another study squirrels seem to have compromised on tree use, rotating some trees and using other trees every year (ref. 24). There is the possibility that after considerable defoliation, ponderosa pines may respond with various chemical compounds for defense that may alter the taste of the inner bark, causing a FT to become an NFT (ref. 25, 26).

Do Feed Trees and Non-Feed Trees Have Different Growth Rates?

Two different tree ring studies were conducted to determine whether FTs and NFTs had different rates of growth, with mixed results. One study showed that the average growth rate of FTs was substantially less than that of NFTs during the three years prior to the coring of the trees (ref. 11). The other study examined growth of FTs and NFTs before squirrels were introduced to a study site at Mt. Trumbull, Arizona, and found that FTs grew more than NFTs before squirrel introductions and FT growth declined relative to NFT growth after introduction (ref. 27).

In summary, the question of how a squirrel selects FTs over NFTs has been extensively examined. Tree chemistry with respect to levels of sugars and terpenes is known to be a factor in FT selection. The dbh range (18.2–76.2 cm) certainly seems to be important given the numbers of trees measured during the various studies conducted. Perhaps the ease of bark removal adds additional detail in the squirrel's selection of a FT.

Seeds from Ovulate Ponderosa Pine Cones

Tassel-eared squirrels will feed on pine seeds almost exclusively when they are available. Squirrels begin eating the maturing pine seeds from the cones in June and continue until the cones open in November (table 4.1). In ponderosa pines, ovulate cone development and maturation require approximately twenty-eight months (ref. 28). All that reproductive effort of cone development and seed maturation is lost as a tassel-eared squirrel shreds the resinous ovulate cone and removes its seeds in a matter of a few minutes (ref. 1, 11).

Each pine seed has approximately one hundred calories (ref. 29). The average ponderosa pine ovulate cone has approximately eighty seeds or 8,000 calories. If a squirrel processed twelve cones in an hour that would represent 96,000 calories. One female Kaibab squirrel averaged seventeen cones/day for eight days of observation (ref. 10).

Tassel-eared squirrels forage on the seeds of the cones; however, cone crops are not always large; therefore this food resource is not a constant in their diets. Fifteen cone crops were rated from 1960 to 1974 as 6/15 good, 2/15 fair, 5/15 poor, and 2/15 very poor. Good crop years never followed each other, but poor years did. The time interval between good and poor seasons was two and one-half years (ref. 10). Two other studies on ponderosa pine ovulate cone production reported that large cone crops occurred in three years out of every ten years (ref. 23, 30).

In 1980, Randall Potter gave a vivid description of how tassel-eared squirrels processed ovulate pine cones and their seeds: "The technique of cone descaling by . . . tassel eared squirrels is quite stereotyped, showing little variation either between squirrels or across cones processed by the same squirrel. Scales are systematically stripped from the cone, beginning at the base and working to the tip. After each scale is removed, the two seeds which lie beneath it are consumed, the cone is rotated slightly to present another scale to the squirrel, that scale is removed, and the entire process is repeated" (ref. 31).

Hall remarked that after ovulate cones open in the fall, releasing their seeds, "squirrels nose about in the duff, retrieving . . . [individual] seeds" (ref. 10). Gathering individual pine seeds is time-consuming and risky as the squirrel is exposed while on the ground. Squirrels have been observed eating individual pine seeds from ovulate pine cones that had already opened in the fall but were still attached to the tree (ref. 15). These two observations provide evidence of just how important pine seeds are to tassel-eared squirrels.

Mycophagy

Consumption of fungi (hypogeous—underground, for example false truffle, and epigeous—aboveground, for example mushroom) by squirrels varies by season (table 4.1) and availability. Fungi have the highest percentage of protein of any food resource (table 4.2). Fungi comprised as much as 80% of the stomach contents of squirrels sampled in November and less than 10% in February (ref. 4). Furthermore, the stomach of one *S. a. aberti* examined contained only fungi (96% hypogeous and 4% lichens) (ref. 32). Another report found that fungi use was highest in August and lowest in January and April (ref. 33). Two different studies examining mycophagy by squirrels reported 36% and 39% for relative use of fungi in the diet over the course of a year (ref. 33, 34). Tassel-eared squirrels consume a wide variety of fungi, with hypogeous species being the most frequently eaten (table 4.8). Squirrels' weights can decline during the winter when availability of fungi is curtailed by snow cover and freezing temperatures (ref. 14, 35). I have on occasion observed squirrels in winter with snow on the ground stop, sniff the ground, and retrieve a buried cone. A false truffle could also be removed in this manner.

— TABLE 4.8 —

Genera of fungi used by tassel-eared squirrels

Genera	Researcher, year
Epigeous fungi	
Agaricus	Keith, 1965; Dodd et al., 2003
Armillaria	Hall, 1981
Amanita	Keith, 1965; Hall, 1981
Boletus	Keith, 1965; Hall, 1981; Pederson et al., 1987
Hypholoma	Keith, 1965
Lepiota	Keith, 1965
Lycoperdon	Keith, 1965
Marasmius	Pederson et al., 1987
Russula	Keith, 1965; Hall, 1981; Pederson et al., 1987; Dodd et al., 2003
Hypogeous fungi	
Brauniella	Dodd et al., 2003
Elaphomyces	Vireday, 1982; Dodd et al., 2003
Endgone	Dodd et al., 2003
Gautieria	Hall, 1981; Vireday, 1982; Dodd et al., 2003
Genabea	Dodd et al., 2003
Geospora	Vireday, 1982; Dodd et al., 2003
Hymenogaster	Vireday, 1982; Dodd et al., 2003
Hysterangium	Vireday, 1982; Dodd et al., 2003
Melanogaster	Dodd et al., 2003
Rhizopogon	Vireday, 1982; Dodd et al., 2003
Sclerogaster	Dodd et al., 2003
Scleroderma	Dodd et al., 2003
Tuber	Keith, 1965; Dodd et al., 2003

Other Foods Obtained from Ponderosa Pine Trees

During late May and early June (table 4.1) staminate or pollen cones are eaten by squirrels. Pollen cones are extremely abundant, but they are a highly ephemeral food source. During the relatively short time of their appearance, squirrels feed so much on them that their feces are golden yellow as are their faces and whiskers.

Keith gave a description of squirrels feeding on terminal pine buds: "squirrels worked slowly and methodically over areas of the tree crown, pulling branches to them as they removed the buds" (ref. 1).

Dwarf mistletoe is a parasite infecting ponderosa pines (ref. 36). The mistletoe sinks its haustoria into the tree branch, causing localized swelling of the tissues, and begins to use the tree's photosynthate production for its growth. The swelling of the pine tissues caused by the invasion plus extra photosynthate shunting by the tree provide a food source for the squirrels, who readily eat the new succulent mistletoe growth (table 4.1). In addition, bark grazing by squirrels occurs for the increased phloem accumulation beneath the bark (ref. 1, 22).

Other Foods Used by Tassel-Eared Squirrels

Miscellaneous foods used by these rodents are quite varied, ranging from seeds of other tree species to animals (table 4.9). Many of the foods listed are from other conifers. This information disputes the label that has been attached to tassel-eared squirrels of obligate herbivores of ponderosa pines. Recently presented evidence offers an additional challenge to that label. Abert's squirrels introduced into the Pinaleño Mountains in southern Arizona are thriving without having a pure stand of ponderosas. In fact, they are a potential threat to Mt. Graham red squirrels as a result of their 1940s introduction (ref. 3, 38). Acorns from Gambel's oak trees are a much sought resource during spring and fall (table 4.1). Gambel's oaks with dbh > 25 cm are the best producers of acorns (ref. 37).

Water

Squirrels obtain their water from food items such as fungi, mistletoe, pine buds, pine seeds, and inner bark, and from stock ponds, intermittent streams after heavy rains, springs, standing water in limestone depressions on rock outcrops, and snow (ref. 1, 10, 15, 16, 39, 40). Seeking freestanding water is risky, as Donald Rasmussen commented in 1971 about Kaibab squirrels: "at least 5 squirrels were observed acting extremely nervous about leaving the edge of the timber stand and hurriedly traveling across an open area to obtain a drink of water from an earthen tank that was 60 to 100 feet from the nearest pine trees" (ref. 41).

— TABLE 4.9 —

Miscellaneous foods used by tassel-eared squirrels

Food category	Researcher, year
Seeds	
Douglas fir (*Pseudotsuga menziesii*)	Nelson, 1918; Ratcliff et al., 1975
Pinyon pine (*Pinus edulis*)	Nelson, 1918; Reynolds, 1966
Gambel oak (*Quercus gambelli*)[1]	Reynolds et al., 1970
Gambel oak (*Quercus gambelli*)[2]	Stephenson and Brown, 1980
Lupine (*Lupinus sp.*)	Hall, 1981
Juniper (*Juniperus ostosperma*)	Soderquist, 1987
Rocky Mountain maples (*Acer glabrum*)[3]	Littlefield, 1984
Southwestern white pine (*Pinus strobiformis*)	Edelman and Koprowski, 2005b[5]
Limber pine (*Pinus flexilis*)	Allred, 2008 (unpublished data)
Leaves, forbs, roots	
Green vegetation (not identified)	Nelson, 1918
Green ponderosa pine needles, grasses (*Poa sp.*), (*Mulenbergia sp.*), (*Geranium sp.*), (*Vicia sp.*)	Stephenson, 1975
Bases of green needle bundles	Austin, 1990
New Mexico locust tree (*Robina sp.*)	Hall, 1981
Fern fronds (not identified)	Hall, 1981
Thistle (*Cirsium sp.*)	Austin, 1990
Roots (not identified)	Nelson, 1918
Inner bark	
Pinyon pine	Reynolds, 1966; Ratcliff et al., 1975; Soderquist, 1987[4]
Engelmann spruce (*Picea englemannii*)	Edelman and Koprowski, 2005b[5]
Terminal (apical) buds	
Douglas fir, southwestern white pine, corkbark fir (*Abides lasiocarpa* var. *arizonica*)	Edelman and Koprowski, 2005b[5]
Staminate cones	
Douglas fir	Edelman and Koprowski, 2005b[5]
Animals—alive and dead	
Bird eggs and young birds (not identified)	Nelson, 1918
Dead jack rabbits (*Lepus californicus*)	Keith, 1965
Dead porcupines (*Erethizon dorsatum*)	Keith, 1965

(Continued top of next page)

— TABLE 4.9 (*con't*) —

Miscellaneous foods used by tassel-eared squirrels

Food category	Researcher, year
Remains of partially decomposed lizard (species not identified)	Keith, 1965
Shed deer (*Odocoileus hemionus*) antlers (teeth marks)	Keith, 1965
Bones of jack rabbits, porcupines, deer, and cattle	Keith, 1965
Diptera or lepidoptera larvae in association with fungi (species not identified)	Stephenson, 1975
Beetles (species not identified), and "parts" of ants (species not identified)	Stephenson, 1975
Dead brown creeper (*Certhis familiaris*)	Hall, 1981
Unusual Lichens (species not identified)	Maser et al., 1978
Soil from a road	Edelman and Koprowski, 2005b[5]

1 —directly from the tree

2 —from the ground after acorn fall

3 —performed captive feeding preference trails with *S. a. ferreus* squirrels and fox squirrels (*S. niger*) where they interface in Colorado

4 —research on Kaibab Plateau—"[pinyon pines] . . . were often more defoliated by squirrels than ponderosa pine"

5 —research on an introduced population of *S. a. aberti* in the Pinaleño Mountains in southern Arizona

Food Caching

Tassel-eared squirrels are on the opposite end of the "caching continuum" when compared to red squirrels with their large caches (middens) of stored cones. Unlike red squirrels that develop, maintain, and protect large middens of cones, tassel-eared squirrels bury cones individually in shallow pits in the litter layer as a potential winter food resource. This behavior was first reported by Bailey in 1931, when he observed a squirrel burying a green ovulate cone (ref. 42). Sometimes one of the cone ends projects from the pit (ref. 43). Burying food items individually is called "scatter hoarding" as opposed to "larder hoarding." Placing green unopened cones in the ground preserves the seeds by retarding their release. On occasion, squirrels do not relocate buried cones and seed germination occurs, qualifying squirrels as tree planters (ref. 44).

Squirrels readily consume mushrooms when they are present. Some mushrooms are nibbled around the edges, while others are turned upside down and the under part of the cap consumed (ref. 45). When there is an abundance of mushrooms, squirrels store them in trees, usually in the forks of branches (ref. 10, 15, 44). Consider the importance of caching a mushroom aboveground where it can dry and be preserved rather than burying it where it will decompose. J. G. Hall witnessed a Kaibab squirrel caching a partially eaten mushroom in a terminal needle cluster of a pine tree (ref. 10). On several windy mornings during the winter, at one of my study sites in the ponderosa pine forest at Lowell Observatory, I noted pieces of dried mushrooms on the fresh snow and observed that tree branches above held several more dried mushrooms still stuck where squirrels had presumably placed them.

Summary

Tassel-eared squirrels are, with few exceptions, confined to ponderosa pine forests and thus forage for foods available to them in ponderosa pine habitats. Inner bark is a year-round food; other foods from ponderosa pines are seasonal. Examples include seeds, pollen cones, and terminal buds. Another food source, the fungi that live either underground or aboveground, varies in abundance seasonally within the forests. Tassel-eared squirrels will also feed on acorns from Gambel's oaks, on bird eggs (though not many records exist), and on carrion, antlers, and bones. Recent discoveries by researchers in conifer forests in southern Arizona where tassel-eared squirrels were introduced about seventy years ago have provided evidence for tassel-eared squirrels feeding on other types of conifers in addition to ponderosa pines.

References for Chapter Four

1. Keith, J. O. 1965. The Abert squirrel and its dependence on ponderosa pine. *Ecology* 46:150–63.
2. Littlefield, V. M. 1984. Habitat interrelationships of Abert squirrels (*Sciurus aberti*) and fox squirrels (*Sciurus niger*) in Boulder County, Colorado. PhD diss., Miami University.
3. Edelman, A. J., and J. L. Koprowski. 2005b. Diet and tree use of Abert's squirrels (*Sciurus aberti*) in a mixed-conifer forest. *Southwestern Naturalist* 50 (4): 461–65.
4. States, J. S., and P. J. Wettstein. 1998. Food habits and evolutionary relationships of the tassel-eared squirrel (*Sciurus aberti*). *In* Ecology and Evolutionary Biology of Tree Squirrels, ed. M. A. Steele, J. F. Merritt,

and D. A. Zegers, 185–94. Special Publications 6. Martinsville: Virginia Museum of Natural History.

5. Pearson, G. A. 1950. Management of Ponderosa Pine in the Southwest. Agriculture Monograph no. 6. Washington, DC: USDA Forest Service.

6. Coughlin, L. E. 1938. The case against the tuft-eared squirrel. U.S. Forest Service. *Rocky Mountain Region Bulletin* 21 (4): 10–12.

7. Allred, W. S. 1989. The effects of Abert squirrel herbivory on ponderosa pines. PhD diss., Northern Arizona University.

8. Gaud, W. S., W. S. Allred, and J. S. States. 1991. Tree selection by tassel-eared squirrels of the ponderosa pine forests of the Colorado Plateau. *In* Proceedings, First Biennial Conference on Research in Colorado Plateau National Parks, ed. P. G. Rowlands, C. van Riper III, and M. K. Sogge, 56–64. Flagstaff: Northern Arizona University.

9. Keith, J. O. 1956. The Abert squirrel (*Sciurus aberti aberti*) and its relation to the forests of Arizona. MS thesis, University of Arizona.

10. Hall, J. G. 1981. A field study of the Kaibab squirrel in Grand Canyon National Park. *Wildlife Monographs* 75.

11. Skinner, T. H., and J. O. Klemmedson. 1978. Abert squirrels influence nutrient transfer through litterfall in a ponderosa pine forest. Research Note RM-353. Fort Collins, CO: USDA Forest Service, Rocky Mountain Research Station.

12. Allred, W. S., and W. S. Gaud. 1994b. Effects of Abert squirrel herbivory on foliage and nitrogen losses in ponderosa pine. *Southwestern Naturalist* 39:350–53.

13. Patton, D. R. 1974a. Estimating food consumption from twigs clipped by the Abert squirrel. Research Note RM-272. Fort Collins, CO: USDA Forest Service, Rocky Mountain Forest and Range Experiment Station.

14. States, J. S., W. S. Gaud, W. S. Allred, and W. J. Austin. 1988. Foraging patterns of tassel-eared squirrels in selected ponderosa pine stands. *In* Proceedings, Management of Amphibians, Reptiles, and Small Mammals in North America, ed. R. C. Szaro, K. E. Severson, and D. R. Patton, 425–31. General Technical Paper RM-166. Fort Collins, CO: USDA Forest Service.

15. Austin, W. J. 1990. The foraging ecology of Abert squirrels. PhD diss., Northern Arizona University.

16. Pederson, J. C., R. C. Farentinos, and V. M. Littlefield. 1987. Effects of logging on habitat quality and feeding patterns of Abert squirrels. *Great Basin Naturalist* 47 (2): 252–58.

17. Allred, W. S., and M. Wright. Unpublished data.

18. Murphy, S. M., and Y. B. Linhart. 1999. Comparative morphology of the gastrointestinal tract in the feeding specialist *Sciurus aberti* and several generalist congeners. *Journal of Mammalogy* 80 (4): 1325–30.

19. Ffolliott, P. F., and D. R. Patton. 1978. Abert squirrel use of ponderosa pine as feed trees. Research Note RM-362. Fort Collins, CO: USDA Forest Service.

20. Capretta, P. J., R. C. Farentinos, V. M. Littlefield, and R. M. Potter. 1980. Feeding preferences of captive tassel-eared squirrels (*Sciurus aberti*) for ponderosa pine twigs. *Journal of Mammalogy* 61:734–37.

21. Pederson, J. C., and B. L. Welch. 1985. Comparison of ponderosa pines as feed and non-feed trees for Abert squirrels. *Journal of Chemical Ecology* 11:149–57.

22. Allred, W. S., and W. S. Gaud. 1994a. Characteristics of ponderosa pines and Abert squirrel herbivory. *Southwestern Naturalist* 39:89–90.

23. Larson, M. M., and G. H. Schubert. 1970. Cone crops of ponderosa pine in central Arizona. Research Note RM-58. Fort Collins, CO: USDA Forest Service.

24. Capretta, P. J., and R. C. Farentinos. 1979. Determinants of selective herbivory in tassel-eared squirrels (*Sciurus aberti*). *In* Preference Behavior and Chemoreception, ed. J. H. A. Kroeze. London: Information Retrieval Ltd.

25. Farentinos, R. C., P. J. Capretta, R. E. Kepner, and V. M. Littlefield. 1981. Selective herbivory in tassel-eared squirrels: Role of monoterpenes in ponderosa pines chosen as feeding trees. *Science* 213:1273–75.

26. Zhang, X., and J. S. States. 1991. Selective herbivory of ponderosa pine by Abert squirrels: A re-examination of the role of terpenes. *Biochemical Systematics and Ecology* 19:111–15.

27. Soderquist, T. R. 1987. The impact of tassel-eared squirrel defoliation on ecotonal ponderosa pine. *Journal of Mammalogy* 68 (2): 398–401.

28. Roeser, J., Jr. 1941. Some aspects of flower and cone production in ponderosa pine. *Journal of Forestry* 39:534–36.

29. Smith, C. C. 1970. The coevolution of pine squirrels (*Tamiasciurus*) and conifers. *Ecological Monographs* 40:349–71.

30. Fowells, H. A., and G. H. Schubert. 1956. Seed crops of forest trees in the pine region of California. Technical Bulletin 1150. Washington, DC: U.S. Department of Agriculture.

31. Potter, R. M. 1980. The development of ponderosa pine cone processing ability in young tassel-eared squirrels (*Sciurus aberti*). PhD diss., Miami University.

32. Maser, C., J. M. Trappe, and R. A. Nussbaum. 1978. Fungal–small mammal interrelationships with emphasis on Oregon coniferous forests. *Ecology* 59 (4): 799–809.

33. Dodd, N. L., J. S. States, and S. S. Rosenstock. 2003. Tassel-eared squirrel population, habitat condition, and dietary relationships in north-central Arizona. *Journal of Wildlife Management* 67 (3): 622–33.

34. Stephenson, R. L. 1975. Reproductive biology and food habits of Abert's squirrels in central Arizona. MS thesis, Arizona State University.

35. Stephenson, R. L., and D. E. Brown. 1980. Snow cover as a factor influencing mortality of Abert's squirrels. *Journal of Wildlife Management* 44 (4): 951–55.

36. Hawksworth, F. G. 1977. The 6-class mistletoe rating system. General Technical Report RM-48. Fort Collins, CO: USDA Forest Service.

37. Reynolds, H. G., W. P. Clary, and P. F. Ffolliott. 1970. Gambel oak for southwestern wildlife. *Journal of Forestry* 68:545–47.

38. Edelman, A. J., and J. L. Koprowski. 2006b. Seasonal changes in home range of Abert's squirrels: Impact of mating season. *Canadian Journal of Zoology* 84:404–11.

39. Farentinos, R. C. 1979. Seasonal changes in home range size of tassel-eared squirrels (*Sciurus aberti*). *Southwestern Naturalist* 24:49–62.

40. Sanford, C. A. 1986. Food habits and related behavior of the Abert squirrel. MS thesis, Northern Arizona University.

41. Rasmussen, D. I. 1971. National and international interest in the Kaibab squirrel: a problem analysis. Rough draft (copy in author's files).

42. Bailey, V. 1931. Mammals of New Mexico. North American Fauna no. 53. Washington, DC: USDA, Bureau of Biological Survey.

43. Trowbridge, A. H., and L. L. Larson. 1942. Abert squirrel-ponderosa pine relationships at the Fort Valley Experimental Forest, Flagstaff, Arizona (copy in author's files).

44. Allred, W. S. Unpublished observation.

45. Bailey, V. 1929. Handwritten field notes on *Sciurus aberti*. Smithsonian Institution Archives, record unit 7176, box 22, folder 8.

NESTS

5

A female Abert squirrel was seen one morning in early May with a mouthful of strips of juniper bark and dry pine needles . . . While I watched, she carefully pushed the needles and juniper bark into the top of her nest and patted them in place . . .

—G. E. Sturdevant, Observations from
Grand Canyon Nature Notes, 1934

Introduction

Abert's squirrels build nests either in the tops of ponderosa pines near the trunk or in the forks of trees. Nests most often face south and east, which increases the amount of solar warming of the nest and its occupant. Branches of the nest tree frequently overlap with branches of adjacent trees, providing alternate routes for leaving and returning to the nest as well as increased protection from storms. Furthermore, birds of prey, such as red-tailed hawks and goshawks, are sometimes thwarted by the mass of branches in the vicinity of the nest (ref. 1, 2, 3, 4). Nest tree site selection has been shown to be associated with sodium and calcium levels of the tree (ref. 5). Some squirrels also use limbs infected by dwarf mistletoe (*Arceuthobium vaginatum* subspecies *cryptopodum*—a ponderosa pine parasite), referred to as witches' brooms, on which the mistletoe has altered the natural growth pattern and architecture of the limb, producing contorted branches interspersed with mistletoe infections (ref. 2, 6, 7).

Abert's squirrels use nests for sleeping both night and day and for nursing and caring of the young by the females. Nests provide protection from foul weather, including snow, rain, strong winds, and falling snow from branches after large storms have cleared. Nests afford the squirrels protection from predators and offer sites for thermoregulation (ref. 1, 2, 4, 8, 9).

Types of Nests

Types of nests used by tassel-eared squirrels are: (1) bolus nests—constructed of ponderosa pine branches primarily on tree branches or tree forks and occasionally on other types of trees, (2) broom nests—constructed on ponderosa pine branches infected with dwarf mistletoe, and (3) cavity nests—built inside trees with rotten or broken limbs or created by woodpeckers (ref. 2, 4, 10, 11).

Bolus Nests

Two nest studies found 98–100% of nests were bolus nests (ref. 2, 12). Robert Farentinos, conducting tassel-eared squirrel research in Colorado, reported a clear 3:1 preference by squirrels of bolus nests over broom nests (ref. 2). Other nest studies found that 80% or more of nests were constructed on the bole-lateral limb junctions. The remaining nests were constructed in forks of branches or in forked boles of trees (ref. 3, 5, 13, 14, 15).

A bolus nest is described as a " ball-like mass of pine twigs" (ref. 2). Nest construction goes on for several days with late spring to early summer the most active time for construction. During fall and winter months nests are refurbished, reinforced, and insulated with thicker layers of branches (ref. 10). Nests are constructed of pine branches that are carried in the squirrel's mouth to the nest construction site and woven into a tight waterproof round-to-oblong shelter (ref. 1). Branches from adjacent pines are sometimes transported to the nest site (ref. 16). Squirrels trample the twigs with their forefeet to flatten and shape the nest (ref. 1).

J. G. Hall spent fifteen summers (1960–74) on the North Rim of the Grand Canyon studying S. a. kaibabensis and their activities. He observed squirrels building nests on several occasions. "One squirrel worked without a break for half an hour while another squirrel worked for forty-five minutes—pulling, pushing, and maneuvering each cut twig into its rightful position" (ref. 17).

I observed a female squirrel in early May in Flagstaff, Arizona, building a nest. She searched for just the right branch, selected the particular section, and quickly severed it with one bite. When the branch became

— TABLE 5.1 —

Materials used by tassel-eared squirrels to line nests

Reporter, year	Materials
Taylor, 1925a	chewed pieces of paper
V. Bailey, 1929	chewed gunny sack and wool socks
Redburn, 1932	chewed strands of an old carpet
Mearns, 1907; McCartney, 1937	grasses pulled up by the roots
Seton, 1953	yucca stalks
Keith, 1965; Hall, 1981; Brown, 1986; Hoffmeister, 1986	newspapers; string; animal fur; plastic bags; shredded bark from pine, aspen, and juniper trees; pieces of cloth and canvas
Allred, unpublished data	deflated birthday balloon
K. Vanwinkle-Swift, personal communication	Tibetan prayer flags
C. Abel, personal communication	pillow case by Kaibab squirrel at North Rim, Grand Canyon National Park

stuck in another branch she tried to move the branch, with no progress. Rather than abandon her choice branch, she quickly ran around and dislodged the stubborn branch, and transported it to her nest site.

New nests are compact and as green as the surrounding foliage on the tree, whereas old or vacated nests are brown and "shaggy" and break down within two seasons postconstruction if not maintained (ref. 17, 18). Usually there is only one entrance, either above or below the centerline of the nest, but nests have been found with two and three entryways (ref. 1, 10). The entryway is a hall that enters the central nesting cavity. Nursery nests are constructed by pregnant females for each new litter. Besides soft grasses, tassel-eared squirrels use a variety of other materials to line their nests (table 5.1).

Fifty nests that were measured by W. P. Taylor on the Kaibab Plateau in 1924 were spherically shaped and had diameters ranging from 38 to 61 cm (ref. 19). In an examination of ninety-seven tassel-eared squirrel nests in north central Arizona, Keith reported that the diameter of the pine cuttings used in the nest construction were 1.2 cm or less; the length varied from 15.2 to 61.0 cm; the inside diameter of the nest averaged 15 cm while the outside diameter averaged 46 cm (ref. 1). When summer and winter nests were compared, summer nests were found to have thinner roofs and walls than winter nests. Several "open" nests showed recent

— TABLE 5.2 —

Nest tree characteristics

Researcher, year	# of nests	Nest tree height (m)	Nest height above ground (m)	Dbh (cm)
Taylor, 1924b[1]	50	NR	9.0–18.3	NR
Seton, 1953	NR	NR	6.1–15.25	NR
Keith, 1965[1]	97	6.0–33.5	4.9–27.0	30.5–104.0
Patton and Green, 1970[1]	10	NR	NR	25.0–60.1
Patton, 1974b, 1975b[1]	302	NR	5.5–25.6	29.5–58.5
Hall, 1981[1]	37	NR	6.0–23.0	30.0–76.0
Pederson et al., 1976[2]	NR	10.6–32.5	6.4–23.0	22.9–116.8
Ffolliott, 1990[1]	NR	NR	10.0–20.0	35.0–60.0
Halloran and Bekoff, 1994[3]	49	16.3–21.7	10.7–16.5	30.0–45.0
Morrell et al., 1999[1]	60	NR	> 10 (91%)	30.3–45.5 (50%)
Allred (unpublished)[1]	28	NR	NR	6.4–73.4
Lema, 2001[1]	NR	12.2–21.4	NR	25.4–63.5

1 —Arizona 3 —Colorado
2 —Utah NR—not reported

activity, leading Keith to conclude that during the warmer summer weather squirrels actually removed the roofs from their nests (ref. 1).

Tassel-eared squirrels construct their nests mostly on the south to east side of trees (ref. 1, 2, 5, 16). A preference with respect to nest orientation for winter nests and summer nests was described in studies in Arizona and Utah. Winter nests were built mostly with south-southeast exposures rather than west exposure. Summer nests were more north or southwest facing (ref. 12, 18). Wind direction has been suggested as another factor in nest placement since nests are often built on the leeward side of the tree trunks (ref. 1, 4). In a study of introduced Abert's squirrels in the Pinaleño Mountains, 38% of their nests had a northern aspect (ref. 20).

Data on squirrel nest placement with regard to height above ground places nests somewhere between 50% and 75% of tree height (ref. 2, 4, 5, 12, 21, 22) (table 5.2), perhaps because ponderosa pines are self-pruning (ref. 23). Squirrels may build nests in the upper third of a tree as a compromise because the lower portion of a tree has fewer branches and the crown has smaller-diameter branches as well as greater exposure to weather and avian predators (ref. 4).

Bolus nests can be located by backlighting the nest in the early morning or late afternoon or by looking for nest clips on the ground beneath ponderosa pine trees. Sometimes these nest clips are accidentally dropped or discarded by squirrels and accumulate on the ground beneath the nest. Nest clips, which have green needles, are much longer (10–38 cm in length) than the terminal pine needle clusters indicative of inner bark feeding (ref. 24). The longer branch could serve as a "handle," allowing the squirrel to force the small branch into the designated place in the nest (ref. 17).

The occurrence of more than one nest per tree is unusual (ref. 10). In a study of 302 nests, Patton located four trees that had two nests (ref. 3, 13). Other researchers either did not report this observation or have not observed multiple nests in trees.

Squirrels use nests from one year to the next with repairs and refurbishing made on a continual basis. Patton checked on the durability of squirrel nests and remarked that a nest that he had previously located in 1965 was "in good condition in July 1974" (ref. 25). Squirrels do build more than one nest within their activity areas in the forest (ref. 26). Keith reported that in the winter months some squirrels kept as many as four nests repaired and livable, and during the summer months squirrels most likely used more than one nest because of their increased home range sizes (ref. 1). A single female *S. a. aberti* was tracked for fifteen days and used five different nests. In another case a male squirrel was tracked for thirty-one days during which time it used six different nests, four in living ponderosas, one in a ponderosa snag, and one in a hollow Gambel's oak (ref. 25). Multiple nest use by Kaibab squirrels has been reported (ref. 17). In a Colorado study, individual squirrels used an average of three nests/year with some nests built in one year and reused two years later (ref. 4). Nest densities (nest/ha) were reported by Farentinos as 0.56/ha (ref. 2), by Patton as 0.63/ha (ref. 3, 13), and by Dodd and colleagues as 0.5–1.9/ha (ref. 26).

Other Types of Nests

Witches' brooms are abnormal growths of pine branches with unusual branching and denser than normal growth patterns due to the invasion of the branches by dwarf mistletoe (ref. 27, 28). It was speculated by Farentinos that building within mistletoe entanglements when available might be a better use of a squirrel's energy and time because of the preexisting platform on which to construct the nest (ref. 2). A nest study conducted by Patton reported 15% of 302 nests on limbs with mistletoe infections (ref. 3, 13). In a huge study of 226 witches' brooms in 144 ponderosa pine trees, 39 brooms were used by squirrels. Of these, 31 were used for feeding and caching of food items, and only 8 for nests (ref. 6, 7).

Tassel-eared squirrels will use existing tree cavities so are considered secondary cavity nesters. Ponderosa pine trees rarely have cavities. In the early 1900s three different researchers proposed that tassel-eared squirrels could be cavity nesters, and in 1932 a Kaibab squirrel was observed nesting in a "hollowed portion" of a ponderosa pine tree (ref. 21, 22, 29, 30). Cavities in Gambel's oak trees are occasionally used for nests (ref. 16, 31). In a tassel-eared squirrel nest study conducted in a mixed forest in Arizona where the squirrels had been introduced, 10% of the nests were in cavities of aspen trees, a single corkbark fir, and one ponderosa pine (ref. 32).

Nest Tree Characteristics

Studies of squirrel nests report that 70%–75% of bolus nests are constructed in trees ranked as codominant trees—trees that conform to the common level of the canopy, receiving full sunlight from above but very little from the sides (ref. 12, 13, 33). The majority of nest trees have three or more interlocking branches from other trees' canopies (ref. 13, 33). Nest trees are in the interior of forest stands of trees rather than at the edges where there are fewer escape routes and where there is less protection from weather (ref. 4, 13, 33). Nests have not been observed in freestanding trees, nor in any tree that overtopped any trees within a cluster (ref. 12). In his 1974 study of 302 tassel-eared squirrel nests, Patton made observations about the trees in which nests were constructed (table 5.3). Eighty-nine percent of the nests examined in that study were in plots having 21–121 trees/ha (ref. 13, 33). The habitat around the nest tree might be as important as the nest tree itself (ref. 12). If the cluster of trees in which the nest is constructed is harvested, squirrels will abandon the nest (ref. 18).

Two nest tree studies, one in Arizona with *S. a. aberti* and one in Colorado with *S. a. ferreus*, established a correlation between nest site selection and the chemistry of trees selected for nest construction. These studies demonstrated that tassel-eared squirrels are sensitive to nutritional aspects as well as secondary compounds produced by trees in which nests are constructed. The biochemistry of nest trees differed from

− TABLE 5.3 −

Observations about 302 tassel-eared squirrel nests
(from Patton, 1974b; 1975b)

Observation	Percent
Nest trees that had a (0–2) dwarf mistletoe infection[1]	98
Trees on study site with forked trunks	80
Nests built in forked-trunk trees	5
Nest trees that were 51–100 years old	66
Nest trees greater than 200 years old	5
Nest trees that were Age Class I (blackjack)[2]	18
Nest trees that were Age Class II	53
Nest trees that were Age Class III & IV[2]	29
Nest trees in Vigor Class B&C[2]	76

1 —mistletoe rating by Hawksworth (1977)

2 —Thomson (1940) age class I – blackjack < 75 years old (yo); age class II – blackjack 75–150 yo;
   age class III – intermediate age class 150–225 yo; age class IV – Yellow pine 225 yo; vigor class A – best;
   vigor class B – medium; vigor class C – light crown; vigor class D – poorest

control trees. Nest tree phloem contained lower levels of copper, iron, and silicon, and significantly lower a-pinene levels. Nest tree phloem contained higher levels of sodium, nonstructural carbohydrates, and calcium, perhaps explaining why pregnant or lactating females selected these trees for nests (ref. 5, 34).

If Abert's squirrels are not in an exclusively ponderosa pine forest, they will utilize other conifers. One study suggests that at least in mixed conifer forests, squirrels might be more dependent on tree size than tree species (ref. 11). Tassel-eared squirrels have also used other tree species for nests (table 5.4).

Summary

Nest sites are chosen and nests are constructed for protection from inclement weather, maximizing of solar exposure in winter, avian predator avoidance, and multiple escape routes. Nests are built within a group of trees with interlocking canopies approximately two-thirds

— TABLE 5.4 —

Other species of trees used by tassel-eared squirrels

Researcher, year	Tree species	Notes
Nelson, 1918[1]	oak	Sierra Madre, Durango, Mexico
Olin, 1961[4]	aspen	bolus nests
Keith, 1965[1]; Reynolds et al., 1970[1]; Patton and Green, Allred, 1970[1]; Leopold 1972[2]; unpublished data[1]	Gambel's oak	cavities in bole/branches and bolus nest of oak leaves
Keith, 1965[1]	cottonwood	bolus nest in branches
Brown, 1986[3]	pine & aspen	cavities most likely created by woodpeckers
Morrell et al., 1999[1]; 2009[1]	Engelmann spruce, corkbark fir, southwestern white	bolus nest
Edelman and Koprowski, 2005a[1]	Douglas fir	bolus nest
Edelman and Koprowski, 2006a[1]	aspen, ponderosa pine, corkbark fir	all cavities (10% of nest on site)

1 —Arizona   3 —Sierra Madre Occidental, Mexico
2 —Yaguirachic, Mexico   4 —location not given

of the distance up the tree from the ground. Tassel-eared squirrels construct bolus and broom nests and occasionally use cavities. Bolus nests are built of terminal ends of tree branches; broom nests are built with terminal ends of branches that are woven around and inside mistletoe infections occurring on branches. Squirrels build and use several nests within their range and maintain some nests for many years.

References for Chapter Five

1. Keith, J. O. 1965. The Abert squirrel and its dependence on ponderosa pine. *Ecology* 46:150–63.
2. Farentinos, R. C. 1972a. Nests of tassel-eared squirrels. *Journal of Mammalogy* 53:900–903.
3. Patton, D. R. 1975b. Abert squirrel cover requirements in southwestern ponderosa pine. Research paper RM-145. Fort Collins, CO: USDA Forest Service, Rocky Mountain Forest and Range Experiment Station.

4. Halloran, M. E., and M. Bekoff. 1994. Nesting behavior of Abert's squirrels. *Ethnology* 97:236–48.
5. Snyder, M. A., and Y. B. Linhart. 1994. Nest-site selection by Abert's squirrel: Chemical characteristics of nest trees. *Journal of Mammalogy* 75:136–41.
6. Garnett, G. N., R. L. Mathiasen, and C. L. Chambers. 2004. A comparison of wildlife use in broomed and unbroomed ponderosa pine trees in northern Arizona. *Western Journal of Applied Forestry* 19 (1): 42–46.
7. Garnett, G. N., C. L. Chambers, and R. L. Mathiasen. 2006. Use of witches' brooms by Abert squirrels in ponderosa pine forests. *Wildlife Society Bulletin* 34 (2): 467–72.
8. Olin, G. 1961. Mammals of the Southwestern Mountains and Mesas. Globe, AZ: Southwestern Monuments Association.
9. Golightly, R. T., and R. D. Ohmart. 1978. Heterothermy in free-ranging Abert's squirrels (*Sciurus aberti*). *Ecology* 59:897–909.
10. Brown, D. E. 1986. Arizona's Tree Squirrels. Phoenix: Arizona Game and Fish Department.
11. Edelman, A. J., and J. L. Koprowski. 2005a. Selection of drey sites by Abert's squirrels in an introduced population. *Journal of Mammalogy* 86 (6): 1220–26.
12. Morrell. T. E., E. A. Point, and J. C. deVos Jr. 1999. Nest site characteristics of sympatric Mount Graham red squirrels and Abert's squirrels in the Pinaleño Mountains, Arizona. Final Report. Department of Biology Technical Report 2. Muncie, IN: Ball State University.
13. Patton, D. R. 1974b. Characteristics of ponderosa pine stands selected by Abert's squirrels for cover. PhD diss., University of Arizona, Tucson.
14. Allred, W. S., and W. S. Gaud. Unpublished data.
15. Ffolliott, P. F. 1990. Small game habitat use in southwestern ponderosa pine forests. *In* Proceedings of Managing Wildlife in the Southwest, ed. P. R. Krausman and N. S. Smith, 107–17. Phoenix: Arizona Chapter, The Wildlife Society.
16. Allred, W. S. Unpublished observation.
17. Hall, J. G. 1981. A field study of the Kaibab squirrel in Grand Canyon National Park. *Wildlife Monographs* 75.
18. Pederson, J. C., R. N. Hasenyager, and A. W. Heggen. 1976. Habitat Requirements of the Abert squirrel (*Sciurus aberti navajo*) on the Monticello District, Manti-LaSal National Forest. Publication 76-9. Salt Lake City: Utah State Division of Wildlife.
19. Taylor, W. P. 1924b. Memorandum for Major Goldman, summary of work, field season 1924, Tucson, Arizona. Smithsonian Institution Archives, record unit 7176, box 29, folder 15.
20. Morrell, T. E., E. A. Point, and J. C. DeVos Jr. 2009. Nest site characteristics of sympatric Mt. Graham red squirrels and Abert's squirrels in the

Pinaleño Mountains. *In* The Last Refuge of the Mt. Graham Red Squirrel, ed. H. R. Sanderson and J. L. Koprowski, 339–57. Tucson: University of Arizona Press.

21. Nelson, E. W. 1918. Smaller North American mammals. *National Geographic* 18 (5).

22. Goldman, E. A. 1928. The Kaibab or white-tailed squirrel. *Journal of Mammalogy* 9:127–29.

23. Harlow, W. M., and E. S. Harrar. 1941. Textbook of Dendrology. American Forestry Series. New York: McGraw-Hill.

24. Rasmussen, D. I., D. E. Brown, and D. Jones. 1975. Use of ponderosa pine by tassel-eared squirrels and a key to determine evidence of their use from that of red squirrels and porcupines. *In* Wildlife Digest. Phoenix: Arizona Game and Fish Department.

25. Patton, D. R. 1975a. Nest use and home range of three Abert squirrels as determined by radio tracking. Research Note RM-281. Fort Collins, CO: USDA Forest Service, Rocky Mountain Forest and Range Experiment Station.

26. Dodd, N. L., S. S. Rosenstock, C. R. Miller, and R. E. Schweinsburg. 1998. Tassel-eared squirrel population dynamics in Arizona: Index techniques and relationships to habitat conditions. Research Branch Technical Report no. 27. Phoenix: Arizona Game and Fish Department.

27. Tinnin, R. O., F. G. Hawksworth, and D. M. Knutson. 1982. Witches' broom formation in conifers infected by *Arceuthobium* spp.: An example of parasitic impact upon community dynamics. *American Midland Naturalist* 107:351–59.

28. Marchand, P. J. 2001. Riding the witches' broom. *Natural History Magazine*, May, 40–41.

29. Cary, M. 1911. North American Fauna no. 33. USDA, Bureau of Biological Survey. Washington, DC: U.S. Government Printing Office.

30. Redburn, R. 1932. A Kaibab squirrel family. *Grand Canyon Nature Notes* 6:66–68.

31. Taylor, W. P. 1925a. Report of winter work at the Southwestern Forest Experiment Station, especially on the life habits and control of the porcupine (*Erethizon epixanthum couesi*), Flagstaff, Arizona. Smithsonian Institution Archives, record unit 7176, box 29, folder 18.

32. Edelman, A. J., and J. L. Koprowski. 2006a. Characteristics of Abert's squirrel (*Sciurus aberti*) cavity nests. *Southwestern Naturalist* 51 (1): 64–70.

33. Patton, D. R. 1975b. Abert squirrel cover requirements in southwestern ponderosa pine. Research Paper RM-145. Fort Collins, CO: USDA Forest Service, Rocky Mountain Forest and Range Experiment Station.

34. Snyder, M. A. 1992. Selective herbivory by Abert's squirrel mediated by chemical variability in ponderosa pine. *Ecology* 73:1730–41.

BEHAVIOR AND SOCIAL INTERACTIONS

6

Their voice is not often heard, but is at once recognized as the husky barking of a big squirrel. Usually it is a soft chuff, chuff, repeated at intervals of a few seconds and only becoming animated when some enemy is sighted and other members of the family are to be warned.

—V. Bailey, *Mammals of New Mexico*, 1931

Introduction

Behavior of the tassel-eared squirrels has been a focus of many researchers, with one of the first observations made in 1894: "It had a loud 'barking' call and feeds on cones of *Pinus ponderosa*, and usually builds its nest of branches in some lightning-blasted trees" (ref. 1).

Much of a squirrel's day is spent searching for and consuming food items, grooming fur, and resting on tree branches. Tassel-eared squirrels hide in trees by flattening on branches, where they may remain motionless for an hour or more, making it very difficult to observe them by looking up into the tree from below. If squirrels are encountered on the ground, they quickly move away. If the squirrels are in a tree and are disturbed, they will bark, cluck, or growl, fluff or flick their tails, and foot thump.

Daily Activity

Diurnal animals, tassel-eared squirrels rise with the sun and are back in their nests by sundown (ref. 2, 3, 4). There is an account of a Kaibab squirrel pushing the limit of being diurnal: "I have no documentation of just when squirrels retire for the night but vividly recall one summer evening on road E-6 when the tail of one ground foraging Kaibab

66

squirrel was seemingly caught up in the golden glow by the horizontal rays of the sun then sinking beyond the hulk of Matthes peninsula" (ref. 5). One report from Colorado states that tassel-eared squirrels leave their nests about forty minutes after sunrise and return to nest for the evening about three hours before sunset (ref. 6). This same report included the amount of time spent outside the nest with the available daylight by season (table 6.1). The amount of time spent in different behaviors varied with the seasons and also depended on the foods available to the squirrels during a particular season. For example, when squirrels were eating seeds from pine cones, they spent more time in nesting behavior and when squirrels were eating inner bark, they spent less time in nesting behavior (ref. 2, 6, 7).

Squirrel behaviors were categorized by William Austin in 1990 based on 296 hours of observations of squirrels during the four seasons over two years (table 6.2). He found that female squirrels foraged more actively in the summer and fall than did males, whereas males were more active in the winter months than females. Females also demonstrated a wider range of foraging activities and choices of food items (ref. 7).

Hall followed a Kaibab squirrel for two successive days from dawn to dusk. That squirrel spent approximately one-third of its time on maintenance and two-thirds in active behavior (ref. 3). A one-year study on the behavior of Abert's squirrels in Flagstaff, Arizona, concluded—just as Hall had with the Kaibab squirrel—that squirrels spent about one-third of their day in maintenance activities. They most often conducted maintenance behaviors in the branches of pine trees rather than on the ground. They spent more time in July and August doing maintenance activities than in the other ten months of the year. Social interactions occurred whenever a squirrel met another squirrel. The amounts of time squirrels spent in the other behavior categories varied seasonally. As temperatures increased, food handling and foraging activities increased, to a point: less foraging time was spent as ambient temperatures increased beyond 21° C. Foraging time increased in the fall and winter while the amount of time spent on maintenance decreased. During the spring and summer with the increase in day length, a reversal was detected, possibly because these seasons offer a much larger variety of foods with higher caloric values. When squirrels are on the ground they spend more time beneath blackjack pines where hypogeous fungi are more common rather than beneath yellow pines, which are more isolated with less available cover (ref. 8, 9). Blackjack ponderosa pine trees are less than 150 years old and have dark bark.

— TABLE 6.1 —

Amount of time spent outside of the nest by tassel-eared squirrels
(from Halloran, 1993)

Season	Time outside nest (hrs/day)	% of available daylight (hrs)
Summer	10.6	76
Fall	7.1	67
Winter	6.3	57
Spring	10.0	69

— TABLE 6.2 —

Eight categories of behaviors observed of tassel-eared squirrels based on 296 hours of observations, divided equally between males and females
(from Austin, 1990)

Category	Activities included
Foraging	All foraging activities including searching and handling
Grooming	Grooming of body and face
Ground movement	Nonforaging movements on the ground
Ground resting	Immobile and quiet on the ground
In nest	Time in nest during daylight
Social	Any interaction between other squirrels
Tree movement	Nonforaging movements in the tree
Tree resting	Immobile and quiet in the nest

As the ponderosas become older the bark color changes to a reddish-orange. These older trees are referred to as "yellow pines" (ref. 10).

A twenty-nine-month study of eight behaviors of seventeen adult *S. a. ferreus* was conducted in the pine forests on Enchanted Mesa near Boulder, Colorado (table 6.3). This research focused on squirrel behavior with respect to the seasonal differences in length of day, ambient temperature, and food supplies. No significant differences between males and females in the amounts of time spent in the different behaviors were reported. The eight behaviors were subcategorized by using an extensive inventory of 112 individual behavior codes. Several examples of the individual behavior codes include feeding on pine bark, feeding on Douglas fir male cone, digging in ground, resting

— TABLE 6.3 —

Eight categories of behaviors of observed tassel-eared squirrels
(from Halloran, 1993)

Category	Explanation
Feeding	Any feeding on any resource on ground or in tree
Food related	Caching food or digging hypogeous fungi or recovering buried cones
Resting	Relaxed posture on tree limbs
Traveling	Any movement not related to food gathering such as running, walking, climbing, jumping
Grooming	Licking or scratching body
Nest related	Building, maintenance, entering or leaving the nest
Other solitary behavior	Bodily functions, drinking water, cheek rubbing, displaying aggressively
Social	Chasing, attacking, copulating

on a stump, leaving nest midday, drinking from rock pool, and mother with juvenile (ref. 6).

From all the studies cited it seems that there is not a definite consensus that daily activities of males and females are different, except on an occasional seasonal basis. Even that difference is not consistent from year to year.

Social Interactions

Tassel-eared squirrels have been described as asocial and as "essentially solitary, silent animals" (ref. 3, 11). Two different studies, one in northern Arizona and the other in Colorado, documented social interactions between tassel-eared squirrels as being rare, with the exceptions of times of abundance or scarcity of foods, and during mating bouts (ref. 8, 12). Another Colorado investigation quantified social interactions during only 4% of the time observed (ref. 6).

Farentinos conducted a two-year study in Colorado with 569 different observations of sixty live-trapped *S. a. ferreus*, individually marked for field identification. During the nonbreeding season, squirrels remained mostly solitary as they foraged for foods. He developed a "Degree of Gregariousness Scale" to plot the numbers of observations of individual squirrels with the approximate distance between them and another squirrel when they were in relatively close proximity to each other during the nonbreeding season. In more than 70% of the observations, squirrels were > 30 m apart. However, during the breeding season the distances between squirrels narrowed significantly (ref. 13).

Squirrels use two different styles of approaches when moving toward an object of interest. The "hesitant approach" is used by a squirrel when an object, such as a baited live trap, is both attractive and threatening at the same time. Dominant males, in the precontact mode before mounting females for copulation, use the "crawl approach," when bodies remain close to the ground without a fluffed tail (ref. 12).

Tassel-eared squirrels respond to various threatening stimuli by demonstrating up to four distinctive alarm behaviors. No differences in alarm displays by squirrels in responses to either avian or terrestrial predators have been observed. Alarm behaviors by squirrels in the order of increasing response to a perceived threat by an individual squirrel are rated from 1 to 4, with 4 involving all of the following behaviors:

1) piloerection (fully fluffed tail)
2) tail flicking (movement in the anterior-posterior direction)
3) forefoot thumping (raising and lowering of forefeet in rapid succession)
4) barking (vocalization) (ref. 13).

Vocalization analyses of five squirrels revealed that the vocalizations were in the 1.0 KHz range, lasting from 0.05 to 0.10 seconds each. Vocalizations were categorized into the following six sounds associated with mating, chasing, alarm, territory, food, and disturbances within the habitat:

1) cluck
2) growl
3) bark
4) screech
5) squeal (adult)
6) squeal (juvenile) (ref. 13).

Mating

A vivid description of a mating bout involving nine tassel-eared squirrels in a mixed conifer forest in Colorado was given by Dale Rice, with the U.S. Fish and Wildlife Service, in 1956. He heard "throaty chucking calls" and observed a number of squirrels running through the forest where he found a single male defending a Douglas fir tree from seven other squirrels. The intruding males who gained access to the tree were repulsed by the defender. The defending squirrel climbed to the top of the tree and approached the female, who was almost hidden from view in the mix of branches. The female clung vertically to the bole of the tree, with her head up, where the male mounted her and copulated for less than ninety seconds. "This was interrupted by several of the other squirrels reinvading the tree; the defending male turned and drove them off again" (ref. 14).

Courtship behavior has not been observed from the males toward the females during mating bouts (ref. 12). The behavior of male squirrels approaching the female for copulation and being repulsed by her was described as "approach-avoidance alarm" (ref. 13). Eleven observed mating bouts of tassel-eared squirrels in Colorado each contained one female squirrel in estrous, one dominant male squirrel, and combinations of subdominant male squirrels forming a train of male squirrels scurrying through the forest. Mating bouts ranged from nine to thirteen hours with the average being slightly more than eleven hours (ref. 15).

During mating the alpha male within the troupe of male squirrels copulated first and most frequently with the estrous female. Male dominance was quantified by noting the number of "wins" during aggressive encounters with the other males present. More than 300 aggressive actions were observed between alpha and subdominant males, usually fast-paced chases occurring on the ground and in the trees. The longest chase observed was 25 m. Fights, though infrequent, did occur if a dominant male caught a subdominant male. Fights were brief, but fur and blood loss did happen on occasions. Occasionally fights that occurred in trees resulted in falls from the branches to the ground. Sometimes during the chases and fights with the subdominants, the dominant male would lose track of the estrus female, leading to a vigorous hunt to relocate her. Subdominants would attempt to mate with the female when the dominant male was occupied with chases and fights and sometimes they were successful in copulating with the female. One amusing behavior that was often repeated occurred when a dominant male was copulating with the female, and one or more of the subdominants would approach and bite the rump of the dominant male, guaranteeing a chase and maybe a fight. Subdominant males had few aggressive encounters between each other. Alpha males were rarely distracted by resting or eating, but subdominant males repeatedly stopped to do both activities (ref. 15).

During some of the mating bouts, estrous females were observed approaching subdominant males and presenting themselves for copulation. This behavior was not observed with the alpha males. Some estrous females displayed avoidance behavior toward alpha males, ranging from pushing away and vocalizations to more aggressive behavior. Some estrous females performed a "face-off threat" by facing an approaching male while remaining motionless with tail in full piloerection, feet well planted to spring forward to advance an attack on the approaching male, with ears flattened backward on her head (ref. 15). On several occasions I have observed estrous females being chased by males. As the males approached the female, who was usually feeding on the ground, she repulsed their attempts by turning and chasing them away or climbing a tree to escape their mating intentions. An immature male was observed attempting to mount an immature female during a mating bout involving adult squirrels (ref. 5).

Nesting Behavior

A study of nesting behavior of *S. a. ferreus* found no difference between males and females in the amount of time spent in nest maintenance such as adding bedding or branches to the nest. The frequency of nest use by females and males did not differ in the amount of time spent inside the nest. Nursing females did use the nest during the day as expected, whereas females without litters were not observed using their nests during the day. Males rarely used nests during the day but day use of nests by males was observed to increase during mating season (ref. 4). John Gurnell in *The Natural History of Squirrels* described squirrels curling into a ball with their tails wrapped around their heads for sleeping position in their nest (ref. 16).

Less nest maintenance was observed during the winter, most likely due to a scarcity of bedding materials and to snow covering potential nest-lining materials. On two occasions during the winter squirrels were observed removing nesting materials from a neighbor's nest when the neighbor vacated the nest for the day (ref. 6).

The first report of several adult tassel-eared squirrels participating in communal nesting was made in 1918 (ref. 17). Communal nesting behavior by Abert's squirrels has been observed in Arizona and Colorado (ref. 4, 18, 19).

Communal nesting was reported as rare (24/363 instances of nest use) in Colorado. When it did occur, unrelated male/female communal nesting of *S. a. ferreus* during the fall and winter was higher than in the spring and summer. Male-male groupings were not observed. Female-female communal nesting accounted for 27% of the observed twenty-four cases (ref. 4).

A twelve-month study in northern Arizona on nesting of *S. a. aberti* was conducted using radiotelemetry. Communal nesting occurred from November to May in 53% of the twenty-eight located nests. Various combinations involving pairs or trios of squirrels within and between age classes and genders were observed (ref. 18).

An extensive study of 251 nesting records of introduced *S. a. aberti* in the Pinaleño Mountains, a habitat of mixed-conifer forest at a high elevation in southern Arizona, reported 25% of the nests were communal. In this study the most common form of communal nesting consisted of groups of two, most frequently male/female. Groups of three and four were also observed. As the ambient temperatures increased, communal nesting decreased, with the reverse happening as temperatures decreased during the winter. Two hypotheses proposed to explain this were: (1) since home range sizes of squirrels are smaller in mixed-conifer forests, there were greater opportunities for social activities such as communal nesting; and (2) the colder temperatures and higher snow accumulations that occur in the Pinaleño Mountains may promote thermoregulatory benefits to communal nestings (ref. 19). Some nest sharing by squirrels during the winter may be explained by the need to conserve heat and reduce hypothermic responses to cold nights and the low caloric winter diet (ref. 20).

In the same study in the Pinaleño Mountains, during the breeding season extending from mid-April through August, no communal nesting was observed with three of four females with known dates of estrus. Several explanations such as the aggressiveness exerted toward males during estrus, warmer ambient temperatures, the possibility of infanticide and cannibalism, and a wider choice of mate selection were presented. Any benefits of thermoregulation were outweighed by costs of diseases, parasite transmissions, competition, and protection of the young (ref. 19).

Movement within the Forest

Squirrel tails are used for shade (*Sciurus* is Latin for "shade tail"), balance, and as a rudder when leaping or jumping from branch to branch or tree to tree. Keith observed an Abert's squirrel leaping more than 2.5 m, and I have observed squirrels leaping between trees that were 3 m apart, quite a feat for an animal that averages a little more than 50 cm nose to tail (ref. 2). Sometimes squirrels jump to the ground from heights unimaginable to us. Two observations of squirrels jumping to the ground from heights of 15 and 24 m were reported. In both cases the squirrels spread their legs, swung their tails in an attempt to maintain balance while falling, and landed on their chest without apparent injury (ref. 2). A dead tassel-eared squirrel was found impaled on a sharp branch on the ground after an apparent jump (ref. 21).

Hall reported female Kaibab squirrels approaching and departing their natal nest by ascending or descending an adjacent tree rather than the nest tree itself. This behavior provides for some nest protection since the nest tree is not identified initially. More interlocking limbs from adjacent trees provide for multiple approaches and departures (ref. 3).

Activities During Storms

Squirrels may remain in their nests following large snowfalls even after weather clears, as snow falls from branches and may land on squirrels if they are on the ground or foraging on branches beneath the snow-packed upper branches. However, reports of tassel-eared squirrels feeding in all types of inclement weather, such as snowstorms, high winds, monsoon rains, and temperature ranges from 13° C to 40° C have been published (ref. 2, 3, 6). Since deep, freshly fallen snow does not support much weight, locomotion by squirrels in these conditions is difficult at best. Nonetheless, Hall reported that Kaibab squirrels can cover 23 cm in a single leap when traveling on light snow at full speed (ref. 3). This particular behavior of snow traveling was observed for S. a. aberti and S. a. kaibabensis (ref. 2, 3). Squirrels feed in trees and wait for a frozen crust to occur on the snow before venturing very far in the deep snow in search for buried foods. In 1918, Edward Nelson, chief of the U.S. Biological Survey, wrote in National Geographic magazine, "In northern Arizona I have known them to stay under cover for a week or two at a time in midwinter." However, no one since Nelson has reported squirrels remaining in their nests for such long periods of time. Tassel-eared squirrels do not hibernate in the winter, remaining active all year though they do seek shelter during storms and harsh winter conditions (ref. 2, 3). Daytime shelter activity is limited, as these animals must have nutrition to remain alive in the winter, the most stressful time of the year due to low food availability, low caloric value of the inner bark, and inclement weather (ref. 2, 22).

Other Behaviors Demonstrated
by Tassel-Eared Squirrels

Researchers in Utah made 183 separate observations of *S. a. navajo* [*aberti*]. The majority of the observations (91%) were in ponderosa pine–oak habitat, with most sightings involving squirrels either running on the ground or feeding/sitting in trees. However, they did report several "unusual behaviors," such as carrying a bone, drinking at a pond, and sitting in a tree killed by fire (ref. 23).

Hall described "solitary play" in Kaibab squirrels. "One form of peculiar activity was observed in solitary adults, and invariably occurred while the squirrel was engaged in some form of behavior on the ground, such as foraging for mushrooms. Suddenly, the squirrel would dash full speed at the nearest tree trunk, launch itself as if to climb but, instead, spring back from the trunk to the ground, scurry wildly about for a second or two, and then either repeat the bouncing routine or simply return to the former sedate activity" (ref. 3). I also have observed this "solitary play" behavior in *S. a. aberti*; perhaps this is practice for predator avoidance given that these squirrels are more vulnerable on the ground.

"Freezing" describes the behavior of squirrels that remain on the same limb for long periods of time without moving. One observer recorded three and one-quarter hours of motionless behavior, and Hall wrote about his experiences with two Kaibab squirrels: "On two occasions I observed squirrels lying motionless for more than four hours before I decided that my patience had been tried sufficiently" (ref. 3, 24). During the heat of the day, squirrels will rest in the shade with their bodies outstretched on a limb (ref. 11), and during the winter tassel-eared squirrels have been observed using the large exposed limbs of yellow pines as sunning perches (ref. 6).

Cheek rubbing by *S. a. ferreus* was observed as a means of self-grooming their faces, especially after eating large quantities of seeds from pine cones or the inner bark of new pine shoots, both of which are filled with sticky resinous sap. Squirrels turned and lowered their heads while sliding their cheeks over or across a tree limb. Another method for removing resin from their faces is by licking their forepaws and then stroking their faces. Squirrels groom their tails with their forepaws and teeth (ref. 25).

A tassel-eared squirrel was observed removing a pine cone placed in a hollow Gambel's oak tree by a red squirrel. After the red squirrel left the tree, the tassel-eared squirrel went into the oak's cavity and took the cone (ref. 26). Three other reports from Arizona and Colorado have documented kleptoparasitic behavior by tassel-eared squirrels removing conifer cones cached in red squirrel middens (ref. 3, 27, 28). One of those studies reported kleptoparasitic behavior by tassel-eared squirrels only of red squirrel middens that were unoccupied (ref. 28).

Tassel-eared squirrels may share trees while feeding on inner bark and ovulate cones. This behavior was observed most frequently in July (ref. 18).

Summary

Strictly diurnal, tassel-eared squirrels rise with the sun and are back inside their nests before sunset. As many as eight categories of tassel-eared squirrel behavior have been described. If one assumes a maximum day length of twelve hours, squirrels spend four of those hours in maintenance behavior, including grooming and resting. The other eight hours, dependent on the seasons, are divided among foraging, feeding, predator avoidance, traveling, nest building/maintenance, and social interactions. Tassel-eared squirrels have been previously described as asocial. However, depending on the season, many social interactions have been observed.

Future Research

An investigation into the significance of mixed-sex communal nest pairings in terms of behavior and evolution of sociality in tassel-eared squirrels should be conducted. This research could provide information to determine whether kin selection is involved within the communal nest pairings (ref. 19).

References for Chapter Six

1. Allen, J. A. 1895. On a collection of mammals from Arizona and Mexico, made by Mr. W. W. Price, with field notes by the collector. *Bulletin of the American Museum Natural History* 7:193–258.
2. Keith, J. O. 1965. The Abert squirrel and its dependence on ponderosa pine. *Ecology* 46:150–63.
3. Hall, J. G. 1981. A field study of the Kaibab squirrel in Grand Canyon National Park. *Wildlife Monographs* 75.
4. Halloran, M. E., and M. Bekoff. 1994. Nesting behavior of Abert's squirrels. *Ethnology* 97:236–48.

5. Hall, J. G. 1967b. The Kaibab squirrel in Grand Canyon National Park—a seven seasons summary—1960–1967. Grand Canyon, AZ: Grand Canyon National Park.

6. Halloran, M. E. 1993. Social behavior and ecology of Abert squirrels (*Sciurus aberti*). PhD diss., University of Colorado.

7. Austin, W. J. 1990. The foraging ecology of Abert squirrels. PhD diss., Northern Arizona University.

8. Sanford, C. A. 1986. Food habits and related behavior of the Abert squirrel. MS thesis, Northern Arizona University.

9. States, J. S. 1985. Hypogeous, mycorrhizal fungi associated with ponderosa pine: Sporocarp phenology. *In* Proceedings of the 6th North American Conference on Mycorrhizae, June 25–29, Bend, Oregon, ed. R. Molina, 271. Corvallis: Oregon State University, College of Forestry.

10. Krauch, H. 1934. Diameter growth of ponderosa pine as related to age and crown development. *Journal of Forestry* 32:68–71.

11. Brown, D. E. 1986. Arizona's Tree Squirrels. Phoenix: Arizona Game and Fish Department.

12. Farentinos, R. C. 1972b. Social dominance and mating activity in the tassel-eared squirrel (*Sciurus aberti ferreus*). *Animal Behavior* 20:316–26.

13. Farentinos, R. C. 1974. Social communication of the tassel-eared squirrel (*Sciurus aberti*): A descriptive analysis. *Z. Tierpsychology* 34:441–58.

14. Rice, D. W. 1957. Sexual behavior of tassel-eared squirrels. *Journal of Mammalogy* 38 (1): 129.

15. Farentinos, R. C. 1980. Sexual solicitation of subordinate males by female tassel-eared squirrels (*Sciurus aberti*). *Journal of Mammalogy* 61 (2): 337–41.

16. Gurnell, J. 1987. The Natural History of Squirrels. New York: Facts on File.

17. Nelson, E. W. 1918. Smaller North American Mammals. *National Geographic* 18 (5).

18. Lema, M. F., W. S. Allred, W. S. Gaud, and N. L. Dodd. 1999. Social behavior of Abert's squirrels in ponderosa pine forests. *In* Proceedings of the Fourth Biennial Conference on Research on the Colorado Plateau, ed. C. van Riper III and M. A. Stuart, 105–12. Flagstaff: Northern Arizona University.

19. Edelman, A. J., and J. L. Koprowski. 2006d. Communal nesting in asocial Abert's squirrels: The role of social thermoregulation and breeding strategy. *Ethology* 112:147–54.

20. Golightly, R. T., and R. D. Ohmart. 1978. Heterothermy in free-ranging Abert's squirrels (*Sciurus aberti*). *Ecology* 59:897–909.

21. States, J. S. Personal communication.

22. Patton, D. R. 1974a. Estimating food consumption from twigs clipped by the Abert squirrel. Research Note RM-272. Fort Collins, CO: USDA Forest Service, Rocky Mountain Forest and Range Experiment Station.

23. Pederson, J. C., R. N. Hasenyager, and A. W. Heggen. 1976. Habitat Requirements of the Abert Squirrel (*Sciurus aberti navajo*) on the Monticello District, Manti-LaSal National Forest. Publication 76-9. Salt Lake City: Utah State Division of Wildlife.

24. Seton, E. T. 1953. Lives of Game Animals. Vol. 4, pt. 1. Boston: Charles T. Branford Co.

25. Halloran, M. E., and M. Bekoff. 1995. Cheek rubbing as grooming by Abert's squirrels. *Animal Behavior* 50:987–93.

26. Patton, D. R. 1974b. Characteristics of ponderosa pine stands selected by Abert's squirrels for cover. PhD diss., University of Arizona.

27. Ferner, J. W. 1974. Habitat relationships of *Tamiasciurus hudsonicus* and *Sciurus aberti* in the Rocky Mountains. *Southwestern Naturalist* 18:470–73.

28. Edelman, A. J., J. L. Koprowski, and J. L. Edelman. 2005. Kleptoparasitic behavior and species richness at Mt. Graham red squirrel middens. *In* Connecting Mountain Islands and Desert Seas: Biodiversity and Management of the Madrean Archipelago II, 2004 May 11–15, comp. G. J. Gottfried, B. S. Gebow, L. G. Eskew, and C. B. Edminster. Proceedings, RMRS-P-36, Tucson, AZ: USDA Forest Service.

REPRODUCTION, EMBRYOLOGY, AND DEVELOPMENT

7

During the spring breeding season, a dominant male and several of his subordinates follow a female . . . This behavior, known as a "mating chase", lasts for about 11 hours . . . After such a long day, one might guess that both sexes would be too tired to breed.

—S. Zeveloff, *Mammals of the Intermountain West*, 1988

This chapter is dedicated to Michael D. Rose (1972–2000). Michael earned an MS at Northern Arizona University with me. His thesis research was on the male tassel-eared squirrel reproductive cycle. Michael died in a boating accident off the coast of California in 2000.

Introduction

The earliest published observation about the mating of tassel-eared squirrels was by Edgar Mearns, a physician and naturalist, who wrote in 1907, "In May, which is the rutting season, whole troops of males are commonly seen chasing the females" (ref. 1). Over the past hundred years, the majority of reproductive research has been devoted to mating activities, including signs of estrus, factors affecting breeding, mating bouts, and copulation. Other reproductive research has focused on gestation, litter sizes, sex ratios, and embryology. Less studied but equally important research areas are characteristics related to reproductive activities; some examples include sperm morphology, spermatogenesis, oogenesis, and anatomical structures.

Estrus

Female tassel-eared squirrels are in estrus for only eighteen hours (ref. 2, 3). During this single day, the estrous females are aggressively pursued by a group of males, both adults and juveniles. The engagement of the female in this pursuit by the males is referred to as a mating bout (ref. 4). Mating activities have been observed in every month of the year, though most mating occurs in spring and early summer (table 7.1).

Female squirrels in estrus exhibit a swelling and reddening of the vulva coupled with an enlargement of the introitus (ref. 2, 4). It takes several days to reach peak estrus when the external vulvar characteristics are visible without binoculars. It is possible that a sexual pheromone is present as male squirrels have been observed investigating areas where the female has passed, such as the ground, the bole, and limbs of trees (ref. 4).

Several hypotheses have been proposed to explain cues that induce estrus. One report connects onset of estrus of female tassel-eared squirrels with the development of the ponderosa pine male pollen (staminate) cones, which are produced during late May to early June and are quite ephemeral, as the pollen is quickly dispersed by the wind and the tiny cones dry and detach from the tree (ref. 3, 5, 6). However, other studies have reported estrus in January, many months before onset of staminate cone production (ref. 7). In addition, embryos and lactating females have

— TABLE 7.1 —
Months reported when tassel-eared squirrels were observed mating

Month	Subspecies	Researcher, year
January	*S. a. aberti*	Allred and Pogany, 1996
Mid-February–June	*S. a. ferreus*	Halloran, 1993
March, April, May	*S. a. aberti* and *S. a. ferreus*	Mearns, 1907; V. Bailey, 1931; Rice, 1957; Hall and Kelson, 1959; Keith, 1965; Farentinos, 1972b; Pogany and Allred, 1995
June–July	*S. aberti*[1] (in Mexico)	Leopold, 1972
April–October	*S. a. aberti*	Cahalane, 1947
Early August	*S. a. kaibabensis*	Hall, 1967b
Late winter/early spring	*S. a. ferreus*	Lechleitner, 1969
November, December	*S. a. aberti*	Allred, unpublished data

1 —subspecies not given

been reported in March from road-killed *S. a. aberti* (ref. 8, 9). Another possible cue for estrus is new pine shoot growth in the late spring (ref. 10). However, since this growth occurs only in the spring it cannot explain pregnancies during the winter (ref. 7, 8). Yet another possible explanation for the onset of estrus is warming temperatures causing the melting of snow, allowing the females to obtain adequate nutrients from buried cones and false truffles (ref. 7, 11). It is possible that mild winters with little snow could similarly affect estrus onset. The onset of estrus in winter or early spring would be of no value unless males are capable of insemination, long considered possible only during the spring and early summer (ref. 3). More recent evidence for insemination capability during most months of the year has been provided (ref. 7, 8, 9).

Climatic influences on life histories of tree squirrels were addressed in 1984 by Lawrence Heaney: "Length of the breeding season is positively correlated with mean annual precipitation and percentage of the year that is frost free" (ref. 12). Global warming and its effects on climate, such as drought and increased ambient temperatures, certainly could increase the percentages of frost-free days across the ranges of tassel-eared squirrels.

The quality of food during the breeding season could affect reproductive outcomes (ref. 3, 13). A study of reproduction in female *S. a. ferreus* found that matings early in the year (February–April) produced smaller litter sizes when compared with matings occurring in May–June, which produced larger litter sizes. There appears to be a trade-off strategy involved with food quality and litter size. Mating early when the food quality is poor for the females results in smaller litter sizes; however, those fledging juveniles have better food quality upon leaving the nest. Breeding late offers the females better food quantity and quality and results in larger litter sizes; however, the emerging juveniles may not be adequately prepared for the oncoming winter. Regardless of the strategy used, the average number of surviving squirrels from either type of litter was one (ref. 14). Females may not breed during years of drought conditions. In 2000, a drought year, Dodd reported that 153 of 160 females in his study failed to produce a litter, providing credence to the idea that environmental conditions affect breeding and reproductive behaviors (ref. 15, 16).

Two biologists, one in 1907 and another in 1924, considered it possible that tassel-eared squirrels could produce two litters of three to four young per year (ref. 1, 17). In 1959, when the same idea was again proposed, it was suggested that if this does occur, it would be limited to the southern range (ref. 18). "One, sometimes two, litters are born each year, one in early May, the second as late as September," Lendell Cockrum, author of *Mammals of the Southwest*, stated in 1982 (ref. 19). Two litters in a year was again hypothesized in two reproductive studies in 1995 and 1998, although these researchers considered it possible even in the tassel-eared squirrel's northern range of distribution in years when there were favorable temperatures, low snowfall, and adequate quality and quantity of food resources (ref. 8, 9). *S. a. kaibabensis* may have more than one litter per year or they may breed at different times of the year (ref. 20). There is no information available on female tassel-eared squirrels in Colorado having more than one litter per year (ref. 21). Aldo Leopold noted in his study of mammals in Mexico that tassel-eared squirrels in northern Mexico breed only during the spring and do not breed again during the summer (ref. 22).

While it hypothetically may be possible for tassel-eared squirrels to produce two litters in a single year under favorable conditions, David Brown, a researcher with the AZGFD, wrote emphatically, "There is no time to raise a second family, and reports in the literature of these squirrels having more than one litter per year are in error" (ref. 3). In fact, there have been no studies confirming that tassel-eared squirrels produce more than one litter in a year.

Copulation

In 1972, Farentinos conducted extensive observations on the mating bouts and copulation activities of *S. a. ferreus* in Colorado (ref. 4). Others have made observations on mating bouts, but his work is by far the most complete. Nine Abert's squirrels in a single tree during a mating bout were photographed by James Tallon and published in the August 1983 issue of *Arizona Highways* (ref. 23). Chapter 6 discusses mating bout activity.

Seventy-three copulation events were observed by Farentinos during six mating bouts. He categorized copulation activity into three phases after the male mounted the female:

First phase—male performed a series of rapid thrusts of his pelvis

Second phase—male performed thrusts that were slower and more penetrating

Third phase—male and female remain motionless with penis still inserted.

Copulation ended when the female pulled away from the male. Copulations that continued for all three phases averaged seventy-two to ninety seconds (ref. 4, 24).

Multiple copulations by different males have been observed (ref. 3, 4). A mixture of semen from several male squirrels could possibly provide for multiple paternities, though males of the genus *Sciurus* possess accessory glands that produce wax-like secretions that plug the vagina after copulation (ref. 25). These vaginal plugs are assumed to prevent further inseminations. Females may have multiple copulations with the alpha male and occasionally will copulate with subdominant males after copulation with an alpha male has ended. No data exists on the DNA of embryos or of squirrels born to term pregnancies, so presently there is no evidence to support multiple paternities.

Gestation and Postnatal Development

Keith conducted the majority of the research involving the gestational period and postnatal development of *S. a. aberti*. He found that gestation lasted between forty to forty-six days (ref. 2, 26). Embryo measurements provided by several researchers are provided in appendix 7.

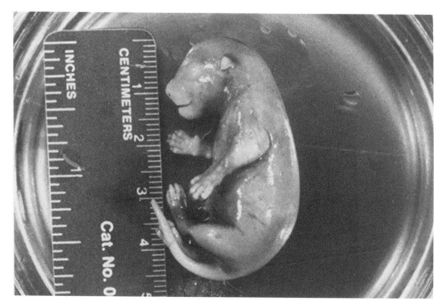

FIGURE 7.1   An embryo of an Abert's squirrel taken from a road-killed female squirrel in July. Photograph by G. C. Pogany and Sylvester Allred.

Seven furless newborn squirrels averaged 12 g in weight and 60 mm in length (appendices 8 and 9) (ref. 26). Their eyes and ears were covered with thin membranes. Each had short vibrissae present on their cheeks and claws on all toes. The sequence of development follows:

> *Two weeks*—squirrels had some hair on their backs, sides, and tails; hair was absent from their chests and abdomens; membranes still covered eyes; ears had tiny openings in their covering membranes
>
> *Five weeks*—average weight 170 g (> 140% increase in weight in thirty-five days)
>
> *Six weeks*—fur resembled adult fur; legs and tails were not proportionate to their bodies because of their lengths; tail fur was flattened rather than erect; ears hung inward toward the face but did become erect when squirrels were focused on a stimulus; eyes open; less sleeping behavior; more active; average weight 195 g
>
> *Seven weeks*—tail broadened out and carried over back as a typical sciurid; ears erect; still nursing mother but began eating other foods such as inner back and mushroom pieces; ventured from nest onto limbs of nest tree; average weight 242 g
>
> *Nine weeks*—ventured to ground; average weight 355 g
>
> *Ten/eleven weeks*—weaned; exploring environment outside of natal nest
>
> *Fifteen/sixteen weeks*—mature size (ref. 26).

Dependence on the mother is approximately seventy days and the first emergence from the natal nest is seven to nine weeks (ref. 3). A study in Colorado with *S. a ferreus* reported maternal care lasting fifteen weeks (ref. 14). James Hill published an observation that tassel-eared squirrels in New Mexico were one-third to one-half grown by August, and Leopold in Mexico reported maternal females with half-grown squirrels in late June and early July (ref. 22, 27). A lactating female *S. a. durangi* was observed in the Sierra Madre Occidental in Mexico in July (ref. 28). Table 7.2 summarizes observed litter sizes, and table 7.3 presents sex ratios of squirrels obtained from five studies.

Females may move their litters to a new nest if disturbed. When transporting young squirrels, mothers pick up their young in their mouths in a fashion similar to that of other mammals. Others have reported this behavior for three of the subspecies of tassel-eared squirrels—*S. a. aberti, S. a kaibabensis,* and *S. a. ferreus* (ref. 2, 14, 29).

− TABLE 7.2 −
Litter sizes reported for tassel-eared squirrels

Researcher, year	# of litters observed	# of individuals in litter
Taylor, 1925a[1]	2	2 and 5
Rasmussen, 1929[2]	5	NG
Keith, 1965[1]	8	2–5, $\overline{X}$= 3.4 ±0.9.
Hall, 1967b[2]	1 2 4 1	1 2 3 4
Stephenson, 1975[1]	NG	$\overline{X}$ = 2.9
Halloran, 1993[3]	12	Ranged 1–5, $\overline{X}$ = 2.9 ± 1.2

1 —*S. a. aberti*
2 —*S. a. kaibabensis*
3 —*S. a. ferreus*
NG—not given

− TABLE 7.3 −
Sex ratios of tassel-eared squirrels

Researcher, year	% of Females/Males
Mearns, 1907[1]	59/41
Keith, 1965[1]	43/57
Farentinos, 1972b[2]	38/62
Stephenson, 1975[1]	55/45

1 —*S. a. aberti*
2 —*S. a. ferreus*

R. A. Redburn, a ranger naturalist at Grand Canyon National Park in 1931, described a female squirrel transporting her young by carrying them in her mouth upside down with their tails extending between her front legs. The young squirrels grasped their mother's fur with their claws, which assisted her in supporting their weight (ref. 30). A mother Kaibab squirrel moved her litter of five babies by carrying each baby squirrel by the nape of the neck and placing it at the base of the new nest tree; she then encouraged her young to climb the tree by repeated nipping at their heels (ref. 31). A litter count study of nests of *S. a. aberti* in northern Arizona using a telescopic camera to peek inside the nest recorded two instances of nest abandonment and relocation of the litter by the same female following the disturbance of the nest by this "peeping" technique (ref. 32).

Lactation

The normal arrangement of the mammae of female tassel-eared squirrels is four pairs: one pectoral pair, two abdominal pairs, and one inguinal pair (ref. 27, 33). The mammae of nonreproductive females are mostly whitish and 1.5 mm in height, whereas lactating female mammae are pigmented and stand 5–9 mm in height (ref. 11). Many researchers conducting either live-trapping studies or road-killed surveys of tassel-eared squirrels have described the pigmentation of the mammae and the areas around the mammae of lactating females (ref. 7, 9, 15, 16, 18). The average volume of milk of three lactating females was 18.5 cc, ranging from 17 to 20 cc (ref. 11).

Female Reproduction

Anatomy

The first study that examined the female reproductive anatomy of tassel-eared squirrels was performed by Richard Stephenson in 1975. The depths and widths of the vagina, cervix, and uterine horns of sixty-nine individuals were measured over the course of a year. All measurements remained fairly constant from July through March. They began to increase in April and May, corresponding with estrus, when, for example, the depth of the vagina of a female in estrus was 14 mm compared with that of a nonestrus female of 6–7 mm. There was a gradual decline in size after estrus (ref. 11).

Oogenesis

Histological examinations of the ovaries of twenty-four road-killed female *S. a. aberti* were conducted by Deborah Guzman, who found that the follicular pattern of development includes four stages: naked follicle → primary oocyte → secondary oocyte → mature egg. The corpus luteum is formed following ovulation. In the analyses, she grouped the different follicular stages into two broad categories. One category consisted of follicles collected from ovaries of squirrels from January to April. These follicles were in the early stages of development and included mostly primary, some secondary, and very few mature follicles. Primary follicles were the most numerous of the follicular stages. The second category of follicles extended from May through December, when the most common follicular stage observed was that of naked follicles, the earliest egg stage, in addition to some early developmental follicular stages. Based on this evidence, females could go through increased follicular development during the early months of the year. There were two peaks in follicular development: February and July–September. Thus Guzman proposed that these dual peaks of ovarian activity could possibly allow a female to produce two litters in a single year (ref. 34).

In an extensive microscopic study, only one corpus luteum was found in all the ovarian tissue sections examined, suggesting that in tassel-eared squirrels, perhaps the corpus luteum does not persist for long because of thus far unexplained hormonal activity (ref. 34).

Male Reproduction

Anatomy

After examining male *S. a. ferreus* in Colorado in 1935, Otis Wade recorded that the "baculum is straight, long and slender; tapering evenly from the broad base to the much narrower neck where the blade begins." The longest baculum collected was 15.1 mm (ref. 35). A 1935 paper written by Otis Wade and Paul Gilbert provides excellent sketches of the baculum of several other tree squirrels (ref. 36). Keith observed males with descending testes during February in 1956. By the middle of March the testes were fully descended and the scrotums were prominent (ref. 2). By September the testes were abdominal and not noticeable (table 7.4). Testicular enlargement extending from September to June, and testicular regression during July and August in another study, supported Keith's earlier findings (ref. 7). The maximum length and weight of the testes of forty-nine squirrels examined were reached by the first week of March (table 7.4) (ref. 11).

Michael Rose examined testes of road-killed male *S. a. aberti* every month for one year, to obtain weights, determine the thickness of the tunica albuginea, calculate the number of Leydig cells, determine the mean diameter of the seminiferous tubules, and determine the number of Sertoli cells and mature spermatozoa present in the lumen of the seminiferous tubules (table 7.5). The number of Sertoli cells, which support the developing spermatozoa, within the seminiferous tubules were not significantly different during the winter and spring seasons. As seminiferous tubule diameter increased, so did the number of Sertoli cells. However

— TABLE 7.4 —

Testicular measurements of S. a. aberti
(from Keith, 1965; Stephenson, 1975)

Researcher, year	Testes volume (mm³)	Testes length (mm)	Weight (g)s
Keith, 1965	465—February 2600—April–July	NG	NG
Stephenson, 1975, n = 49	NG	15.1–15.5—July–January 26—March	0.147—0.186 2.0

NG—not given

— TABLE 7.5 —

Testicular measurements of S. a. aberti
(from Rose, 1997)

Season	Weight (g) n = 171	Tunic albuginea thickness (o.u.)*	Leydig cell (o.u.)* n = 32	Seminiferous tubules (o.u.)* n = 32	# mature spematozoa in lumen of seminiferous tubules (o.u.)*
Spring	3.43 ± 0.15	7.1–10.8	9.4 ± 0.15	263.0–560.0	7–22
Regression	0.63 ± 0.06	15.8–22.5	3.8 ± 0.21	143.3 ± 3.7	——
Winter	2.24 ± 0.15	4.0–9.6	9.4 ± 0.15	250.5–302.0	8–18

* microscopic examinations using a microscope at 1000X with a microscopic grid of 100 X 100 ocular units (o.u.)

during testicular regression, the Sertoli cell numbers decreased by only 36%. During the winter season, he found that there were essentially the same number of mature spermatozoa present in the lumen of the seminiferous tubules as in the spring season. This research provides the crucial histological evidence that males can mate with females in estrus even during the coldest months of the year (ref. 10).

Cowper glands increase in size in April and attain maximum size by the end of May (ref. 1, 11). Cowper glands have long coiled ducts approximately one-half the diameter of the gland, coiling around the gland once and then descending to the bulb of the penis and emptying into the bulbar gland (ref. 11). The prostate gland begins noticeably enlarging in March, reaching its maximum size and weight by May (ref. 11).

Spermatogenesis

Sperm were present in the cauda of the epididymis of all males examined by Stephenson in March, April, and May 1973 and January, April, and May 1974. No sperm were found in the specimens collected in other months (ref. 11). However, a later study concluded, "Males maintain a prolonged regimen of spermatogenesis even during the winter months . . . Even when testicular regression ensues (July and August), primary spermatogenic elements are still retained." This residual spermatogenic activity found in male Abert's squirrels was defined as "maintenance meiosis," which enables the germ cells to develop rapidly through the two periods of meiosis, making spermatogenesis possible at most times of the year. Since the onset of estrus and the incidence of gestation is regulated in females according to environmental cues, it was hypothesized that tassel-eared squirrels have a "female-driven system" of reproduction (ref. 8).

Sperm Morphology

A study of the sperm morphology of *S. a. aberti* and *S. a. kaibabensis* was conducted and, based on various measurements, no distinction between the two subspecies could be determined with respect to sperm shape or size. However, using a silver staining technique limited to the post-acrosomal sheath region of the sperm, the sperm of the two subspecies were clearly distinguishable, possibly because of differential uptake of silver by proteins on the post-acrosomal sheath (ref. 37). Sperm of *S. a. chuscensis* were compared with sperm of *S. a. aberti* and *S. a. kaibabensis*. *S. a. chuscensis* sperm had a smaller surface area than either of the other two subspecies and there was no uptake of silver on the post-acrosomal sheath (ref. 38).

Reproductive Anomalies

In a study involving 418 road-killed squirrels the following anomalies were observed: one female with only two pair of mammae, four males with only one testis each; and a single female with only one ovary (ref. 39).

Future Research

In spite of a century of observations and studies there are numerous gaps in the understanding of reproductive physiology in tassel-eared squirrels. Examples of investigations that warrant attention: (1) Do multiple paternities occur with tassel-eared squirrels? (2) Are speciation mechanisms (e.g., protein differences on sperm) occurring that could produce separate species of tassel-eared squirrels due to the geographical separation of the subspecies? (3) Are trends occurring with respect to global warming and early onset of estrus in females? (4) Are tassel-eared squirrels capable of successfully producing and raising two litters in a given year? (5) What are the nutritional and environmental cues that induce estrus?

References for Chapter Seven

1. Mearns, E. A. 1907. Mammals of the Mexican Boundary of the United States. Pt. 1. U.S. National Museum Bulletin 56. Washington, DC: Smithsonian Institution.
2. Keith, J. O. 1965. The Abert squirrel and its dependence on ponderosa pine. *Ecology* 46:150–63.
3. Brown, D. E. 1986. Arizona's Tree Squirrels. Phoenix: Arizona Game and Fish Department.
4. Farentinos, R. C. 1972b. Social dominance and mating activity in the tassel-eared squirrel (*Sciurus aberti ferreus*). *Animal Behavior* 20:316–26.
5. Rasmussen, D. I. 1971. National and international interest in the Kaibab squirrel. Rough draft (copy in author's files).
6. Fowells, H. A., and G. H. Schubert. 1956. Seed crops of forest trees in the pine region of California. Technical Bulletin 1150. Washington, DC: U.S. Department of Agriculture.
7. Allred, W. S., and G. Pogany. 1996. Early estrus in a female Abert squirrel (*Sciurus aberti aberti*). *Southwestern Naturalist* 41:90.
8. Pogany, G. C., and W. S. Allred. 1995. Abert's squirrels of the Colorado Plateau: Their reproductive cycle. *In* Proceeding of the Second Biennial Conference of Research in Colorado Plateau National Parks, ed. C. van Riper III, 293–305. NPS/NRNAU/NKTP-95/11. Flagstaff: Northern Arizona University.
9. Pogany, G. C., W. S. Allred, and T. Barnes. 1998. The reproductive cycle of Abert's squirrel. *In* Ecology and Evolutionary Biology of Tree Squirrels, ed. M. A. Steele, J. F. Merritt, and D. A. Zegers, 53–59. Special Publications 6. Martinsville: Virginia Museum of Natural History.
10. Rose, M. D. 1997. Histological examination of the male reproductive cycle in the Abert squirrel, *Sciurus aberti*. MS thesis, Northern Arizona University.
11. Stephenson, R. L. 1975. Reproductive biology and food habits of Abert's squirrels in central Arizona. MS thesis, Arizona State University.

12. Heaney, L. R. 1984. Climatic influences of life-history tactics and behavior of North American tree squirrels. *In* The Biology of Ground-Dwelling Squirrels, ed. J. O. Murie and G. R. Michener, 43–78. Lincoln: University of Nebraska Press.

13. Austin, W. J. 1990. The foraging ecology of Abert squirrels. PhD diss., Northern Arizona University.

14. Halloran, M. E. 1993. Social behavior and ecology of Abert squirrels (*Sciurus aberti*). PhD diss., University of Colorado.

15. Dodd, N. L., S. S. Rosenstock, C. R. Miller, and R. E. Schweinsburg. 1998. Tassel-eared squirrel population dynamics in Arizona: Index techniques and relationships to habitat conditions. Research Branch Technical Report no. 27. Phoenix: Arizona Game and Fish Department.

16. Dodd, N. L. 2003b. Landscape-scale habitat relationships to tassel-eared squirrel population dynamics in north-central Arizona. Technical Guidance Bulletin 6. Phoenix: Arizona Game and Fish Department.

17. Taylor, W. P. 1924c. Progress report on animal forest work, Division of Biological Investigations, Bureau of Biological Survey. Conducted in cooperation with the Southwestern Forest Experiment Station, Flagstaff, Arizona. Smithsonian Institution Archives, record unit 7176, box 29, folder 14.

18. Hall, E. R., and K. R. Kelson. 1959. The Mammals of North America. 2 vols. New York: Ronald Press.

19. Cockrum, E. L. 1982. Mammals of the Southwest. Tucson: University of Arizona Press.

20. Hall, J. G. 1967b. The Kaibab squirrel in Grand Canyon National Park—a seven seasons summary—1960–1967. Grand Canyon, AZ: Grand Canyon National Park.

21. Lechleitner, R. R. 1969. Wild Mammals of Colorado—Their Appearance, Habits, Distribution, and Abundance. Boulder, CO: Pruett Publishing Co.

22. Leopold, A. S. 1972. Wildlife of Mexico: The Game Birds and Mammals. Berkeley: University of California Press.

23. Tallon, J. 1983. Photograph. *Arizona Highways* 59 (8): 38.

24. Rice, D. W. 1957. Sexual behavior of tassel-eared squirrels. *Journal of Mammalogy* 38 (1): 129.

25. Farentinos, R. C. 1980. Sexual solicitation of subordinate males by female tassel-eared squirrels (*Sciurus aberti*). *Journal of Mammalogy* 61 (2): 337–41.

26. Keith, J. O. 1956. The Abert squirrel (*Sciurus aberti aberti*) and its relation to the forests of Arizona. MS thesis, University of Arizona.

27. Hill, J. E. 1942. Notes on mammals of northeastern New Mexico. *Journal of Mammalogy* 23:75–82.

28. Baker, R. H., and J. K. Greer. 1962. Mammals of the Mexican State of Durango. Publication of the Museum. *University of Michigan Biological Series* 2:25–154.

29. Hall, J. G. 1981. A field study of the Kaibab squirrel in Grand Canyon National Park. *Wildlife Monographs 75.*

30. Redburn, R. A. 1931. A mother squirrel transports its young. *Grand Canyon Nature Notes* 5 (8): 80–81.

31. Rasmussen, D. I. 1929. The Kaibab squirrel (copy in author's files provided by William Hurst).

32. Sieg, M. J. 2002. Landscape composition and Abert squirrel survivorship, predator-based mortality, home range size and movement. MS thesis, Northern Arizona University.

33. Raught, R. W. 1967. Tree squirrels. *In* New Mexico Wildlife Management, 95–100. Santa Fe: New Mexico Game and Fish Department.

34. Guzman, D. 1997. A histological analysis of the female Abert squirrel, *Sciurus aberti aberti*, reproductive cycle. MS thesis, Northern Arizona University.

35. Wade, O. 1935. Notes on the northern tuft-eared squirrel *Sciurus aberti ferreus* True, in Colorado. *American Midland Naturalist* 16 (2): 201–2.

36. Wade, O., and P. T. Gilbert. 1935. The baculum of some Sciuridae and its significance in determining relationships. *Journal of Mammalogy* 16:52–63.

37. Pogany, G. C., and W. S. Allred. 1992. Sperm morphology as a tool for taxonomy. *In* Proceedings Fifth U.S./Mexico Border States Conference on Recreation, Parks, and Wildlife. Las Cruces, New Mexico, September 17–19, pp. 44–47. Tucson: University of Arizona.

38. Pogany, G. C., and W. S. Allred. Unpublished data.

39. Allred, W. S. Unpublished data.

8

MORTALITY AND
PARASITES

The most important factors regulating populations may be the availability of food . . . Habitat has been influenced over much of the squirrel's range by the intervention of people in the ponderosa pine woodland.

—D. M. Armstrong, *Rocky Mountain Mammals*, 1987

Introduction

In 1947, Vernon Cahalane wrote in *Mammals of North America* that "[r]uthless hunting or the destruction of the yellow pine forest could wipe out the . . . Kaibab squirrels" (ref. 1). Although Cahalane was addressing only one of the six subspecies of tassel-eared squirrels, his remarks are still applicable to the mortalities and population levels of all tassel-eared squirrels, as they are obligate herbivores in ponderosa pine forests in the southwestern United States and Mexico. Presently three of the six subspecies are considered small game animals and are hunted in three states. Forest thinning and wildfires reduce ponderosa pine habitat. Other mortality factors, some natural and some human induced, are discussed in this chapter. Examples of tassel-eared squirrel mortality causes are diseases, parasites, predation, and highway deaths.

Predation

Predators of tassel-eared squirrels are both aerial and terrestrial. Numerous researchers have either speculated or collected indirect evidence on potential predators or witnessed predation directly on tassel-eared squirrels (table 8.1). Squirrels are most vulnerable to avian and terrestrial predators when they are foraging in the litter layer of the forest floor.

— TABLE 8.1 —

Actual or potential predators of tassel-eared squirrels cited in the literature

Predator	Researcher, year
Avian	
Red-tailed hawk (*Buteo jamaicensis*)	V. Bailey, 1931[1]
Northern goshawk (*Accipiter gentiles*)	Rasmussen, 1941[1]; Reynolds, 1963[1]; A. M. Bailey and Niedrach, 1965[2]; Keith, 1965[1]; Farentinos, 1972c[1]; Reynolds et al., 1992[1]; Lema, 2001[1]; Drennan and Beier, 2003[1]
Swainson's hawk (*Buteo swainsoni*)	Keith, 1956[1]
Great horned owl (*Bubo virginianus*)	Farentinos, 1972c[2]
Peregrine falcon (*Falco peregrinus*)	Hall, 1981[1]
Golden eagle (*Aquila chrysaetos*)	
Cooper's hawk (*Accipter cooperi*)	
Terrestrial	
Coyote (*Canus latrans*)	Farentinos, 1972c[2]
Red fox (*Vulpes fulva*)	
Bobcat (*Lynx rufus*)	Hall, 1981[1]
Gray fox (*Urocyon cinereoargenteus*)	
Mountain lion (*Felis concolor*)	
Rattlesnake (*Crotelus sp.*)	
Gopher snake (*Pituophis sp.*)	
Mountain lion (*Felis concolor*)	Turkowski, 1980[1,3]
Coyote (*Canus latrans*)	
Bobcat (*Lynx rufus*)	

1 —Arizona
2 —Colorado
3 —data from a scat analysis

Avian Predators

In an article in *Arizona Wildlife* in 1927, Glen Sturdevant stated that hawks were the principle predator of Kaibab squirrels within the Grand Canyon National Park and advocated for management of the hawks as necessary to avoid loss of squirrels: "[W]hen one form tends to prey upon another to the point of extermination, it is necessary to reduce the numbers of the preying species" (ref. 2). Vernon Bailey wrote in

1931, "Enemies are numerous, and it is doubtful if half the squirrels ever see a second summer." He examined the crop of a red-tailed hawk and found the remains of tassel-eared squirrel, thus reporting the first account of an avian predator on tassel-eared squirrels (ref. 3). Donald Rasmussen in 1941 spotlighted the predation of goshawks and hawks on squirrels by including a diagram depicting a food chain centered on the ponderosa pine forests with direct links between Kaibab squirrels and red-tailed hawks in his treatise "Biotic Communities of the Kaibab Plateau" (ref. 4).

Abert's squirrels are listed as an important prey species for northern goshawks (*Accipiter gentilis*) in the southwestern United States in the current U.S. Forest Service management plan recommendations (ref. 5). In the first published account of a northern goshawk feeding on an Abert's squirrel, the observer suggested that goshawks could serve as regulators of fluctuating Abert's squirrel populations (ref. 6). In 1965, Alfred Bailey and Robert Niedrach hypothesized in *Birds of Colorado* that tassel-eared squirrels provided the majority of food for the unfledged young of goshawks in their graphic details of the feeding of a *S. a. ferreus* by a goshawk to her young (ref. 7). Goshawks in northern Arizona were found to feed mostly on cottontails (*Sylvilagus* spp.) and Abert's squirrels during the winter and during the goshawk breeding season (ref. 8).

In Colorado Farentinos noted that most of the goshawk predation events on *S. a. ferreus* occurred in fall and winter months. Five unsuccessful attacks by goshawks were witnessed in his study (ref. 9). During his many years of conducting research on tassel-eared squirrels, Patton observed "a sort of face-to-face battle" between a tassel-eared squirrel and a goshawk. "The squirrel did not retreat and the goshawk flew off. One advantage the squirrel had was a number of small branches that prevented the goshawk from getting a good opening to the squirrel" (ref. 10).

Conducting ecological research in northern Arizona, Keith wrote in 1956, "On one occasion I observed a Swainson's hawk attack a group of squirrels. It was unsuccessful and the squirrels showed little concern over the hawk after the initial attack" (ref. 11). Other failed attempts by a juvenile red-tail and a juvenile Cooper's hawk on two different Kaibab squirrels have been reported (ref. 12, 13). Hall observed Kaibab squirrels with a family of Cooper's hawks: "squirrels seemed unconcerned but watchful" (ref. 13). Tassel-eared squirrel skulls have also been found in pellets of great horned owls (ref. 9).

Terrestrial Predators

An unsuccessful attack on a *S. a. ferreus* by a coyote was witnessed in Colorado. Red foxes were also observed on the same study sites but no evidence of squirrel predation was found (ref. 9). In a report submitted to the Grand Canyon National Park, Hall listed potential predators of Kaibab squirrels (table 8.1) (ref. 12). A carnivore scat analysis from the Beaver Creek watershed in central Arizona found that 5% of the 367 scat samples collected from mountain lions, coyotes, and bobcats contained *S. a. aberti* remains (ref. 14). A bobcat was observed with a fresh-killed Abert's squirrel within the city limits of Flagstaff in 2009 (ref. 15).

Mortality from Habitat Loss

As early as 1928, overgrazing by deer on the Kaibab Plateau was reported to cause Kaibab squirrels to be more vulnerable to predation by hawks (ref. 16). Since 1942 many studies have concluded that loss of habitat due to timber harvest practices is detrimental to squirrel numbers and recruitment (ref. 17, 18, 19, 20). Wildfires due to fire suppression, drought, lightning, and human carelessness have destroyed extensive squirrel habitat (ref. 21).

Season and Mortality

Winter is the most critical time for survival because the only reliable food—inner bark—is of lower caloric value (ref. 18). Inner bark caloric values are > 1,000 calories /g lower in winter when compared with inner bark caloric values in the spring and summer (ref. 20).

Cold weather and snow together with a decrease in available food supplies caused a decline in *S. a. ferreus* populations in Colorado (ref. 9). A ten-year study on mortality of *S. a. aberti* in Arizona found that mortality rates ranged from 22 to 66%. The low range was in a winter when squirrels could obtain "high quality foods" such as pine seeds and hypogeous fungi because there were only fourteen days when snow depth was 10 cm or greater. The high range occurred in a year when snow depth was 10 cm or greater for eighty-five days. The snow depth and length of the time the snow remained on the ground explained 70% of the variation in morality during the study (ref. 22). The same inverse relationship between snow cover duration and squirrel survivorship was found in another squirrel study, which also reported a positive relationship between squirrel survivorship and "dietary fungal diversity" (ref. 23).

Food shortages, poor-quality food, and the fact that tassel-eared squirrels do not hibernate, thus feeding every day, certainly create a narrow survival ledge to walk in the winter.

Highway Mortalities

Two investigators concluded that deaths by automobiles were high for both the Abert's and the Kaibab squirrels (ref. 1, 13). "Both the Kaibab and Abert squirrel have never learned to beware of automobiles, and the mortality from this cause is comparatively high," Cahalane wrote in 1947 (ref. 1). And Keith reported that tassel-eared squirrels seem to be confused by approaching vehicles and are "commonly killed" as they attempt to cross roads or highways (ref. 11). Hall described Kaibab squirrels' road-crossing behavior as being "obviously confused and befuddled, dashing first this way and then that, all too often making its final rush right beneath the wheels of the car" (ref. 12). In a 1965 article about Kaibab squirrels, Nat Dodge remarked, "During the past thirty years the number of road kills has decreased in spite of the increase in numbers of automobiles using the north rim roads." He considered this a sign, as did William Hurst, a former regional forester, of the decline in the population numbers of the Kaibab squirrel (ref. 24, 25). One study on road-killed squirrels found that from September to November there were more than 50% more males (n = 44) than females (n = 21) killed by vehicles in northern Arizona (ref. 26). In some forested areas of northern Arizona where the Arizona Department of Transportation has conducted tree thinning projects to reduce shady areas and ice accumulation on highways during the winter, squirrels might not be crossing highways as frequently, since squirrels tend to avoid areas where there are few trees or trees without interlocking canopies.

Road-killed tassel-eared squirrels have been used by numerous researchers in their projects on reproduction, diet, DNA, and parasites (ref. 26, 27, 28, 29, 30, 31, 32, 33, 34, 35, 36).

Hunting

Faunal remain records found in many ruins across the Southwest indicate that tassel-eared squirrels were used as food and their pelts for clothing (appendix 4) (ref. 2). In Arizona, Colorado, and New Mexico, tassel-eared squirrels are considered small game animals with specific seasons and bag/possession limits. This includes *S. a. aberti*, *S. a. ferreus*, and *S. a. kaibabensis*. On the Navajo reservation, *S. a. chuscensis* is listed as a sensitive species and is protected (ref. 37). Utah and Wyoming prohibit the hunting of tassel-eared squirrels. Utah Division of Wildlife Resources gave *S. a. aberti* an S1S2 ranking, which indicates "extreme rarity," with the species being vulnerable to extinction (ref. 38). Wyoming Game and Fish Department classifies *S. a. aberti* as a Species of Special Concern, with a Native Species Status of 3 because of its restricted range (ref. 39). In Mexico, *S. a. durangi* and *S. a. barberi* are considered rare and have a status of "species subject to special protection" (ref. 40).

Parasites

Ectoparasites of tassel-eared squirrels fall into four groups of arthropods: fleas, lice, mites, and ticks. The first report regarding fleas and tassel-eared squirrels was given by Karl Jordan, who conducted his studies in New Mexico in the 1920s (ref. 41). Keith wrote, "All thirty-four [*S. a. aberti*] squirrels collected were infested . . . and they often bit and scratched to relieve this irritation." He noted that fleas were never in extreme numbers (ref. 11). Five different species of fleas were found on twenty-nine tassel-eared squirrels examined in New Mexico. Red squirrels (*Tamiasciurus hudsonicus*) shared four of the five flea species, suggesting the possibility of cross-transmission between the two squirrel species when both are in the same area (ref. 41). Others have reported finding lice, mites, and ticks on tassel-eared squirrels (table 8.2).

Endoparasites in tassel-eared squirrels include nematodes and coccidians. There have been no reports of Platyhelminthes in tassel-eared squirrels. An unidentified nematode was found in the body cavity of a single Abert's squirrel (ref. 11). A second study revealed two different nematodes, both of which were first reports, in 21 of 29 squirrels examined in New Mexico (table 8.2) (ref. 42).

Three different coccidian species have been found in the GI tracts of tassel-eared squirrels (table 8.2) (ref. 42, 43, 44). During one of the studies, 3 of 12 of the *S. a. kaibabensis* and 5 of 11 of the *S. a. aberti* GI tracts were observed with ulcerated intestinal linings from the coccidian infections (ref. 44).

— TABLE 8.2 —

Ectoparasites and endoparasites of tassel-eared squirrels

Ectoparasite	Location	Researcher, year
Fleas		
Opistodasys (Ceratophyllus) robustus	New Mexico	Jordan, 1925
Opistodasys robustus	Arizona	Keith, 1956
Oropsylla idahoensis	Arizona	Skinner, 1976
Monopsyllus eumolpi	Utah	Pederson et al., 1987
Hystrichopsylla dippiei		
Ceratophyllus vison (2/29)	New Mexico	Patrick and Wilson, 1995
Eumolpianus eumolpi (5/29)		
Opistodasys robustus (2/29)		
Orchopeas caedens caedens (1/29)		
Orchopeas neotomae (3/29)		
Lice (found in nest)		
Order Psocoptera	Arizona	Skinner, 1976
Mites (found in nest)		
Order Acarina	Arizona	Skinner, 1976
Ticks		
Dermacentor andersoni	Utah	Pederson et al., 1987; Emmons, 1988[1]
Endoparasites		
Nematodes		
Unidentified specimen in body cavity	Arizona	Keith, 1956
Enterobius sciuri (5/29)	New Mexico	Patrick and Wilson, 1995
Citellinema quadrivittati (16/29)		
Coccidians		
Eimeria ontarioensis	Arizona (Apache County)	Hill and Duszynski, 1986
E. tamiasciuri		
E. tamiasciuri (11/29)	New Mexico	Patrick and Wilson, 1995
E. tamiasciuri (3/40)	Arizona	M. Wright, W. S. Allred, and P. Wilber, unpublished data, 1996
E. toddi (6/40)		

* numbers in parentheses represent the number of squirrels with a particular infection
1—listed tassel-eared squirrels as one of numerous mammalian host species for Colorado tick fever

Other Causes of Mortality

Only three diseases are mentioned in all the tassel-eared literature reviewed. One is induced and the others are transmitted by fleas and mosquitoes. Shock disease was first described in tassel-eared squirrels as being "characterized by . . . degeneration of the liver, a failure of the storage of glycogen in that organ, and a terminal development of an abnormal blood sugar" (ref. 45). Shock disease results in death and seems to be related to stresses encountered by squirrels when they are live-trapped (ref. 12, 17). A Grand Canyon National Park naturalist observed a squirrel "suffering from 'fits' or shock just before its death" (ref. 12). Sylvatic plague caused by the bacterium *Yersinia pestis* and vectored by fleas is lethal to squirrels (ref. 27). In the fall of 2008, the Coconino County Department of Health in Flagstaff, Arizona, confirmed that two dead tassel-eared squirrels tested positive for West Nile virus (ref. 46).

Even with careful handling, baiting, and placement of traps, researchers conducting squirrel trapping invariably have squirrels die (ref. 17). The deaths of eight squirrels due to various causes such as heat prostration and an improperly fitting radio collar were reported from a study in Utah (ref. 47). Three Kaibab squirrels died after being trapped when they were being transported to Mt. Logan (ref. 48). One trapping study was delayed due to goshawk harassment of trapped squirrels (ref. 49). In one project including more than 2,500 captures, thirty-two squirrels died in trapping incidents, a 1.3% mortality rate (ref. 49). John Koprowski, a tree squirrel researcher at the University of Arizona, reported that in trapping and handling more than 3,500 individuals of seven different species of tree squirrels, the mortality rate was < 0.01%, a remarkable survival success rate for trapped squirrels (ref. 50).

Keith described two unusual deaths of tassel-eared squirrels. One had chipped incisors, which produced malocclusions preventing the squirrel from eating, leading to starvation; and the second had its chest and esophagus pierced by a porcupine's quill (ref. 17). A dead Abert's squirrel was found impaled on a tree branch sticking up from the ground, most likely from a fall or misjudgment in leaping from one tree to another (ref. 51).

Life Span

The average life span of a tassel-eared squirrel in the wild is about three to four years (ref. 17). A colleague raised an abandoned juvenile *S. a. aberti* that lived in captivity for nine years (ref. 52). In one long-term squirrel study conducted by Patton, a male squirrel lived seven years and one female lived eight years (ref. 10). Table 11.4 in chapter 11 provides a life table of fifty-eight Kaibab squirrels (ref. 53).

Summary

Mortalities from diseases, parasites, predation, and loss of habitat due to wildfires are normal within animal populations. Mortalities from vehicles, hunting, and loss of habitat from timber harvesting are human-caused.

Future Research

Some research questions that will require more studies on mortalities of tassel-eared squirrels are: (1) Do the six subspecies of tassel-eared squirrels share any common ectoparasites or endoparasites? (2) What are the primary causes of mortalities of the two subspecies of tassel-eared squirrels that live in ponderosa pine forests of Mexico? (3) What other intestinal pathogens might be harbored in the GI tracts of tassel-eared squirrels? (4) What are the viral pathogens of tassel-eared squirrels? (5) Are there shared parasites with other squirrel species that live in areas adjacent to tassel-eared squirrels? (6) Are forest thinning practices along highways influencing the number of road-killed squirrels? (7) What are the effects of forest restoration practices on squirrel population levels? (8) In September 2008 in Flagstaff, Arizona, two Abert's squirrels were found at necropsy to be infected with the West Nile virus. Is this a fatal pathogen or do some tassel-eared squirrels have a resistance? This study could be conducted with road-killed squirrels.

References for Chapter Eight

1. Cahalane, V. H. 1947. Mammals of North America. New York: Mac-Millan Co.
2. Sturdevant, G. E. 1927. The Kaibab and Abert squirrel. *Arizona Wildlife* 1 (8) (March): 2–3.
3. Bailey, V. 1931. Mammals of New Mexico. North American Fauna no. 53. U.S. Department of Agriculture, Bureau of Biological Survey. Washington, DC: U.S. Government Printing Office.
4. Rasmussen, D. I. 1941. Biotic communities of the Kaibab Plateau, Arizona. *Ecological Monographs* 11:229–75.
5. Reynolds, R. T., R. T. Graham, H. M. Reiser, R. L. Bassett, P. L. Kennedy, D. A. Boyce Jr., G. Goodwin, R. Smith, and E. L. Fisher. 1992. Management

recommendations for the northern goshawk in the southwestern United States. General Technical Report RM-217. Fort Collins, CO: USDA Forest Service, Rocky Mountain Forest and Range Experiment Station.

6. Reynolds, H. G. 1963. Western goshawk takes Abert squirrel in Arizona. *Journal of Forestry* 61:551.

7. Bailey, A. M., and R. J. Niedrach. 1965. Birds of Colorado. Vol. 1. Denver: Denver Museum of Natural History.

8. Drennan, J. E., and P. Beier. 2003. Forest structure and prey abundance in winter habitat of northern goshawks. *Journal of Wildlife Management* 67 (1): 177–85.

9. Farentinos, R. C. 1972c. Observations on the ecology of the tassel-eared squirrel. *Journal of Wildlife Management* 36 (4): 1234–39.

10. Patton, D. R. Personal communication.

11. Keith, J. O. 1956. The Abert squirrel (*Sciurus aberti aberti*) and its relation to the forests of Arizona. MS thesis, University of Arizona.

12. Hall, J. G. 1967b. The Kaibab squirrel in Grand Canyon National Park—a seven seasons summary—1960–1967. Grand Canyon, AZ: Grand Canyon National Park.

13. Hall, J. G. 1981. A field study of the Kaibab squirrel in Grand Canyon National Park. *Wildlife Monographs* 75.

14. Turkowski, F. J. 1980. Carnivora food habits and habitat use in ponderosa pine forests. Research Paper RM-215. Fort Collins, CO: USDA Forest Service.

15. Shannon, J. P. 2009. Personal communication.

16. Goldman, E. A. 1928. The Kaibab or white-tailed squirrel. *Journal of Mammalogy* 9:127–29.

17. Trowbridge, A. H., and L. L. Larson. 1942. Abert squirrel–ponderosa pine relationships at the Fort Valley Experimental Forest, Flagstaff, Arizona (copy in author's files).

18. Keith, J. O. 1965. The Abert squirrel and its dependence on ponderosa pine. *Ecology* 46:150–63.

19. Patton, D. R., R. L. Wadleigh, and H. G. Hudak. 1985. The effects of timber harvesting on the Kaibab squirrel. *Journal of Wildlife Management* 49 (1): 14–19.

20. Pederson, J. C., R. C. Farentinos, and V. M. Littlefield. 1987. Effects of logging on habitat quality and feeding patterns of Abert squirrels. *Great Basin Naturalist* 47 (2): 252–58.

21. Keith, J. O. 2003. The Abert's Squirrel (*Sciurus aberti*): A Technical Conservation Assessment. Golden, CO: USDA Forest Service, Rocky Mountain Region.

22. Stephenson, R. L., and D. E. Brown. 1980. Snow cover as a factor influencing mortality of Abert's squirrels. *Journal of Wildlife Management* 44 (4): 951–55.

23. Dodd, N. L., J. S. States, and S. S. Rosenstock. 2003. Tassel-eared squirrel population, habitat condition, and dietary relationships in north-central Arizona. *Journal of Wildlife Management* 67 (3): 622–33.
24. Dodge, N. N. 1965. Whitetail squirrel. *Pacific Discovery* 18:23–26.
25. Hurst, W. Personal communication.
26. Minard, A. 2000. Morphological and genetic investigations of Abert squirrels (*Sciurus aberti aberti*). MS thesis, Northern Arizona University.
27. Brown, D. E. 1986. Arizona's Tree Squirrels. Phoenix: Arizona Game and Fish Department.
28. Guzman, D. 1997. A histological analysis of the female Abert squirrel, *Sciurus aberti aberti*, reproductive cycle. MS thesis, Northern Arizona University.
29. Rose, M. D. 1997. Histological examination of the male reproductive cycle in the Abert squirrel, *Sciurus aberti*. MS thesis, Northern Arizona University.
30. Allred, W. S. 1995. Black-bellied form of an Abert squirrel (*Sciurus aberti aberti*) from the San Francisco Peaks area, Arizona. *Southwestern Naturalist* 40:420.
31. Pogany, G. C., and W. S. Allred. 1992. Sperm morphology as a tool for taxonomy. *In* Proceedings Fifth U.S./Mexico Border States Conference on Recreation, Parks, and Wildlife. Las Cruces, New Mexico, September 17–19, pp. 44–47. Tucson: University of Arizona.
32. Allred, W. S., and G. Pogany. 1996. Early estrus in a female Abert squirrel (*Sciurus aberti aberti*). *Southwestern Naturalist* 41:90.
33. Pogany, G. C., and W. S. Allred. 1995. Abert's squirrels of the Colorado Plateau: Their reproductive cycle. *In* Proceeding of the Second Biennial Conference of Research in Colorado Plateau National Parks, ed. C. van Riper III, 293–305. NPS/NRNAU/NKTP-95/11. Flagstaff: Northern Arizona University.
34. Pogany, G. C., W. S. Allred, and T. Barnes. 1998. The reproductive cycle of Abert's squirrel. *In* Ecology and Evolutionary Biology of Tree Squirrels, ed. M. A. Steele, J. F. Merritt, and D. A. Zegers, 53–59. Special Publications 6. Martinsville: Virginia Museum of Natural History.
35. Minard, A., and W. S. Allred. 1999. Analyses of Road-Killed Abert Squirrels in Northern Arizona. April. Poster. Flagstaff: Arizona/Nevada Academy of Sciences.
36. Allred, W. S., and M. Wright. Unpublished data.
37. Navajo Nation. 2008. Sensitive Species List. Window Rock, AZ: Division of Natural Resources, Department of Fish and Wildlife. www.navajofishandwildlife.org.
38. Inventory of sensitive species and ecosystems in Utah. 1997. Salt Lake City: Utah Division of Wildlife Resources. September 30.
39. http://gf.state.wy.us/.

40. Ramirez-Pubido, J., J. Arroyo-Cabrales, and A. Castro-Campillo. 2005. Current status and relationship of nomenclatural land mammals of Mexico. *Zoological Record Mexicana*, n.s., 21 (1): 21–82.

41. Jordan, K. 1925. New Siphonaptera. *Novitates Zoologicae* 32:96–112.

42. Patrick, M. J., and W. D. Wilson. 1995. Parasites in the Abert's squirrel (*Sciurus aberti*) and red squirrel (*Tamiasciurus hudsonicus*) of New Mexico. *Journal of Parasitology* 81 (2): 321–24.

43. Hill, T. P., and D. W. Duszynski. 1986. Coccidia (Apicomplexa: Eimeriidae) from Sciurid rodents (*Eutamias, Sciurus, Tamiasciurus* spp.) from the western United States and northern Mexico with descriptions of two new species. *Journal of Protozoology* 33 (2): 282–88.

44. Allred, W. S., M. Wright, and P. Wilber. Unpublished data.

45. Green, R. G., C. L. Larson, and J. F. Bell. 1939. Shock disease as the cause of the periodic decimation of the snowshoe hare. *American Journal of Hygiene* 30:83–102.

46. Coconino County Health Department. 2008. Cases: 08-6093 and 08-6094. Reports of West Nile virus infected Abert's squirrels. Flagstaff, Arizona (copies in author's files).

47. Pederson, J. C., R. N. Hasenyager, and A. W. Heggen. 1976. Habitat Requirements of the Abert Squirrel (*Sciurus aberti navajo*) on the Monticello District, Manti-LaSal National Forest. Publication 76-9. Salt Lake City: Utah State Division of Wildlife.

48. Brown, D. E., and J. W. Evans. 1972. Kaibab squirrel stocking. Progress Report, project W-53-R-22, work plan 6, job 4. Phoenix: Arizona Game and Fish Department.

49. Dodd, N. L., S. S. Rosenstock, C. R. Miller, and R. E. Schweinsburg. 1998. Tassel-eared squirrel population dynamics in Arizona: Index techniques and relationships to habitat conditions. Research Branch Technical Report no. 27. Phoenix: Arizona Game and Fish Department.

50. Koprowski, J. L. 2002. Handling tree squirrels with a safe and efficient restraint. *Wildlife Society Bulletin* 30 (1): 101–3.

51. States, J. S. Personal communication.

52. Keller, R. Personal communication.

53. Patton, D. R. 1997. Wildlife Habitat Relationships in Forested Ecosystems. 2nd ed. Portland, OR: Timber Press.

9

GENETICS

Upon first consideration, the various described forms of the tassel-eared squirrel seem to be very distinctive and sharply differentiated. Further examination, however, tends to emphasize the fact that they represent a curiously variable group, with somewhat parallel lines of variation in widely separated localities . . .

—E. D. McKee, "Distribution of the Tassel-Eared Squirrels," 1941

Introduction

The earliest genetic study, which produced the first karyotype of tassel-eared squirrels, was conducted in 1967 (ref. 1). The term "genetic polymorphism" was used to explain coat color of tassel-eared squirrels in Colorado (ref. 2). Several genetic studies have examined T-cell receptor genes, phylogeny of mitochondrial DNA, and the major histocompatibility complexes of tassel-eared squirrels (ref. 3, 4, 5). The most recent study involving tassel-eared squirrel genetics was performed in 2000 and involved using ground squirrel DNA primers in Abert's squirrel variability studies (ref. 6).

Karyotypes and Chromosomes

Charles Nadler and Dallas Sutton assembled and compared the karyotypes of five North American Sciuridae in 1967. They included specimens from *S. a. aberti*, *S. niger rufiventer* (fox squirrel), *S. griseus griseus* (California gray squirrel), and two subspecies of eastern gray squirrels, *S. carolinensis carolinensis* and *S. carolinensis pennsylvanicus*. The *S. aberti* (subspecies not given) karyotype was analyzed from the bone marrow of a single male specimen from an "unknown locality." The results revealed a diploid number of forty chromosomes for all specimens examined consisting of fourteen metacentric, twenty-four submetacentric, one unpaired metacentric chromosome (X), and one unpaired acrocentric chromosome (Y) (ref. 1).

Chromosomes are described based on the location of the centromere on the chromosomes. Centromeres are constriction areas and serve as attachment points for the spindle fibers during mitosis and meiosis. If the centromere is directly in the center it is referred to as "metacentric"; if near the end it is "acrocentric"; and if it is located between the center and the end it is "submetacentric" (ref. 7).

The centromeres of the autosomes of *S. n. rufiventer, S. c. carolinensis*, and *S. aberti* are all in the same location, making them indistinguishable from one another. *S. g. griseus* differs slightly from the other three species with respect to the Y chromosome and the "presence of secondary constrictions" on several other chromosomes (ref. 1).

David Forsyth conducted an analysis of the forty chromosomes of the karyotypes of *S. a. aberti* and *S. a. kaibabensis* in 1991 (figures 9.1a and 9.1b). The analysis involved fifteen specimens of *S. a. aberti* (five females, ten males) and ten specimens of *S. a. kaibabensis* (two females, eight males). He obtained samples from blood, spleen, and bone marrow. He gave an excellent description of each of the nineteen pairs of autosomes and the sex chromosomes, describing several identifying characteristics of each, such as arm lengths, arm length ratios, and size comparisons. The chromosomes of *S. a. aberti* and *S. a. kaibabensis* were described as "conserved," meaning that no major changes have occurred between the two subspecies since the time of separation, leading to a hypothesis that neither subspecies had diverged significantly from each other and that "hybrid progeny produced by secondary contact [between the two subspecies] would most likely be fertile" (ref. 8).

In a small preliminary sperm morphology study designed to differentiate the two subspecies *S. a. aberti* and *S. a. kaibabensis* taxonomically, there was not a significant difference in sperm shape or size between the two subspecies, lending support to Forsyth's hypothesis that these subspecies have not diverged significantly (ref. 8, 9). Another examination using silver staining was conducted with sperm of the two subspecies. The various proteins on the acrosomal sheath of a sperm will bind silver differentially. Even though the silver staining of the postacrosomal sheaths of the sperm of the two subspecies was identical, the respective density was clearly different between the two. This difference could have been due to the small sample size of sperm used or to the collection technique, and needs further study (ref. 9).

Forsyth's study used the Giemsa trypsin banding method to allow microscopic examination of chromosomes. Trypsin causes the chromosomes to swell, and the Giemsa stains the chromosome bands so they become visible. The Giemsa trypsin banding patterns of the chromosomes for *S. a. aberti* and *S. a. kaibabensis* were homologous with very little variation, which was attributed to the degree of chromosomal contraction and staining intensity. Forsyth also examined the constitutive heterochromatin, DNA that is tightly coiled within the nucleus, and the nucleolus organizer region, an area on chromosomes where the nucleolus forms, for both subspecies and found that both appeared to be similar (ref. 8).

Serum Proteins

Transferrin

Transferrin is a glycoprotein that carries iron found in plasma. Serum proteins of five species of the genus *Sciurus* (*S. argentinus, S. griseus, S. niger, S. carolinensis,* and *S. aberti*) were examined with electrophoresis. *S. aberti* had a single band of transferrin that was similar in mobility to *S. niger*; no other similarities were noted in this study (ref. 10).

Albumin

Albumin is a plasma protein that maintains osmotic pressure. Serum albumins from four ground squirrels (*Eutamias dorsalis dorsalis*—cliff chipmunk; *E. umbrinus fremonti*—Unita chipmunk; *E. u. montanus*— Unita chipmunk; and *Ammospermophilus lectcurus pennipes*—white-tailed antelope squirrel) and a tassel-eared squirrel (*S. a. ferreus*) were analyzed to determine if a distinction between the five squirrels could be found from the different samples. *S. a. ferreus* had a specific albumin component that was distinctly different from that of the other squirrels examined. No significant differences in albumins were found between any of the squirrels with respect to their gender. Based on this study of albumin from blood samples, it was concluded that certain protein fractions could be useful in discriminating between individual species and subspecies (ref. 11).

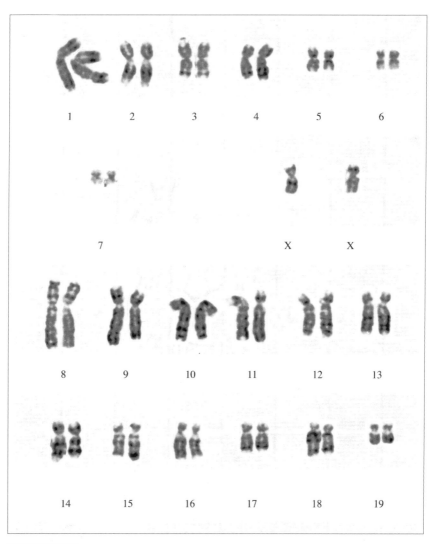

FIGURE 9.1a   Karyotype of a female Abert's squirrel. Used with permission from David Forsyth.

T-cell Receptor Genes

A T-cell receptor (*tcr*) is a molecule located on surfaces of T lymphocytes (T-cells), a type of white blood cell and an important component of the immune system. *Tcr* is responsible for recognition of antigens (foreign proteins) that have been bound to molecules of the major histocompatibility complex. In 1990 Peter Wettstein and colleagues performed an analysis of the *tcr* alpha (*a*) and beta (*b*) genes of sixty

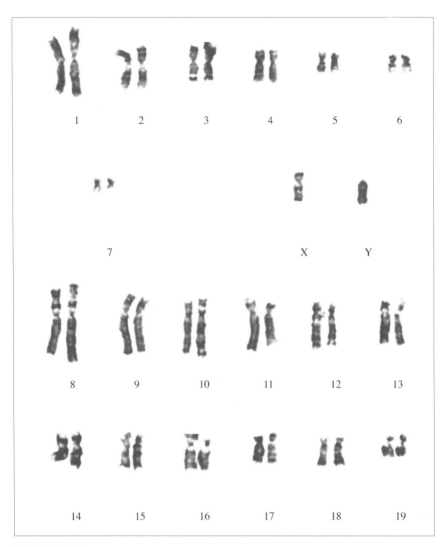

Karyotype of a male Abert's squirrel. Used with permission from David Forsyth.

S. a. aberti and sixty-two *S. a. kaibabensis* to determine if relationships existed between the availability of false truffles and the expression of the genes that regulate the immune system. False truffle production is related to environmental conditions and false truffles serve as one of the food resources of tassel-eared squirrels. It was determined that the level of *tcra* heterozygosity for Kaibab squirrels was directly related to false truffle availability. Interestingly, the *tcrb* heterozygosity was inversely related to false truffle production in Kaibab and Abert's squirrels.

— TABLE 9.1 —

False truffle availability and levels of *tcra* and
tcrb heterozygosity in Abert's and Kaibab squirrels

Subspecies	False truffle availability	*Tcra* heterozygosity	*Tcrb* heterozygosity
S. a. aberti	Low	Varied	High
	High	Varied	Low
S. a. kaibabensis	Low	Low	High
	High	High	Low

However, Abert's squirrel *tcra* heterozygosity differed from the Kaibab *tcra* heterozygosity in that it varied over the years with false truffle availability. A possible explanation for this difference is that Abert's squirrels have greater polymorphism in the *tcr* genes. Nutritional stress caused by decreased food resources might result in a less efficient immune system. Individual squirrels that express genes for a strengthened immune system under certain stressful environmental and nutritional conditions have a selective advantage for survival (table 9.1) (ref. 12).

Major Histocompatibility Complex

The major histocompatibility complex (MHC) is a large genomic region of importance in the immune system. Classes I and II of the MHC are used to present foreign antigens to T-cells. An investigation of the DNA of twenty-two *S. a. kaibabensis* was conducted to determine the existence of polymorphic sequences of these class I and II genes (ref. 4). In a parallel study, the DNA from twelve *S. a. aberti* was examined. The majority of the banding patterns of class I and II were identical to *S. a. kaibabensis*. The findings of both studies suggest that even though the two subspecies are separated geographically, there has been little divergence within these particular genes (ref. 5). Both studies found greater polymorphisms in class II than in class I (ref. 4, 5).

Genetics and Pelage Color

A "little subpopulation" of white-bellied Kaibab squirrels on the southern end of Walhalla Plateau, North Rim of Grand Canyon National Park, was reported by Hall, who remarked, "The genetics of the situation remains an enigma" (ref. 13). From his examinations of white-bellied

Kaibab squirrels and black-bellied Abert's squirrels, he observed that "only the belly color has been affected." The tail color remained typical for each subspecies of squirrel, suggesting that it was probably controlled by a stable gene or genes (ref. 13). Other investigators studying pelage length and colors have speculated that polymorphisms of coat color in tassel-eared squirrels are the results of mutations involving at least two gene loci or the result of a single gene variation at the specific agouti locus (ref. 5, 14, 15). Atypical coat colors such as white-bellied Kaibab squirrels and black-bellied Abert's squirrels might result from "de novo retroviral insertions or deletions" (ref. 5).

Nucleotide Diversity Using Mitochondrial DNA

Mitochondrial DNA (mtDNA) of four subspecies of tassel-eared squirrels was studied to determine the evolutionary relationships. The researchers labeled the subspecies Abert, Chuska, Ferreus, and Kaibab for reference purposes. Their findings revealed two major assemblages of the four subspecies: the Abert/Kaibab group and the Chuska/Ferreus group (ref. 3).

The mtDNA clones of the Abert specimens exhibited the greatest nucleotide divergence when compared to the mtDNA clones of Ferreus, suggesting that their respective lineages had been separated approximately 572,000 years. Furthermore, one-half of the Chuska samples shared one mtDNA clone with a single Abert clone sample. This finding was explained by the possibility of a "relatively recent intermixing . . . of Abert and Chuska populations resulting in what appears to be an Abert → Chuska migration." The four subspecies were ranked with respect to nucleotide diversity as Chuska > Abert > Ferreus > Kaibab. The greater diversity of Chuska was attributed to the possible recent Abert contact within the range of the Chuska. The higher Abert diversity over the other two subspecies was credited to habitat sizes of the respective subspecies and to their isolation from each other (ref. 3).

An analysis of the mtDNA of the six subspecies of tassel-eared squirrels was conducted to explain the fragmented distributional pattern of the tassel-eared squirrels in the southwestern United States and Mexico. The researchers reported "two major phylogeographic assemblages." One was labeled "eastern" and contained tassel-eared squirrels from Mexico, northern New Mexico, Colorado, and Utah. The second assemblage, deemed "western," contained tassel-eared squirrels from Arizona and southwestern New Mexico. Based on the assumption that the historical distribution of tassel-eared squirrels was tightly linked with the distribution of ponderosa pine forests, the data pointed to the direct influence of climatic changes during the Pleistocene on the evolutionary genetics of tassel-eared squirrels and partially supports the distribution of the six subspecies (ref. 16, 17).

Cytochrome b Gene

The cytochrome b gene is used as a taxonomic tool to determine divergence within and between taxonomic groups of organisms. The complete mtDNA cytochrome b gene from each of the six subspecies of tassel-eared squirrels (n = 612) was sequenced in 1995. A molecular phylogeny of the squirrels was constructed to determine if there was a relationship in subspecific genetic structures and geographic patterns. Three genetic assemblages were identified: Assemblage 1—*S. a. barberi* and *S. a. durangi*; Assemblage 2—*S. a. aberti* and *S. a. kaibabensis*; and Assemblage 3—*S. a. ferreus*. The samples of *S. a. chuscensis* were split, with one specimen being identical to *S. a. aberti* and the other specimens clustering with *S. a. ferreus*. There was limited divergence of nucleotide sequences between members of Assemblage 1 and Assemblage 2 (ref. 18). The samples of *S. a. chuscensis* suggested a recent "influx" of *S. a. aberti* mtDNA, which had been previously reported (ref. 3).

The amount of time estimated for separation between the six subspecies ranged from 940,000 to 1,520,000 years. Assemblage 3 of *S. a. ferreus* exhibited a much greater divergence of sequences than Assemblage 1 and 2, highlighting *S. a. ferreus* as possessing the greatest genetic base. Based on the levels of cytochrome b divergence of the three assemblages, this investigation presented an argument against any significant role of late-Pleistocene glaciation in the pattern of tassel-eared squirrel dispersals. Glacial activity was acknowledged as perhaps having had an influence in the mixing of *S. a. aberti* and *S. a. chuscensis*, resulting in a higher level of nucleotide diversity in the *S. a chuscensis* samples. Nucleotide diversity between subspecies was scored as *chuscensis* >> *aberti* > *barberi* ~ *kaibabensis* ~ *ferreus*. There was no relationship established between the diversity of the assemblages and their respective habitat size (ref. 18).

Microsatellites

Microsatellites are variable number tandem repeats (VNTRs) found in the noncoding regions of nuclear DNA consisting of 1–6 base pairs. Microsatellites are used to determine the relatedness of alleles within and between species (ref. 19). An attempt was made to adapt microsatellites from the Northern Idaho ground squirrel (*Spermophilus brunneus brunneus*) for use in Abert's squirrels. The genetic differences or variability between individuals of the same species can be determined by examination and comparison of the VNTRs at each gene locus. The microsatellites of the unrelated taxon, the Northern Idaho ground squirrel, were used in this study because none had been developed for *S. a. aberti* and because previous studies had demonstrated that some microsatellites have broad taxonomic limits (ref. 6). Even with two hundred samples, this investigation was ineffective, perhaps because these microsatellites were not broad enough taxonomically since the two squirrel species are not closely related (ref. 6, 19).

Summary

Genetic research of tassel-eared squirrels began about fifty years ago with a study that produced the first karyotype of *S. a. aberti*. The genetics of the immune system of tassel-eared squirrels is of particular importance today because the ponderosa pine forests are being thinned in restoration projects to reduce catastrophic fires. As tree densities are reduced, populations of squirrels can become fragmented, leading to founder effects with respect to the gene pool. Populations with large numbers of squirrels and broad geographic distributions (e.g., Abert's squirrels [*S. a. aberti*]) tend to have more robust gene pools than smaller populations with restricted geographical ranges (e.g., Kaibab and Chusca squirrels). If isolated populations do not have genetic variations within the available gene pool, local extinctions could occur if pathogens are encountered within populations without resistance.

Future Research

(1) Determine whether more differences or more similarities exist between the chromosomes of the various sciurids (ref. 1). (2) Expand the preliminary study on the differing levels of silver staining on the post-acrosomal sheath of the sperm and add other subspecies of tassel-eared squirrels (ref. 6). (3) Expand the chromosome studies of the Abert's and Kaibab squirrels to the other four subspecies of tassel-eared squirrels (ref. 5). (4) Explore whether there is a link with pelage color, hair length, and climatic conditions in the northern ranges of tassel-eared squirrels as some researchers have suggested (ref. 17). (5) Conduct

more research on squirrel coat color polymorphism and the degree of aridity in an area (ref. 2). (6) Develop microsatellites specific for use in genetic variability studies with tassel-eared squirrels. (7) Investigate further several relationships that have been established between false truffle availability and the heterozygosity of T-cell receptor genes of Abert's and Kaibab squirrels (ref. 9). (8) Determine whether any reproductive isolation mechanisms exist within the six subspecies of tassel-eared squirrels.

References for Chapter Nine

1. Nadler, C. F., and D. A. Sutton. 1967. Chromosomes of some squirrels (mammalia—Sciuridae) from the genera *Sciurus* and *Glaucomys*. *Experientia* 23:249–51.
2. Ramey, C. A., and D. J. Nash. 1976b. Coat color polymorphism of Abert's squirrel, *Sciurus aberti*, in Colorado. *Southwestern Naturalist* 21 (2): 209–17.
3. Wettstein, P. J., P. Lager, L. Jin, J. S. States, T. Lamb, and R. Chakraborty. 1994. Phylogeny of mitochondrial DNA clones in tassel-eared squirrels, *Sciurus aberti*. *Molecular Ecology* 3:541–50.
4. Wettstein, P. J., and J. States. 1986a. The major histocompatibility complex of tassel-eared squirrels. I. Genetic diversity associated with Kaibab squirrels. *Immunogenetics* 24:230–41.
5. Wettstein, P. J., and J. States. 1986b. The major histocompatibility complex of tassel-eared squirrels. II. Genetic diversity associated with Abert squirrels. *Immunogenetics* 24:242–50.
6. Minard, A. 2000. Morphological and genetic investigations of Abert squirrels (*Sciurus aberti aberti*). MS thesis, Northern Arizona University.
7. Tamarin, R. 1998. Principles of Genetics. 6th ed. Dubuque, IA: McGraw-Hill.
8. Forsyth, D. R. 1991. A comparative cytogenetic investigation of *Sciurus aberti aberti* and *Sciurus aberti kaibabensis*. MS thesis, Northern Arizona University.
9. Pogany, G. C., and W. S. Allred. 1992. Sperm morphology as a tool for taxonomy. *In* Proceedings Fifth U.S./Mexico Border States Conference on Recreation, Parks, and Wildlife. Las Cruces, New Mexico, September 17–19, pp. 44–47. Tucson: University of Arizona.
10. Hight, M. E. 1972. The use of serum proteins in studying phylogenetic relationships of the Sciuridae. PhD diss., Wayne State University.
11. Seaman, R. N., and D. J. Nash. 1977. An electrophoretic description of five species of squirrel. *Comparative Biochemical Physiology* 58B:309–11.

12. Wettstein, P. J., R. Chakraborty, J. States, and G. Ferrari. 1990. T-cell receptor genes in tassel-eared squirrels (*Sciurus aberti*). I. Genetic polymorphism and divergence in the Abert and Kaibab subspecies. *Immunogenetics* 32:219–30.

13. Hall, J. G. 1981. A field study of the Kaibab squirrel in Grand Canyon National Park. *Wildlife Monographs* 75.

14. Hancock, D. C., Jr., and D. J. Nash. 1982. Dorsal hair length and coat color in Abert's squirrel (*Sciurus aberti*). *Great Basin Naturalist* 42:597–98.

15. Searle, A. G. 1968. Comparative Genetics of Coat Colour in Mammals. London: Academic Press.

16. Lamb, T., T. R. Jones, and P. J. Wettstein. 1997. Evolutionary genetics and phylogeography of tassel-eared squirrels (*Sciurus aberti*). *Journal of Mammalogy* 78 (1): 117–33.

17. Hoffmeister, D. F., and V. Diersing. 1978. Review of the tassel-eared squirrels of the subgenus *Otosciurus*. *Journal of Mammalogy* 59:402–13.

18. Wettstein, P. J., M. Strausbauch, T. Lamb, J. States, R. Chakraborty, L. Jin, and R. Riblet. 1995. Phylogeny of six *Sciurus aberti* subspecies based on nucleotide sequences of cytochrome b. *Molecular Phylogenetics and Evolution* 4 (2): 150–62.

19. Jarne, P., and P. J. L. Lagoda. 1996. Microsatellites, from molecules to populations and back. *Trends in Ecology and Evolution* 11:424–29.

THE KAIBAB SQUIRREL

10

A January morning, just after sun-up, can be numbing in the pine forests of northern Arizona, at 8,000 feet above sea level. On such a morning it seems almost impossible to conceive of any creature surviving the twelve black, bitterly cold hours just past. . . . Emerging from the lofty needle-and-twig nest in which he spent the night, a large tree squirrel now moves quickly towards the outermost twigs of an upper branch . . . in the top of a favorite tree for breakfast.

—J. G. Hall, "White Tails and Yellow Pines," 1967

This chapter is dedicated to Dr. Joe Hall for his extensive research on the Kaibab squirrel.

Introduction

The Kaibab squirrel was named after the geographical area where it lives, the Kaibab Plateau. *Kaibab*, a Piute word, means "mountain lying down." In 1882 Clarence Dutton, with the U.S. Geological Survey, wrote, "The Kaibab is the loftiest of the four plateaus through which the Grand Canyon extends . . . We, who through successive summers have wandered through its forests and parks, have come to regard it as the most enchanting region it has ever been our privilege to visit" (ref. 1).

The Kaibab Plateau is 95 km long and 55 km wide with much of its elevation at 1,830 m. The Kaibab Plateau was described by Rasmussen as unique because it is "the largest and best-defined of the block plateaus" (ref. 2). Approximately one-third of the Kaibab Plateau is covered by ponderosa pine forest, the chief plant indicator for the Merriam's Transition Life Zone in the southwestern United States. The ponderosa pine forest is about 90% (81,000 ha) in the Kaibab National Forest with the remaining approximately 8,000 ha within Grand Canyon National Park (ref. 3).

Fifty-three years after Woodhouse's discovery and description of the Abert's squirrel, John Stewart, a trapper, collected squirrels from the Kaibab Plateau; from Stewart's collection C. Hart Merriam described and named this squirrel *Sciurus kaibabensis*. Merriam stated that the Kaibab specimens he examined "differ strikingly from the well known Abert squirrel . . . [and were] scarce and wild" (ref. 4). Kaibab squirrels have black bodies with a snowy white tail. Abert's squirrels have white bellies, grayish ventral surfaces, and a gray tail on top with white fur underneath. Both subspecies have the rufous dorsal patch extending down their backs. A small population of Kaibab squirrels living in Grand Canyon National Park have white bellies typical of the Abert's squirrel and, conversely, black-bellied Abert's squirrels have been reported near Flagstaff (ref. 5, 6).

Kaibab squirrels have most likely been confined on the plateau since the Pleistocene epoch (ref. 7). Hoffmeister wrote in *Mammals of the Grand Canyon* that perhaps a small number of Abert's squirrels crossed the canyon and river, colonizing the North Rim, probably during the late Pleistocene (ref. 8). Another group of researchers wrote, "Collectively, the genetics, morphologic, and paleoclimatic data offer strong support for a late-Pleistocene origin for *S. a. kaibabensis* via northward dispersal from Arizona" (ref. 9). Based on analysis of mitochondrial DNA, it has been estimated that *S. a. aberti* and *S. a. kaibabensis* have been separated for 235,000 years (ref. 10).

The Kaibab squirrels have been described as "prisoners of geography" (ref. 11). A Natural Landmark Brief for the U.S. Department of the Interior, National Park Service, written in 1962, stated, "In a local way it is as significant as are the finches of the Galapagos Islands which gave Darwin key insights into the importance of isolation in evolution" (ref. 12).

In 1921, an article written by E. Hough in the *Saturday Evening Post*, titled *The President's Forest*, described a trip to the Kaibab Plateau. Hough was told he would see white-tailed squirrels. "I never expected to see a white-tailed squirrel any more than I expected to see a purple cow or pink deer. . . . Sure enough we passed a placard on a tree 'Range of white-tailed squirrel' . . . And sure enough again, the forest service made good on its sign in less than a quarter of a mile! Came a flash of white from under a fallen tree, and there crossed our road a smallish dark animal with a spectacular banner over its back" (ref. 13).

"The white-tailed squirrel is very showy and conspicuous, whether on the ground or in a tree. When on the ground, the large waving white tail may, at first glance, give the impression that the animal is a skunk, but its identity is quickly revealed in part by its agility and grace of movement," E. A. Goldman wrote in 1928 (ref. 14). An article in *Nature Magazine* described the Kaibab squirrel: "Next to the Canyon itself it is, in my opinion, the most distinctive thing in the park ... They are handsome squirrels and doubtless are the most photographed rodents in the nation ..." (ref. 15). And Hall described the Kaibab squirrel as "[o]ne of the most appealing, and incidentally, one of the rarest, mammals found in North America" (ref. 5).

Historical Overview of Kaibab Squirrel Protection

In 1893, President Benjamin Harrison established the Grand Canyon Forest Reserve within the Territory of Arizona, preventing anyone from making any settlements within the area (ref. 16). Although the proclamation also prevented entry into the area, except for authorized government officials, it was not until November 1906 that the animals living within the established boundaries became protected. This protection was accomplished when President Theodore Roosevelt established the Grand Canyon National Game Preserve, which was contained within the original forest reserve created by President Harrison (ref. 17). Roosevelt's proclamation specifically stated, "the President of the United States is hereby authorized to designate such areas in the Grand Canyon Forest Reserve as should, in his opinion, be set aside for the protection of game animals and be recognized as a breeding place." Section 2 of this Proclamation prohibited "hunting, trapping, or capturing of game animals" (ref. 17).

The boundaries of the Grand Canyon National Game Preserve are completely contained within the North Kaibab Ranger District of the Kaibab National Forest, which was created by an executive order of President Roosevelt in July 1908. The order stated, "It is not intended by this order to modify the proclamations heretofore issued establishing the Grand Canyon National Game Preserve" (ref. 18). The following animals were considered as nongame and thus not protected: "mountain lions, wolves, coyotes, wild cats, skunks, and rabbits" (ref. 19). Specifically the Kaibab squirrel was not one of the listed animals allowed to be hunted within the preserve, thus should be assumed to be excluded from hunting and therefore protected by this document.

Grand Canyon National Park was established in 1919, protecting all animals within its boundaries. The park shares a common boundary with the Kaibab National Forest and comprises approximately 10% of the range of the Kaibab squirrel.

In 1924, R. H. Rutledge, the district forester for the Kaibab National Forest, issued a Statement of Policy for the Administration of the Kaibab National Forest, in which he declared, "A general program for the development and maintenance of the value of the forest for recreation . . . will include the protection of the Kaibab squirrel to increase their numbers if possible" (ref. 20). In 1936, the Forest Service in its "Rules for Management of Wildlife on the Grand Canyon National Game Preserve" gave permission to the forest supervisor to authorize hunting of "porcupines, gophers, ground squirrels, skunks, wildcats, foxes, coyotes, mountain lions, and goshawks" (ref. 19). Again the Kaibab squirrel is excluded from this list and thus assumed to be protected.

The National Natural Landmark (NNL) designation suggested in 1962 was granted in October 1965 by the U.S. Department of the Interior to 800 km² of ponderosa pine forests (ref. 11). This area was referred to as Kaibab Squirrel Area NNL and was within the boundaries of the North Kaibab Forest and Grand Canyon National Park. Regional Forester William D. Hurst signed a timber management plan in June 1972 specifically stating, "In the Kaibab Squirrel Management Unit, timber production will be subordinate to squirrel habitat maintenance and improvement" (ref. 21). In April 1976, the U.S. Forest Service and the Arizona Game and Fish Commission (AZGFC) signed a cooperative agreement in which both parties agreed to develop and manage wildlife resources within the Kaibab National Forest "north of the Colorado River" (ref. 22). The management of habitat for wildlife species "is the responsibility of the Forest Service" (ref. 22).

Kaibab squirrels are protected within the North Rim boundary of Grand Canyon National Park, but since the AZGFC considers the Kaibab squirrel a small game animal, this squirrel is hunted within the North Kaibab National Forest—90% of its range—and in the Mt. Logan Wilderness Area from early October to December 31, with a bag limit of five squirrels/day (ref. 23).

Although the Kaibab squirrel lives nowhere else in the world, presently there are no accurate estimates of the number of Kaibab squirrels in existence, either in the Kaibab National Forest or Grand Canyon National Park. The reports that discuss Kaibab squirrel population size (table 10.1) are all rough estimates at best or, as Taylor admitted, "a wild guess" (ref. 24).

— TABLE 10.1 —

Population estimates for the Kaibab squirrel

Population Estimates	Researcher, year
4,800–9,600	Taylor, 1926b
2,900	Rasmussen, 1941
3,000–4,000	Hall, 1967b
1,000	Fisher et al., 1969
4,000 +	Webb, 1970 (cited by Rasmussen, 1971)
5,000 and 10,000	Hall, 1972
22,000	Turbak, 1987a

The Controversy of the Status—
Endangered or Threatened?

As early as 1924 there was concern that these squirrels might be in peril of extinction. Reports of raptors feasting on the squirrels led to investigation by Goldman of the Bureau of Biological Survey (BBS) (ref. 25). He traveled on horseback for eleven days through the ponderosa pine forests looking for squirrels and evidence of squirrel activity. He observed thirteen squirrels and saw many signs, such as chewed cones and terminal shoot ends from inner bark feeding activities. He concluded that Kaibab squirrels were not "in any real danger of extermination." The next year Goldman rode for thirteen days within the ponderosa pine forest looking for Kaibab squirrels. This time he observed only two squirrels and reported that feeding signs were also fewer. He noted that since it had been unusually dry no mushrooms were available and deer and livestock grazing had reduced the ground cover, thus making squirrels on the ground more vulnerable to raptor predation. He requested, as he had the year before, that when hawks were observed to have taken squirrels as prey that they be shot and their bodies sent to the BBS for inspection (ref. 26).

The following year a report filed by Taylor with the BBS stated that even though past reports had been made that suggested the possibility of extinction of the Kaibab squirrel because of their low numbers in the forest, nothing was observed "that indicates any danger of the white-tailed squirrel's extermination at this time." His report was based solely on observations of a forest ranger who had conducted a roadside census of Kaibab squirrels (ref. 27).

In a conservation article published in 1941 in *Audubon Magazine* titled "Our Rarer Mammals," Grover Allen wrote, "Owing to its striking and conspicuous coloration, this fine squirrel might easily become shot out but fortunately is now given a complete legal protection, so that its numbers are at present much increased over those of some years ago. At the same time, it should be remembered that its welfare depends also on that of the yellow pine, so that any impairment of the stands of this tree would endanger the squirrels as well" (ref. 28).

In May 1964, the controversy about the management of Kaibab squirrels was brought to the attention of the American people when the *Washington Post–Times Herald* and the *National Parks Magazine* each published articles attacking the decision by three of the five commissioners of the AZGFC to allow public hunting of the Kaibab squirrels for the first time (ref. 29).

The chairman of the Audubon Naturalist Society, I. R. Barnes, wrote a weekly column in the *Washington Post–Times Herald*. He used his column, "The Naturalist," to provoke public outrage at the May decision in June 1964, in an article he titled "Arizona gambles with the Kaibab squirrel." Barnes wrote, "This will be the first time in history that the Kaibab squirrel has not been fully protected. . . . [AZGFC] should rescind its decision to permit hunting of the rare Kaibab squirrel" (ref. 30). Within a week an editorial, "Exit the Kaibab Squirrel," continued the criticism in the same newspaper:

> One of the most attractive animals in the West is the Kaibab squirrel, which is found only in a narrow range along the North Rim of the Grand Canyon in Arizona. Tourists have traveled miles to watch these handsome little fellows scampering in the pines. Now the Arizona Game and Fish Commission in its wisdom has decided to declare an open season on Kaibab squirrels and let hunters kill one apiece. Since the Kaibabs are already extremely scarce, Arizona hunters will now slaughter the rest, or most of them. It is a commentary of the quality of humankind that men derive pleasure from killing anything so charming and harmless as a Kaibab squirrel, especially since the dead animal is not needed for its food or pelt. So the Kaibab squirrel will follow the Carolina parakeet, the passenger pigeon, and presently the whooping crane into oblivion in order that a few Arizonans may have the pleasure of shooting them. We hope that for every Kaibab squirrel shot, a score of tourists will give Arizona a wide berth. Perhaps the Arizona Game and Fish Commission will regret the destruction of one more natural asset. (ref. 31)

Later that summer an editorial titled "Assault on Common Sense" in *National Parks Magazine* maintained the criticism: "If an Oscar were to be awarded for the nation's unwisest decision of the year in the field of American game management, the Arizona Game and Fish Commission would probably qualify as front runner for 1964 to the date of this writing. The Commission has sanctioned an 8-day open season on the rare and scientifically important Kaibab squirrel . . . Readers of this Magazine who feel that the Kaibab squirrel ought to be completely protected at all times may write to the Honorable Paul Fannin, Governor of Arizona, State Capitol Building, Phoenix, Arizona, and tell him so" (ref. 32).

By August 1964, under the intense public criticism and pressure, the AZGFC rescinded the proposed hunt of Kaibab squirrels, turkeys, and Chukar partridges, stating that since the turkey population was too low, the entire hunt season was closed. The Kaibab squirrels received a reprieve, at least temporarily (ref. 33).

Even though the AZGFC rescinded the hunt, *Audubon Magazine*, in its November–December 1964 issue, continued the anti-hunting campaign with the article "Why Shoot the Kaibab Squirrel?"

> Because of its unusual markings, its evolutionary example, its extremely limited range and its rarity, *Sciurus kaibabensis* is a species of unusual interest to scientists all over the world . . . The Arizona Game and Fish Department seemed downright surprised when a storm of protest arose [over hunting of the Kaibab squirrel during the turkey hunting season]. On August 21 the commission announced that the entire hunt in the North Kaibab had been cancelled for 1964 because of a shortage of wild turkeys. Conservationists throughout the country breathed a sigh of relief. (ref. 34)

In 1965, Dodge wrote that he was very concerned that the AZGFC even considered allowing hunting of Kaibab squirrels and prophetically warned about "the possibility of a repetition in the future" (ref. 35).

At the 45th annual meeting of the American Society of Mammalogists in 1965, a resolution concerning the Kaibab squirrel was presented, which among other thing asked the U.S. Congress "to place the Kaibab squirrel under its protection as a species of national interest." Copies of this resolution relating to the Kaibab squirrel were sent to the governor of Arizona, the director and members of the AZGFC, the secretaries of Agriculture and the Interior, the chief of the U.S. Forest Service, and the director of the National Park Service (ref. 36). Dr. Joe Hall supported this resolution in a letter, stating that his opposition to hunting Kaibab squirrels was based on the low population numbers and inadequate field data on the squirrel's natural history and reproductive biology (ref. 36).

In a March 1967 memorandum to the forest supervisor of the Kaibab National Forest, William Hurst, the regional forester of Region 3, wrote, "The Forest Service has a moral, as well as a legal, obligation to protect this animal. Initially, we should outline his range as precisely as possible . . . every activity undertaken within his range should be carefully evaluated, giving the needs of the squirrel prime consideration. Coupled with this, we should search out all the information we can on his habitat requirements. If this information is inadequate, which I suspect it is, we should give leadership to a research program to learn more about the squirrel. There is undoubtedly, a limiting factor in his environment and we must learn what it is—and soon" (ref. 37). In a later memorandum Hurst was more specific in his request: "I am asking you to meet as a team and reflect in the Timber Management Plan now under development the adjustments necessary to protect the Kaibab squirrel habitat. For one thing, it would appear desirable to alter our objective of even age management on the North Kaibab. In addition, the harvesting process must assure leaving groups of trees that constitute the squirrels' feeding, nesting and protective habitat" (ref. 38).

The Kaibab squirrel was included in *The Red Book—Wildlife in Danger*, published by the Commission of the International Union for Conservation of Nature and Natural Resources, and in *Threatened Wildlife of the United States*, published by the U.S. Department of the Interior in 1973 (ref. 39, 40). The latter publication proposed continuation of complete legal protection, preservation of habitat (Gambel oaks and ponderosa pine), and encouragement of efforts to have a captive breeding program. Nothing came of the proposed measurements for protection of the Kaibab squirrel.

Presently there are no population studies on this unique tree squirrel. Loss of habitat caused by forest fires, logging activities, drought conditions, and hunting pressures certainly affect population numbers. Grand Canyon National Park serves as the only refuge for the Kaibab squirrels, since in 1984, twenty years after the AZGFC rescinded hunting, the prediction Dodge made in 1965 came true when Kaibab squirrel hunting was again approved, this time by a unanimous vote (ref. 41). Unfortunately, this time the decision was barely noted except by hunters.

Transplants of Kaibab Squirrels

Eight Kaibab squirrels (one male and seven females) were transplanted by the AZGFD to Mt. Logan, Arizona, during the spring of 1972 (ref. 42). The objective of this transplantation was to stock Mt. Logan with twenty to forty Kaibab squirrels obtained from the Kaibab National Forest. No tassel-eared squirrels were on Mt. Logan and "a successful introduction meant that the Kaibab subspecies would not be restricted to one geographical locale" (ref. 43). By 1977, twenty-one Kaibab squirrels had been released in the Mt. Logan area (ref. 42, 43). This transplant project was successful. Kaibab squirrels were sighted by AZGFD personnel in 2008 (ref. 44).

Summary

The importance of habitat for the Kaibab squirrel was summarized by Joe Hall: "*Pinus ponderosa* is to the Kaibab squirrel both the alpha and the omega. If their life history, which now bristles with unsolved riddles, is eventually better understood, the understanding will no doubt hinge on intricacies of the give-and-take between white tails and yellow pines" (ref. 45). Kaibab squirrels are unique animals living on the sky island of the Kaibab Plateau. Kaibab squirrels have over the years received more attention in the press than any other squirrel because of their visual appeal and more importantly because of the controversy regarding their possible threatened or endangered status. Since we do not have accurate information on Kaibab squirrel numbers, hunting of them should be prohibited by the AZGFC.

Future Research

(1) Conducting a population survey of Kaibab squirrels in the Kaibab National Forest and Grand Canyon National Park is a top priority. (2) Another research area is an examination of effects on the Kaibab squirrel of lost habitat due to fires and thinning within the Kaibab National Forest and Grand Canyon National Park. (3) It must be determined whether the Kaibab squirrel needs protection.

In the spring of 2009 the National Natural Landmark program presented a bronze plaque to the Kaibab Plateau Visitor Center in recognition of this unique North American squirrel (ref. 46).

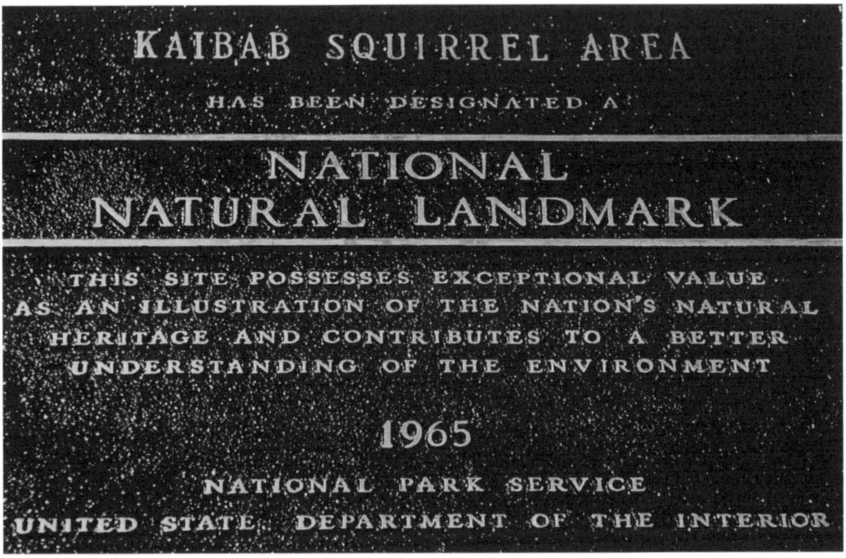

FIGURE 10.1 Plaque designating the Kaibab Squirrel Area a Natural National Landmark. Photograph by Sylvester Allred.

References for Chapter Ten

1. Dutton, C. E. 1882. Tertiary History of the Grand Canyon, with Atlas. Washington, DC: U.S. Geological Survey.
2. Rasmussen, D. I. 1941. Biotic communities of the Kaibab Plateau, Arizona. *Ecological Monographs* 11:229–75.
3. Hall, J. G. 1981. A field study of the Kaibab squirrel in Grand Canyon National Park. *Wildlife Monographs* 75.
4. Merriam, C. H. 1904. Two new squirrels of the *aberti* group. *Proceedings of Biological Society of Washington* 17:129–30.
5. Hall, J. G. 1967b. The Kaibab squirrel in Grand Canyon National Park— a seven seasons summary—1960–1967. Grand Canyon, AZ: Grand Canyon National Park.
6. Allred, W. S. 1995. Black-bellied form of an Abert squirrel (*Sciurus aberti aberti*) from the San Francisco Peaks area, Arizona. *Southwestern Naturalist* 40:420.
7. MacClintock, D. 1970. Squirrels of North America. New York: Van Nostrand Reinhold Co.
8. Hoffmeister, D. F. 1971. Mammals of the Grand Canyon. Chicago: University of Illinois Press.
9. Lamb, T., T. R. Jones, and P. J. Wettstein. 1997. Evolutionary genetics and phylogeography of tassel-eared squirrels (*Sciurus aberti*). *Journal of Mammalogy* 78 (1): 117–33.

10. Wettstein, P. J., R. Chakraborty, J. States, and G. Ferrari. 1990. T-cell receptor genes in tassel-eared squirrels (*Sciurus aberti*). I. Genetic polymorphism and divergence in the Abert and Kaibab subspecies. *Immunogenetics* 32:219–30.

11. Turbak, G. 1987a. Prisoner of geography. *National Wildlife* 25 (2): 14–16.

12. Salyer, J. C. 1962. Kaibab squirrel—Kaibab Plateau pine forest, Arizona. Evaluation for Natural Landmark Designation. U.S. Fish and Wildlife Service (copy in author's file).

13. Hough, E. 1921. The president's forest. *Saturday Evening Post* 194:6–7.

14. Goldman, E. A. 1928. The Kaibab or white-tailed squirrel. *Journal of Mammalogy* 9:127–29.

15. McCartney, E. S. 1937. Calling on the Kaibab squirrel. *Nature Magazine* 29 (5): 271–72.

16. Proclamation by the President [Benjamin Harrison] of the United States to create the Grand Canyon Game Reserve, February 20, 1893. http://memory.loc.gov/ammem/amrvhtml/conshome.html.

17. Proclamation by the President [Theodore Roosevelt] of the United States to create the Grand Canyon Game Preserve, November 28, 1906. U.S. Statutes at Large 34:3263. http://memory.loc.gov/ammem/amrvhtml/conshome.html.

18. Executive Order of the President [Theodore Roosevelt] of the United States to create the Kaibab National Forest, July 2, 1908. Monthly Catalogue, July. United States Public Documents, no. 163. Washington, DC: U.S. Government Printing Office. http://memory.loc.gov/ammem/amrvhtml/conshome.html.

19. Miller, R. 1996. History of the intent and management of the Grand Canyon Game Preserve. Unpublished report prepared for Arizona Game and Fish Department, Flagstaff (copy in author's files).

20. Rutledge, R. H. 1924. Statement of policy for the administration of the Kaibab National Forest (copy in author's files).

21. Hurst, W. D. 1972. Timber management plan, North Kaibab block, Kaibab National Forest, Region 3 (copy in author's files).

22. USDA Forest Service, 1976. Cooperative agreement with Arizona Game and Fish Commission (copy in author's files).

23. Arizona Game and Fish Department. 2008. 2008–2009 Arizona Hunting and Trapping Regulations. Phoenix: AZGFD.

24. Taylor, W. P. 1924c. Progress report on animal forest work, Division of Biological Investigations, Bureau of Biological Survey. Conducted in cooperation with the Southwestern Forest Experiment Station, Flagstaff, Arizona. Smithsonian Institution Archives, record unit 7176, box 29, folder 14.

25. Goldman, E. A. 1924. Report on conditions affecting the Kaibab squirrel (August 16–26, 1924). Smithsonian Institution Archives, record unit 7176, box 25, folder 4.

26. Goldman, E. A. 1925. Memorandum concerning the Kaibab squirrel (June 6–18, 1925). Smithsonian Institution Archives, record unit 7176, box 25, folder 9.

27. Taylor, W. P. 1926b. Memorandum of the White-Tailed Squirrel (*Sciurus kaibabensis*) of the Grand Canyon National Game Preserve. Division of Biological Investigations, Bureau of Biological Survey, U.S. Department of Agriculture. Smithsonian Institution Archives, record unit 7176, box 29, folder 19.

28. Allen, G. M. 1941. Our rarer mammals. *Audubon Magazine* 43 (March–April): 151–60.

29. Arizona Game and Fish Commission. 1964a. Minutes and proceedings, May 23 (copy in author's files).

30. Barnes, I. R. 1964. Arizona gambles with the Kaibab squirrel. The Naturalist. *Washington Post–Times Herald*, June 28.

31. Exit the Kaibab squirrel. 1964. *Washington Post–Times Herald*, editorial, July 5.

32. Assault on common sense. 1964. August. *National Parks* 38:16.

33. Arizona Game and Fish Commission. 1964b. Minutes and proceedings, August 15 (copy in author's files).

34. Buchheister, C. W. 1964. Why shoot the Kaibab squirrel? *Audubon Magazine*, November–December, 359–60.

35. Dodge, N. N. 1965. Whitetail squirrel. *Pacific Discovery* 18:23–26.

36. American Society of Mammalogists. 1965. Report of Conservation of Land Mammals Committee, 1965, 45th annual meeting, Winnipeg, Manitoba, Canada (copy in author's files).

37. Hurst, W. D. 1967. Memorandum—wildlife habitat management. U.S. Department of Agriculture, Forest Service (copy in author's files provided by William Hurst).

38. Hurst, W. D. 1971. Memorandum—Kaibab squirrel study. U.S. Department of Agriculture, Forest Service (copy in author's files provided by William Hurst).

39. Fisher, J., N. Simon, and J. Vincent. 1969. The Red Book—Wildlife in Danger. London: Collins.

40. U.S. Department of the Interior. 1973. Threatened Wildlife of the United States. Resource Publication 114 (Revised Resource Publication 34). Washington, DC: U.S. Government Printing Office.

41. Arizona Game and Fish Commission. 1984. Minutes and proceedings, April 28 (copy in author's files).

42. Brown, D. E., and J. W. Evans. 1972. Kaibab squirrel stocking. Progress Report. Project W-53-R-22, work plan 6, job 4. Phoenix: Arizona Game and Fish Department.
43. Brown, D. E. 1986. Arizona's Tree Squirrels. Phoenix: Arizona Game and Fish Department.
44. Goodwin, John. AZGFD. Personal communication.
45. Hall, J. G. 1967a. White tails and yellow pines. *National Parks* 41:9–11.
46. Kaibab National Forest. 2009. News Release. www.fs.fed.us/r3/kai.

11

ECOLOGY

Tassel-eared squirrels were fairly common in the yellow pine association, and were most active early in the morning. . . . The squirrels were feeding on the bark of the yellow pine twigs and the ground under several young trees was covered with branch-tips. . . . One was seen chased by the much smaller chickaree.

—J. E. Hill, "Notes on Mammals of
Northeastern New Mexico," 1942

*This chapter is dedicated to Dr. Jim Keith for
all of his research with Abert's squirrels.*

Introduction

The importance of the relationship between the tassel-eared squirrel and the ponderosa pine forest was first noted in 1925 when Taylor stated, "Its attractive presence could ill be spared from the woods" (ref. 1). Bailey wrote of a conversation he had regarding tassel-eared squirrels on the South Rim of the Grand Canyon: "[T]he gardener at El Tovar Hotel told me he saw one of the big squirrels bring the cone of a yellow pine into the hotel flower garden and bury it among his snapdragons. This seems to fix the storing habit among these squirrels sufficiently to place them on the list of useful tree planters" (ref. 2). Later Bailey wrote again about the importance of squirrels and their cone-burying habits: "If it were not for the squirrels, the pine cones would lie on the ground or scatter their seeds to be eaten by mice and jays. Consequently, although many branches are trimmed and many seeds are eaten by these small tenants of the forest, it is still evident that they are great planters and thus conservators, of the forest trees on which they depend for their living" (ref. 3). Abert's squirrels bury pine cones with their "legs rapidly cross-ing and re-crossing with their familiar covering up and patting down motions" (ref. 4). Tassel-eared squirrels are considered to be beneficial to the forest because they act as "seed spreaders" (ref. 5). When green ovu-late cones are buried by squirrels and not later located and eaten, many seeds may germinate (ref. 6).

All the feeding activities of tassel-eared squirrels, obligate herbivores in ponderosa pine forests, from digging for false truffles to consuming seeds from ovulate cones, directly affect the forests (ref. 7). Digging opens the litter layer to the parent soils while seed eating can in some cases elim-inate an entire tree's reproductive effort for a year. Feeding on inner bark with the concomitant loss of green needles influences nutrient cycling. Numerous ecological studies have examined the complex relationship between the tassel-eared squirrels and the ponderosa pine forests.

Ecology of Tassel-Eared Squirrels and Ponderosa Pines

Tassel-Eared Squirrels and Ponderosa Pine Tree Morbidity and Mortality

Tree mortality due to defoliation of ponderosa pine trees by tassel-eared squirrels as they feed on inner bark has been evaluated in a number of studies with differing conclusions. Taylor reported excessive defolia-tion by squirrels during their feeding activities to be rare. He examined 942 trees and noted that only three trees appeared to be severely dam-aged and that "branch-cutting" activities could be beneficial or neutral to the tree rather than being considered harmful (ref. 8). Two years later Taylor wrote, "One tree was observed from which most of the foliage had been trimmed by squirrels. As with the Abert most of the work of the white-tail [Kaibab] was apparently diffuse . . . if the animals did become superabundant they might do serious damage to the western yellow pine, through their branch-cutting and cone-scaling activities" (ref. 9). In another report the next year, Taylor wrote that squirrels "ordinarily do little damage but in a few areas squirrels have defoliated and caused the death of some trees" (ref. 10).

Hall attributed the death of one ponderosa pine tree to squirrel clip-ping activities but he cautioned that this was an isolated case in all of his work with the Kaibab squirrel over ten years. He noted that trees that had been fed on by Kaibab squirrels for inner bark did show a difference

PLATE 1   Col. Abert's squirrel by John Woodhouse Audubon. Plate 153 from the first octavo edition of *The Quadrupeds of North America*. Hand-colored stone lithograph by J. T. Bowen, 1854. Used by permission of Minniesland.com, LLC.

PLATE 2   Dr. Samuel W. Woodhouse, 1854. Courtesy of Museum of Northern Arizona Photo Archives (Negative Number MS 189-1-5).

PLATE 3   San Francisco Peaks in northern Arizona where Dr. Woodhouse first discovered and named the Abert's squirrel. Photograph by Sylvester Allred.

PLATE 4 Distinctive tassels at the tips of the ears of an Abert's squirrel during the fall. Photograph by Steve Mull. Used with permission.

PLATE 5 Absence of tassels during summer of an Abert's squirrel. Photograph by Steve Mull. Used with permission.

PLATE 6   Distinctive white eye rings, agouti-colored face, white chest, and black vibrissae of an Abert's squirrel. Photograph by Steve Mull. Used with permission.

PLATE 7 Rufous-colored dorsal patch, agouti dorsal sides, grayish-white tail of an Abert's squirrel. Photograph by Steve Mull. Used with permission.

PLATE 8 Melanistic Abert's squirrel from the South Rim of the Grand Canyon. Photograph by Steve Mull. Used with permission.

PLATE 9   Kaibab squirrel from North Rim of the Grand Canyon.
Photograph by Sylvester Allred.

PLATE 10   Variations in the pelage colors of S. a. ferreus from Colorado.
Photograph taken at the zoological collection of the Denver Museum of Nature
and Science by Sylvester Allred.

PLATE 11   Juvenile melanistic Abert's squirrel taken at South Rim of the Grand Canyon. Photograph by Steve Mull. Used with permission.

PLATE 12   Re-curved claws on the feet of an Abert's squirrel. Photograph by Steve Mull. Used with permission.

PLATE 13   Ideal ponderosa pine forest habitat for tassel-eared squirrels with a mix of tree sizes and interlocking canopies with some open spaces. Photograph by Sylvester Allred.

PLATE 14   Unsuitable ponderosa pine habitat for tassel-eared squirrels due to the homogeneous stand and no interlocking canopies. Photograph by Sylvester Allred.

PLATE 15   A feed tree in the foreground compared to a non-feed tree in the background. Photograph by Sylvester Allred.

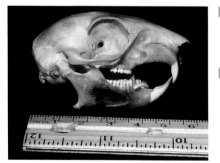

PLATE 16 (Above) Abert's squirrel selecting branch for feeding in ponderosa pine tree. Photograph by Bill Noble. Used with permission.

PLATE 17 (Left) Skull of an Abert's squirrel. Photograph taken at the Museum of Vertebrate Zoology at University of California–Berkeley by Sylvester Allred.

PLATE 18 Early spring feeding signs of tassel-eared squirrels with clipped terminal shoots, peeled twigs, and intact terminal buds. Photograph by Sylvester Allred.

PLATE 19 Numerous terminal shoots discarded by feeding tassel-eared squirrels during the winter. Photograph by Sylvester Allred.

Abert's squirrel feeding in tree. Photograph by Sylvester Allred.

Peeled twigs from inner bark feeding by tassel-eared squirrels. Photograph by Sylvester Allred.

PLATE 24   Ponderosa pine staminate (pollen) cones. Photograph by Sylvester Allred.

PLATE 25   Bark grazing on a ponderosa pine branch infected with dwarf mistletoe. Photograph by Sylvester Allred.

PLATE 26 Abert's squirrel eating juniper berries. Photograph by Steve Mull. Used with permission.

PLATE 27   Kaibab squirrel eating acorns in a Gambel's oak tree. Photograph by Sylvester Allred.

PLATE 28   Acorns of the Gambel's oak tree. Photograph by Sylvester Allred.

PLATE 29 False truffles (*Rhizopogon ochracerubens*) in the litter layer of the ponderosa pine forest. Photograph by Jack States. Used with permission.

PLATE 30 A squirrel dig in the litter layer in the ponderosa pine forest. Photograph by Sylvester Allred.

Abert's squirrel eating a false truffle. Photograph by Steve Mull. Used with permission.

PLATE 32 A mushroom (*Russula sp.*) in the ponderosa pine forest. Photograph by Sylvester Allred.

PLATE 33 A mushroom placed in a ponderosa pine tree by a tassel-eared squirrel. Photograph by Sylvester Allred.

PLATE 34 Abert's squirrel drinking from a water source. Photograph by Steve Mull. Used with permission.

PLATE 35 Nest clipping materials beneath tassel-eared squirrel nest. Note the longer branch component. Photograph by Sylvester Allred.

PLATE 36 Tassel-eared squirrel bolus nest. Note placement and interlocking canopies of other trees. Photograph by Sylvester Allred.

PLATE 37 (Inset) Tassel-eared squirrel bolus nest in a Gambel's oak tree. Photograph by Sylvester Allred.

PLATE 38 (Above) Cavity in a Gambel's oak tree. Potential nest site of tassel-eared squirrels. Photograph by Sylvester Allred.

PLATE 39 Abert's squirrel grooming. Photograph by Steve Mull. Used with permission.

PLATE 40 Winter scene in a ponderosa pine forest with squirrel tracks.
Photograph by Sylvester Allred.

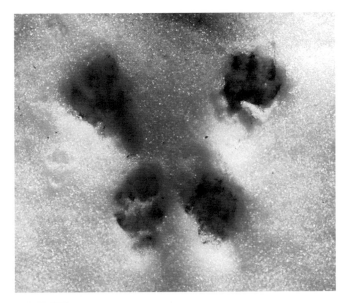

PLATE 41   Abert's squirrel tracks in the snow. Photograph by Sylvester Allred.

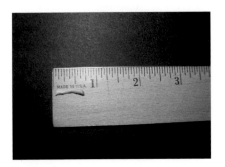

PLATE 42   Tassel-eared squirrel baculum. Photograph taken at the zoological collection of the Denver Museum of Nature and Science by Sylvester Allred.

PLATE 43   Abert's squirrel sitting after crossing the road. Photograph by Sylvester Allred.

PLATE 44   Lactating Abert's squirrel. Photograph by Steve Mull. Used with permission.

PLATE 45   Very young Abert's squirrels found on the ground near nest tree after their mother was killed by a car. Photograph by Sylvester Allred.

PLATE 46 Female goshawk feeding young. Photograph by David Ponton and Patricia L. Kennedy. Used with permission.

PLATE 47   Mature ponderosa pine ovulate cones lost from tree during inner bark feeding activities. Photograph by Sylvester Allred.

PLATE 49   Ponderosa pine seedlings sprouting from buried cone not located by tassel-eared squirrel. Photograph by Sylvester Allred.

PLATE 48   Immature cones (conelets) on ponderosa pine terminal shoot. Photograph by Sylvester Allred.

PLATE 50   Oak seedling that sprouted from a buried acorn. Photograph by Sylvester Allred.

PLATE 51   A "backyard tassel-eared squirrel" in Flagstaff, Arizona. As the ponderosa pine forest is encroached upon, squirrels frequently interface with city residents. Photograph by Sylvester Allred.

PLATE 52 Scarlet macaw feathers from Mexico are attached to a tassel-eared squirrel pelt from the Utah area in this ceremonial skirt, which would be tied with the buckskin straps on the sides. This 900+-year-old artifact is further described in appendix 4. Photograph by Sylvester Allred from the Edge of the Cedars State Park Museum, Blanding, Utah. Used with permission.

in growth though the difference was small when total tree growth was considered. He concluded that defoliation induced by squirrel herbivory was not significant if the feed trees were in prime habitat (ref. 11).

In a study of effects of herbivory of an introduced population of Kaibab squirrels to Mt. Trumbull, tree rings were used to determine that prior to the introduction, feed trees had more growth than non-feed trees. The study concluded that defoliation by squirrel herbivory "may place considerable stress on ecotonal forests" (ref. 12).

A 1942 article reported that "one or two trees were obviously at the point of death due to continued defoliation by squirrels" (ref. 13). In 1950, G. A. Pearson at the Fort Valley Experimental Station near Flagstaff, Arizona, wrote in *Management of the Ponderosa Pine in the Southwest* that few trees had been killed by squirrel herbivory, but trees that were heavily fed upon could be further damaged or weakened and be susceptible to damage by insects such as Pandora moths (*Coloradia pandora*) and bark beetles (*Dendroctonus* sp.) (ref. 14). The authors of a 1970 study of ponderosa pine cone crops in Arizona mentioned only one tree in their study that was killed by tassel-eared squirrel herbivory (ref. 15).

Ponderosa pine trees that are heavily defoliated by squirrels as they feed on inner bark have decreased photosynthetic activity. The resulting decrease causes the tree to produce less glucose, with a concomitant decrease in nutrition necessitating longer feeding times by squirrels to obtain the same amount of nutrition from that tree. This inefficiency could possibly cause the squirrels to abandon that tree for more nutritious trees since this places a time-energy constraint on the squirrels (ref. 16).

A study of green foliage losses due to Abert's squirrel herbivory compared to foliage losses of ponderosa pines during snowstorms was conducted in northern Arizona. During heavy snowstorms trees are often killed by having their trunks bend and break whereas no trees in this study were killed by squirrel herbivory, though 166 trees were killed by two snowstorms during one year. In a forest stand of 5.6 ha, 1.4% of the entire green biomass was lost in five days in a single snowstorm. In this four-year study, during a year when squirrels consumed the most inner bark because no ovulate cones were produced, loss of green needles to squirrel herbivory was 1.1% for the entire year (ref. 17).

Pearson wrote, "rodents are an important factor in retarding pine regeneration, beginning as they do with the seed supply" (ref. 14). M. M. Larson and G. H. Schubert stated, in a ten-year cone crop study that examined the influence of Abert's squirrels on cone production of 241 ponderosa pine trees that were over 30 cm dbh, "Abert squirrels are extremely destructive to cone crops . . . only the largest and best cones were taken by squirrels." Ovulate cone production was reduced by 20% by squirrels over the ten-year study. In addition, immature ovulate cones (conelets) lost to terminal shoot removal by squirrels were observed, but the researchers concluded that the conelet loss was not serious to the overall reproductive loss to the trees (ref. 15). A fourteen-month study in ten ponderosa pine stands in central Arizona reached the same conclusion regarding conelet losses due to squirrel herbivory: "Squirrels . . . are insignificant predators of ponderosa pine conelets during the developmental stage" (ref. 18). Rather than squirrels, ponderosa pine cone beetles (*Conophthorus ponderosae*), ponderosa pine-cone worms (*Dioryctria* sp.), and abortion were found to be the major factors in conelet mortality (ref. 18).

Twig-clipping activities for inner bark consumption by Abert's squirrels were observed for twenty-five months in a ponderosa pine stand at Lowell Observatory in Flagstaff, Arizona. Of the nearly 60,000 terminal shoots lost from trees by twig-clipping squirrels, almost 9% had conelets attached. There were an additional 1,800 unattached conelets in the litter beneath the trees. Twenty percent of the cone crop was estimated to be lost when conelet-bearing pine shoots and individually excised conelets were removed during inner bark consumption (ref. 19).

A personal observation by an ecologist in Flagstaff was shared with me in 2009: "I just observed [an Abert's squirrel] stripping the leaves and bark from a section of a ponderosa seedling about 4 m outside my office window. I went outside and found needles, small pieces of outer bark, and the stripped cut section. I also found a fresh cut on a seedling about 4 m from where s/he was. The seedling was about 20 cm tall and multibranched, so this particular seedling will survive the loss of a branch, but my previous observations indicate that [tassel-eared squirrels] also decapitate ponderosa seedlings" (ref. 20).

Alternation of Feed Tree Selection

Pearson observed tassel-eared squirrels alternating their twig clipping between trees over several years, in effect rotating the use of feed trees (ref. 14). However, Larson and Schubert in 1970 found that squirrels clipped the same trees from one year to the next (ref. 15). A few years later, another study provided data supporting Pearson's original observations, that there was an alternation of trees between years. This study lasted four years and involved 1,300 trees (ref. 21). Tassel-eared squirrels on study sites in Colorado alternated tree use over the years (ref. 22). Most studies reflect an alternation of feed tree selection.

Tassel-Eared Squirrels as Agents of Selection of Ponderosa Pine Trees

Abert's squirrels have been proposed as possible mediators in the natural selection process of ponderosa pine trees since their herbivory could potentially decrease the fitness (an individual contribution to the gene pool of future generations) of some trees by removal of staminate and ovulate cones as well as affect the overall growth of the tree. It was argued that this influence might not be negative since other herbivores, such as insects, also feed on ponderosa pines, and a combination of differing genetic polymorphisms within the forest stand could be beneficial overall (ref. 22, 23).

Feed tree selection by *S. a. aberti* in Arizona and *S. a. ferreus* in Colorado was compared in a 1998 study. The trees in the two states were substantially different in their biochemistry, and feed trees were chemically different from non-feed trees, leading the authors to conclude, "The results presented here provide evidence of geographical differentiation of squirrel-pine interactions, and imply that such differentiation can lead to different evolutionary outcomes" (ref. 24).

Nitrogen Cycling

Nitrogen cycling resulting from increased green-needle litter from tassel-eared squirrel herbivory was examined in a one-year study. The majority of the nitrogen (82%) was in the lost green needles caused by squirrel pruning during feeding. Feed trees had more than 15 kg/ha/year of foliage transferred to the litter layer when compared to non-feed trees, which lost 9.0 kg/ha/year of foliage. The highest amounts of herbivory occurred toward the end of winter continuing into the spring, which coincided with the highest levels of nitrogen in the trees' tissues (ref. 25).

Nitrogen and green foliage losses decreased 62% (80 kg/ha to 30 kg/ha) from ponderosa pine trees when abundant cones were available. One tree with a dbh of 39.0 cm (selected because it had the largest number of terminal shoots removed) had its effective photosynthetic canopy reduced to the size expected of a tree with a dbh of 33.0 cm, a reduction in photosynthetic surface area of 15% (ref. 26). Nitrogen loss from the ponderosa pine trees, however, certainly benefits understory vegetation and neighboring

— TABLE 11.1 —

Measurements of five elements found in tassel-eared
squirrel–induced green litter (% dry weight of the foliage)
(Allred et al., 1987)

Nitrogen	Phosphorus	Potassium	Magnesium	Calcium
1.2	0.14	0.52	0.11	0.96

trees. In another nutrient cycling study, squirrel-induced green litter was collected and analyzed for five elements. The induced litter averaged 91 g/ feed tree on a 1.5-ha study plot (table 11.1) (ref. 27).

Ecology of Tassel-Eared Squirrel Digs

Abert's squirrels dig in the forest litter layer and into the soil for recovery of false truffles, buried ovulate cones, and acorns, displacing soil in the process. Forests are benefitted by tassel-eared squirrels as they excavate soil in their foraging activities. These digs provide places for litter to collect, for seeds to germinate, and for spiders to construct webs, thus creating microhabitats. Digs provide water channels into the soil through the litter layer, allowing faster movement of water into the root zone. Soil displacement redistributes nutrients and promotes inoculation of pine roots by mycorrhizal spores found in the fecal pellets of squirrels (ref. 28).

Ecology of Tassel-Eared Squirrels and Fungi

Mycorrhizal fungi live in a mutualistic relationship with ponderosa pine roots. In this type of relationship both parties derive a benefit. The fungi encase the pine roots with sheaths that act like sponges to absorb and store water and nutrients, which are available for use by the tree. The fungi are provided a habitat on the tree's roots and glucose from photosynthesis. Unlike epigeous fungi (mushrooms) with above-ground spores that are easier to disperse, mycorrhizal fungi are hypogeous with their spore-filled fruiting bodies (false truffles), produced beneath the litter layer, preventing easy spore dispersal.

Squirrels consume false truffles by digging beneath the blackjack pines where the truffles are more abundant. As squirrels free-range within the forest, their fecal pellets, containing between two hundred million and one billion mycorrhizal spores/g of fecal material, are scattered through the forest. Spores are not affected by passage through the GI tract of squirrels; thus squirrels serve as mycorrhizal spore vectors.

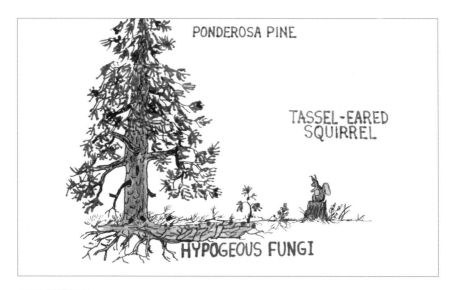

FIGURE 11.1 Tassel-eared squirrel, hypogeous fungi, and ponderosa pine interactive model. Drawn by J. S. States. Used with permission.

When these hypogeous fungi spores contact pine roots, they form new mycorrhizal associations with the trees (ref. 29, 30).

In 1985, Jack States, a mycologist at Northern Arizona University, clearly demonstrated that ingestion of fungi as a food resource (mycophagy) by squirrels distributes spores of six different hypogeous fungi (ref. 31). Another study proposed that forest and fungi successional stages are assisted by squirrel mycophagy because squirrels spread the new species' spores within the forest (ref. 32).

Therefore, the three organisms (tree, squirrel, fungi) provide for each other through their tripartite relationship (ref. 29, 30, 33, 34). Disturbance of one member will eventually result in the disturbance of the other two. False truffles are specifically clustered under the more dense canopies of blackjack ponderosa pines rather than under the mature yellow pines (ref. 35). This positive correlation with canopy cover and hypogeous fungi production should be considered with any management practices conducted within ponderosa pines forests.

Tassel-Eared Squirrel Interactions with Other Animals

Tassel-eared squirrel introductions by AZGF in the 1940s correlated to reduced numbers of Mt. Graham red squirrels (*Tamiasciurus hudsonicus grahamensis*), an endangered species, in the Pinaleño Mountains in southern Arizona. The reduction of red squirrels is attributed to competition for food resources with tassel-eared squirrels (ref. 36, 37). There is concern that tassel-eared squirrels might eventually competitively exclude the Mt. Graham red squirrel (ref. 36). In a study in Colorado, red squirrels (*T. h. fremonti*) and tassel-eared squirrels interacted at the interfaces of ponderosa pine and Douglas fir trees. Tassel-eared squirrels were observed feeding on Douglas fir cones that had been previously cut by red squirrels, and red squirrels were observed feeding on ponderosa pine cones (ref. 38). Kaibab squirrels and red squirrels were observed in competition within ponderosa pine forests at Grand Canyon National Park. Hall wrote in 1981, "I noted that the 2 species are intolerant of each other and . . . that in about three-fourths of the confrontations the smaller red squirrel took the role of aggressor and drove off the Kaibab squirrel" (ref. 11).

Another Mt. Graham study reported that competition between Mt. Graham red squirrels and tassel-eared squirrels was reduced because red squirrels nested in smaller diameter trees, built and nested in nests lower in the trees, tended to select nest trees in areas of greater tree density, and used a variety of nest types (bolus, cavity, and ground) (ref. 39). In the most recent study at Mt. Graham, it was found that *T. h. grahamensis* were very interactive with tassel-eared squirrels in mixed stands of conifers such as ponderosa pines, Douglas firs, lodgepole pines, and spruce trees. Red squirrels chased tassel-eared squirrels from their middens (ref. 40). A recent study suggests that Abert's squirrels could negatively affect Mt. Graham red squirrels directly by competing for food and shelter resources and indirectly by increasing the number of avian predators (ref. 41).

S. a. ferreus and eastern fox squirrels (*S. niger*), considered an exotic species, interface in some of the mountains in Colorado, but population levels of *S. niger* are low and do not at this time appear to be a threat to tassel-eared squirrels because they are not in direct competition for resources (ref. 42). As a result of introductions of fifty-four *S. a. aberti* by AZGFD during the early 1940s into the Catalina Mountains, Lange speculated that Arizona gray squirrels (*S. arizonensis catalinae*) living there may have been adversely affected (ref. 43).

A 1938 U.S. Forest Service paper titled "The case against the tuft-eared squirrel" gave seven conclusions regarding tassel-eared squirrels and ponderosa pine forests. One conclusion was that the squirrels "destroy young birds and eggs, which in the case of insectivorous

— TABLE 11.2 —
Observations of direct or indirect interactions between tassel-eared squirrels and other animals

Researcher, year	Observation
Mearns, 1907	observed a tassel-eared squirrel claim Steller's jay's (*Cyanocitta stelleri*) nest and build a nest on top of it
Ligon, 1927	cautioned that if pregnant cows ate the green needles clippings from squirrel herbivory, the calves might have problems (note: this is the only report in the literature relating harmful effects of ingestion of green needles)
F. M. Bailey, 1932	observed a Mearns' woodpecker (*Melanerpes formicivorus*) chase a tassel-eared squirrel from the woodpecker's acorn cache in an old yellow ponderosa
McKee, 1934	observed an Abert squirrel and a raven fighting over a tray of pinyon nuts; the squirrel chased the raven away
F. M. Bailey, 1939	numerous observations between Steller's jays and ravens with regard to foods and caching of foods
Seton, 1953	observed an Abert squirrel raiding the seed caches of *M. formicivorus*
Keith, 1956	observed a chipmunk (*Eutamias sp.*) that used an abandoned Abert's squirrel nest to raise its young
Keith, 1956	observed western bluebirds (*Sialia mexicanna*) preventing Abert's squirrels from climbing trees where the birds had built their nests
Sutton and Sutton, 1970; Allred (unpublished observation)	observed fallen green needle clusters resulting from tassel-eared squirrel herbivory being fed upon by jackrabbits during winters when heavy snow accumulations prevented the jackrabbits from foraging on other plants
Sutton and Sutton, 1970	observed porcupines using abandoned tassel-eared squirrel nests as resting platforms
Hall, 1981	observed two "encounters" of Kaibab squirrels with a coyote and a bobcat
D. E. Brown, 1986	observed tassel-eared squirrels competing with thick-billed parrots (*Rhynchopsitta pachyrhyncha*) for cavities in pine snags created by woodpeckers, in the Sierra Madre Occidental, Mexico
Allred (unpublished observation)	observed a Kaibab squirrel with three porcupine quills in her nose
D. and M. Best, personal communication	observed mule deer eating fallen needle clusters on the top of snow from tassel-eared squirrel herbivory

— TABLE 11.3 —

Causes attributed to population fluctuations in tassel-eared squirrels

Cause	Researcher, year
Physical condition entering the winter season	Keith, 1965
Juvenile recruitment	Farentinos, 1972c
Food quality	Patton, 1974a; States et al., 1988
Cover	Patton, 1975b
Severity of the winter	Stephenson and Brown, 1980
Suitable habitat	Pederson et al., 1987

birds affects protection of the trees from insects" (ref. 44). Table 11.2 lists numerous observations relating to direct and indirect interactions between tassel-eared squirrels and other animals.

Population Ecology

A population density study in the spring of 1970 on tassel-eared squirrels at a 72-ha study plot in Colorado determined that there were 3.33 squirrels/10 ha (n = 24). During the fall the density increased to 5.56 squirrels/10 ha (n = 40). This increase was attributed to increased recruitment of juveniles after the spring reproductive season. One-half of the forty squirrels were juveniles. During the winter the population declined dramatically to 3.06 squirrels/10 ha (n = 22). This data demonstrates population fluctuation over the course of a year (ref. 45). Previous studies over the past century on population levels have described tassel-eared populations ranging from abundant to rare and declining. Wide fluctuations in squirrel numbers have been attributed to numerous causes (table 11.3).

Patton developed a life table for a cohort of fifty-eight Kaibab squirrels. This, the only tassel-eared squirrel life table ever developed, followed the squirrels for over six years (table 11.4) (ref. 46).

Summary

As one member of the well-described squirrel–mycorrhizal fungi–ponderosa pine triad, tassel-eared squirrels are integral to the stable ecology of the ponderosa pine forest. These animals are crucial at every

— TABLE 11.4 —
Life table for fifty-eight *S. a. kaibabensis*, sexes combined[1]

Age (x) (years)	Frequency fx[2]	Survival lx[3]	Mortality (dx)	Mortality Rate (qx)	Survival Rate
0–1	58	1000	552	0.552	0.448
1–2	26	448	207	0.462	0.538
2–3	14	241	69	0.286	0.714
3–4	10	172	86	0.500	0.500
4–5	5	86	52	0.605	0.395
5–6	2	34	34	1.000	———

1 —from Patton's original field data. Used with permission.
2 —number of squirrels remaining in each age class from an initial population of 58.
3 —number of squirrels converted to a base cohort of 1000.

ecosystem level—from spreading spores to planting trees as they bury cones, and as prey for the goshawk. Though tassel-eared squirrels are essential ecological members in their natural habitat, when they have been introduced into other ecosystems concerns have been raised that they may outcompete the indigenous red squirrel species and consequently have a negative effect on the ecology of their nonnative habitats.

Future Research

(1) More long-term studies on feed tree growth compared with non-feed tree growth are needed to determine if there is a difference due to squirrel herbivory. (2) Although there have been studies on the chemicals that ponderosa pine trees use to defend themselves against herbivory, more studies could be conducted on phenolic compounds and peroxidase activities, similar to the study of squirrel herbivory on the China fir (*Cunninghamia lanceolata*) (ref. 47). (3) Research on the biochemistry of feed trees and non-feed trees should be conducted with the other subspecies of tassel-eared squirrels and the ponderosa pine forests they inhabit (ref. 24). (4) A study should be conducted of tassel-eared squirrel response to the forest thinning and restoration practices around Flagstaff, Arizona. (5) Monitoring of the populations of introduced tassel-eared squirrels should be continued to determine the status of the populations and any

impacts to the forests and other tree squirrel species within those forests. (6) Research should be conducted to determine the ecological relationships between red squirrels and Kaibab squirrels (both natural populations) on the Kaibab Plateau. (7) Another study could be conducted to determine the ecological relationships between Abert's squirrels and red squirrels (both natural populations) in the San Francisco Peaks area. (8) More studies should be initiated to determine the effects of introduced Abert's squirrels on the Mt. Graham red squirrel (ref. 41).

References for Chapter Eleven

1. Taylor, W. P. 1925b. Report of winter work at the Southwestern Forest Experiment Station. The Abert squirrel. Flagstaff, Arizona. Smithsonian Institution Archives, record unit 7176, box 29, folder 18.

2. Bailey, V. 1929. Handwritten field notes on *Sciurus aberti*. Smithsonian Institution Archives, record unit 7176, box 22, folder 8.

3. Bailey, V. 1931. Mammals of New Mexico. North American Fauna no. 53. U.S. Department of Agriculture, Bureau of Biological Survey. Washington, DC: U.S. Government Printing Office.

4. Bailey, F. M. 1932. Abert squirrel burying pine cones. *Journal of Mammalogy* 13:154–66.

5. Ramey, C. A. 1972. Squirrels with tassel ears. *Colorado Outdoors* 21:36–38.

6. Allred, W. S. Unpublished observation.

7. Keith, J. O. 1965. The Abert squirrel and its dependence on ponderosa pine. *Ecology* 46:150–63.

8. Taylor, W. P. 1924b. Memorandum for Major Goldman, summary of work, field season 1924, Tucson, Arizona. Smithsonian Institution Archives, record unit 7176, box 29, folder 15.

9. Taylor, W. P. 1926b. Memorandum of the white-tailed squirrel (*Sciurus kaibabensis*) of the Grand Canyon National Game Preserve. Division of Biological Investigations, Bureau of Biological Survey, U.S. Department of Agriculture. Smithsonian Institution Archives, record unit 7176, box 29, folder 19.

10. Taylor, W. P. 1927. The biological side of business of forest and forage production. *Journal of Forestry* 25:386–414.

11. Hall, J. G. 1981. A field study of the Kaibab squirrel in Grand Canyon National Park. *Wildlife Monographs* 75.

12. Soderquist, T. R. 1987. The impact of tassel-eared squirrel defoliation on ecotonal ponderosa pine. *Journal of Mammalogy* 68 (2): 398–401.

13. Trowbridge, A. H., and L. L. Larson. 1942. Abert squirrel-ponderosa pine relationships at the Fort Valley Experimental Forest, Flagstaff, Arizona (copy in author's files).

14. Pearson, G. A. 1950. Management of Ponderosa Pine in the Southwest. Agriculture Monograph no. 6. Washington, DC: USDA Forest Service.
15. Larson, M. M., and G. H. Schubert. 1970. Cone crops of ponderosa pine in central Arizona. Research Note RM-58. Fort Collins, CO: USDA Forest Service.
16. Capretta, P. J., and R. C. Farentinos. 1979. Determinants of selective herbivory in tassel-eared squirrels (*Sciurus aberti*). *In* Preference Behavior and Chemoreception, ed. J. H. A. Kroeze. London: Information Retrieval, Ltd.
17. Allred, W. S., and W. S. Gaud. 1993. Green foliage losses from ponderosa pines induced by Abert squirrels and snowstorms: A comparison. *Western Journal of Applied Forestry* 8:16–18.
18. Schmid, J. M., J. C. Mitchell, and S. A. Mata. 1986. Ponderosa pine conelet and cone mortality in central Arizona. *Great Basin Naturalist* 46 (3): 445–48.
19. Allred, W. S., W. S. Gaud, and J. S. States. 1994. Effects of herbivory by Abert squirrels (*Sciurus aberti*) on cone crops of ponderosa pine. *Journal of Mammalogy* 75:700–703.
20. Vankat, J. 2009. Personal observation.
21. Ffolliott, P. F., and D. R. Patton. 1978. Abert squirrel use of ponderosa pine as feed trees. Research Note RM-362. Fort Collins, CO: USDA Forest Service.
22. Snyder, M. A. 1993. Interactions between Abert's squirrel and ponderosa pine: The relationship between selective herbivory and host plant fitness. *American Naturalist* 141:866–79.
23. Snyder, M. A. 1992. Selective herbivory by Abert's squirrel mediated by chemical variability in ponderosa pine. *Ecology* 73:1730–41.
24. Snyder, M. A., and Y. B. Linhart. 1998. Subspecific selectivity by mammalian herbivore: Geographical differentiation of interactions between two taxa of *Sciurus aberti* and *Pinus ponderosa. Evolutionary Ecology* 12:755–65.
25. Skinner, T. H., and J. O. Klemmedson. 1978. Abert squirrels influence nutrient transfer through litterfall in a ponderosa pine forest. Research Note RM-353. Fort Collins, CO: USFS, Rocky Mountain Research Station.
26. Allred, W. S., and W. S. Gaud. 1994b. Effects of Abert squirrel herbivory on foliage and nitrogen losses in ponderosa pine. *Southwestern Naturalist* 39:350–53.
27. Allred, W. S., W. S. Gaud, J. S. States, and W. J. Austin. 1987. Abert squirrel herbivory: Implications for nutrient cycling. Abstract no. 134. American Society of Mammalogists, 67th annual meeting, University of New Mexico, Albuquerque.
28. Allred, W. S., and W. S. Gaud. 1999. Abert squirrel (*Sciurus aberti*) as a soil excavator. *Southwestern Naturalist* 44:88.
29. Kotter, M. M., and R. C. Farentinos. 1984a. Formation of ponderosa pine

ectomychorrhizae after inoculation with feces of tassel-eared squirrels. *Mycologia* 76:758–60.

30. Kotter, M. M., and R. C. Farentinos. 1984b. Tassel-eared squirrels as spore dispersal agents of hypogeous mycorrhizal fungi. *Journal of Mammalogy* 65:684–87.

31. States, J. S. 1985. Hypogeous, mycorrhizal fungi associated with ponderosa pine: Sporocarp phenology. *In* Proceedings of the 6th North American Conference on Mycorrhizae, June 25–29, Bend, Oregon, ed. R. Molina, 271. Corvallis: Oregon State University, College of Forestry.

32. Maser, C., and Z. Maser. 1988. Interactions among squirrels, mycorrhizal fungi, and coniferous forests in Oregon. *Great Basin Naturalist* 48 (3): 358–69.

33. States, J. S. Personal communication.

34. Vireday, C. C. 1982. Mycophagy in tassel-eared squirrels (*Sciurus aberti aberti* and *S. a. kaibabensis*) in northern Arizona. MS thesis, Northern Arizona University.

35. States, J. S., and W. S. Gaud. 1997. Ecology of hypogeous fungi associated with ponderosa pine. I. Patterns of distribution and sporocarp production in some Arizona forests. *Mycologia* 89:712–21.

36. Minckley, W. L. 1968. Possible extirpation of the spruce squirrel from the Pinaleño (Graham) Mountains, south-central Arizona. *Journal of the Academy of Science* 5:110.

37. Spicer, R. B. 1985. Status of the Mt. Graham red squirrel, *Tamiasciurus hudsonicus grahamensis*, of southeastern Arizona. Phoenix: Arizona Game and Fish Department.

38. Ferner, J. W. 1974. Habitat relationships of *Tamiasciurus hudsonicus* and *Sciurus aberti* in the Rocky Mountains. *Southwestern Naturalist* 18:470–73.

39. Morrell, T. E., E. A. Point, and J. C. deVos Jr. 1999. Nest site characteristics of sympatric Mount Graham red squirrels and Abert's squirrels in the Pinaleño Mountains, Arizona. Final Report. Department of Biology Technical Report 2. Muncie, IN: Ball State University.

40. Hutton, K. A., J. L. Koprowski, V. I. Greer, M. I. Alanen, C. A. Schauffert, and P. J. Young. 2003. Use of mixed conifer and spruce-fir forests by an introduced population of Abert's squirrels (*Sciurus aberti*). *Southwestern Naturalist* 48:257–60.

41. Edelman, A. J., and J. L. Koprowski. 2009. Introduced Abert's squirrels in the Pineleño Mountains: A review of their natural history and potential impacts on the red squirrel. *In* The Last Refuge of the Mt. Graham Red Squirrel, ed. H. R. Sanderson and J. L. Koprowski, 358–76. Tucson: University of Arizona Press.

42. Keith, J. O. 2003. The Abert's Squirrel (*Sciurus aberti*): A Technical

142   CHAPTER ELEVEN

Conservation Assessment. Golden, CO: USDA Forest Service, Rocky Mountain Region.

43. Lange, K. I. 1960. Mammals of the Santa Catalina Mountains, Arizona. *American Midland Naturalist* 64 (2): 436–58.

44. Coughlin, L. E. 1938. The case against the tuft-eared squirrel. U.S. Forest Service. *Rocky Mountain Region Bulletin* 21 (4): 10–12.

45. Farentinos, R. C. 1972c. Observations on the ecology of the tassel-eared squirrel. *Journal of Wildlife Management* 36 (4): 1234–39.

46. Patton, D. R. 1997. Wildlife Habitat Relationships in Forested Ecosystems. 2nd ed. Portland, OR: Timber Press.

47. Huang, Feng-Hou, Song-Gen Huang, Po-Han Hsu, and Yen-Li Chung. 1982. A preliminary study by peroxidase analysis of two genotypes of China fir (*Cunninghamia lanceolata*) differing in their susceptibility to squirrel damage. *Quarterly Journal of Chinese Forestry* 15 (4): 21–22.

12

CENSUS AND MONITORING METHODS AND TECHNIQUES

> In conducting population studies... one is continually confronted with the problem of locating and observing a satisfactory number of individuals. They are very wary and it is seldom possible to watch them for an extended period. It is, moreover, desirable to study these animals at closer range than afforded by stalking. Live-trapping proved to be the only way by which the individuals could be closely examined without killing them.
>
> —L. Baumgartner, "Trapping, Handling, and Marking Fox Squirrels," 1940

Introduction

Every research project on the tassel-eared squirrel that involves observation, monitoring, or direct contact requires a method or technique that should be consistent and reproducible. This chapter discusses the many methods and techniques used in the history of tassel-eared squirrel studies, from the first census studies when Taylor used bulky wooden traps in the 1920s near Flagstaff, Arizona, to the current remote precision monitoring with new technology (ref. 1).

Squirrel Census Methods

Evidence of Feeding Activities

Squirrels primarily use inner bark for food in the winter, and the discarded pine shoots are readily seen and can be counted. As squirrels feed, the terminal needle clusters are discarded and fall to the forest floor. Terminal shoots of pine twigs discarded by feeding squirrels in the winter might be linked to their population levels and provide an index of squirrels. In a study to evaluate this link, Keith found the average number of terminal shoots used by squirrels to be fifty/day. Therefore, he proposed that the population of squirrels in a given area could roughly be calculated by dividing the collected pine shoots by fifty per day, but he cautioned that this method would present problems with remote sites in the winter. Additionally, he stated that when squirrel levels were high, there might be confusion caused because of feeding overlaps of the numerous squirrels (ref. 2).

In years when there is a decrease in ovulate cones and hypogeous and epigeous fungi, Jordan Pederson and colleagues in Utah argued that larger numbers of terminal shoots would be found since the only available food source is inner bark. They suggested that in these years there would be more than fifty discarded terminal shoots daily and that using Keith's method could create a bias in the population estimate (ref. 3).

The Arizona Game and Fish Department developed descriptors to differentiate tassel-eared squirrel clips from red squirrel and porcupine pine clippings since in some areas all three animals use ponderosa pine trees for a food source. The terminal end of the discarded clippings of tassel-eared squirrels usually has several years of accumulated green needles, including current year needles, with the cut angle of the clipping of 33°–45°. Peeled twigs that result from the squirrel's removal of the outer and inner bark during their feeding activities accompany the green needle clippings on the ground (ref. 4).

A squirrel census method used on the Kaibab Plateau, developed by Brown for the AZGFD, involved selecting plots measuring 0.19 ha each. Clipped pine shoots were cleared from these plots every September for eight years. Every spring the terminal clips that resulted from squirrel herbivory on inner back were counted. This number was divided by the days of snow cover and then multiplied by 100 to establish a clipping index, and squirrel observations were made when the terminal-clipping census was being conducted. A significant relationship could not be established between numbers of squirrels observed and the clipping index. However, Brown stated that "randomly located clipping-count transects could provide at least gross indices of tassel-eared squirrels." He advised that in years of little or no snow covering the ground or in years with variations in the squirrel's diet, this method may be lacking in its ability to accurately predict squirrel densities. This clipping index produced a strong link over four years with squirrel hunter successes measured by questionnaires and by foot collection boxes. Hunter success and clip counts might be "a reliable survey technique" assuming hunter success equates to squirrel densities (ref. 5, 6).

A squirrel index using inner bark feeding signs has too many inherent problems to be resolved before this method can be considered valid. Some of the problems have been collecting consistent feeding data from remote sites during winter, distinguishing tassel-eared squirrel clippings from terminal branches lost for other reasons, assessing the quantities of clippings during times when squirrels have only inner bark for food, and reconciling squirrel observations with the numbers of clipped terminal shoots. Feeding signs indicate the presence of squirrels and their preferences for particular trees in certain parts of their territories.

Using feeding signs in combination with other techniques might prove more reliable. Hall used discarded terminal shoots, cone cores, highway mortalities, observations, and trapping data to estimate Kaibab squirrel densities. He stated that the Kaibab squirrel population on his study plots on the Kaibab Plateau declined three times in five years when the number of feeding trees increased, leading him to conclude that the increase in feeding trees does not automatically mean an increase in squirrel numbers. The number of clippings found beneath trees would be more accurate than the number of feeding trees, though he advised that in years of poor cone crops, squirrels would increase their use of inner bark, creating a problem in estimating squirrel densities (ref. 7).

Several other techniques for predicting squirrel densities have been evaluated. Fungi digs in January provided a very good correlation for one year but were not effective the next January because of heavy snowfall. Ponderosa pine seed consumption confirmed by cone cores on the litter layer provided "consistent and strong relationships." However, cone cores found after the summer's end into the fall were not reliable indicators. A combination of cone cores collections and track pan data found some improvement in population estimates though not enough to produce a squirrel density prediction for management purposes. During the spring the squirrel density correlation with twig clipping was rated as "marginally acceptable." That technique was improved when baited track pans were added. Overall, combining feeding signs of clipped twigs and digs for buried cones and false truffles during April "ranked the best" (ref. 8, 9).

Hunter Success

The AZGFD has used hunter success in conjunction with twig clipping and squirrel tracks in the snow to estimate squirrel density. The first hunter success surveys were conducted on a contact basis at check stations when hunters were asked about their squirrel hunting success (ref. 10). Later, AZGFD sent questionnaires to hunters after the squirrel hunting season (ref. 11). In addition, AZGFD has set up collection boxes and requested that hunters remove one foreleg from each squirrel killed so the ages of the squirrels killed could be determined (ref. 12).

Forest Characteristics

A mark and recapture method was used to establish an index of Kaibab squirrels using three forest characteristics (basal area, number of trees/ha, timber volume/ha) and the number of squirrel nests in the trap site area within a virgin ponderosa pine forest. The most significant and consistent finding was that the basal area of ponderosa pine trees with greater than 15 cm dbh was the best predictor of quality squirrel habitat. Since this study was conducted in a virgin ponderosa pine forest, "the validity of strict extrapolation of the relations found to a managed forest is unknown" (ref. 13). Computer modeling corroborated that basal area was indeed the best predictor of tassel-eared squirrel densities (ref. 14).

Nest Counts

Counting squirrel nests with new green twigs used in nest construction during the fall was proposed as a method to estimate squirrel densities. Green branches indicate fresh nests or reworked nests in current use, and this information could be used as an index of squirrel numbers. Old brown nests degrade slowly and should not be used in establishing squirrel densities and, furthermore, neither should summer or winter nests as squirrels construct and maintain several nests during these seasons (ref. 2).

Table 12.1 presents nest densities for several research projects. However, no significance between active squirrel nest density and squirrel density was found by Dodd and colleagues, who concluded that attempts to correlate nest densities with squirrel densities involved a tremendous amount of observer time and were rampant with observer bias (ref. 8).

Track Pans

A study to index several different small mammals including *S. a. aberti* employed an inexpensive census method using rainproof track pans.

– TABLE 12.1 –

Nest densities for tassel-eared squirrels established by various researchers

Researcher, year	Nest density (nests/ha)	State where research was conducted
Farentinos, 1972a	0.56	Colorado
Patton, 1975b	0.63	Arizona
Allred, 1989 (unpublished data)	2.8	Arizona
Halloran and Bekoff, 1994	0.47	Colorado
Dodd et al., 1998	0.5–1.9	Arizona

Plastic rain drainpipe was used to hold an aluminum plate that had been sprayed with a mixture of alcohol and carpenter's chalk. When the alcohol evaporated, the chalk adhered to the pan. Any movement on the track pan by animals removed the chalk, leaving an imprint. The method provided a very strong positive correlation when compared with the catch-per-unit-effort technique (# of captures/100 trap nights). Track stations were more effective at demonstrating the presence of squirrels than were live-traps (ref. 15).

Tracks in Snow

Several studies have used snowfalls to track squirrels in their territories (ref. 8, 16, 17). Snow depths > 30 cm provide excellent conditions for tracking (ref. 8). A combination of fresh squirrel tracks found in the snow with observed terminal clips on an established route through the forest was used to develop a rough guide to Abert's and Kaibab squirrel numbers (ref. 16, 17, 18, 19). It was recommended that AZGFD discontinue tracking squirrels because of variations in snow depth from none to very deep, lack of personnel needed to accomplish the tracking, required use of snowmobiles to examine all sites, and required long-term time commitment to account for variations in track numbers on each site (ref. 19).

Squirrel Observations Made During Other Animal Surveys

A method for census of tassel-eared squirrels used by the AZGFD was described in which squirrel counts were conducted in conjunction with elk and turkey surveys within the various forests of Arizona. Though the results were mixed in reliability, it was nonetheless recommended that these types of surveys continue until other more reliable methods could be explored (ref. 20, 21).

Time-Area Count and Strip-Count Techniques

Robert Kufeld, a researcher with AZGFD, compared the time-area technique with the strip-count technique to determine which would work best for tassel-eared squirrels. He concluded that the time-area technique, which produced "twice as many squirrels," worked best (ref. 22, 23, 24).

The time-area technique involves following a transect with known stations. At each station the observer remains quiet for a timed period while making observations in all directions for squirrels. The researcher then travels to another station while recording additional observations along the way. The transects are run four times/day.

The strip-count technique involves walking a transect at a slow pace and observing both sides of the transect for squirrels. This technique is conducted four times daily.

Methods of Determining Age

Tail Collections

During the 1963 and 1964 hunting seasons, the AZGFD collected hunter-killed tassel-eared squirrel tails to determine if a method developed for aging gray squirrels by tail pelage characteristics could be used for aging tassel-eared squirrels. It was determined that this technique could not be used with tassel-eared squirrels because the ventral white surfaces of the tails of Abert's squirrels do not exhibit changes in marking with age (ref. 22, 25, 26).

Epiphyseal Cartilage and Teeth

The AZGFD collected forelegs from hunter-killed squirrels to determine if it was possible to distinguish juveniles from adults based on a technique of X-raying the forelegs of gray and fox squirrels for presence or absence of the epiphyseal cartilages that are present in juveniles and absent in adults. This technique was also "reasonably accurate" for tassel-eared squirrels (ref. 22, 25, 27, 28). Use of this information, number of juveniles, and number of adults provides age ratios for the harvested squirrels and could be used as an indicator of population fluctuations. A study on gray squirrels (*S. carolinensis*) found that if juvenile squirrels killed by hunters accounted for less than 62% of the killed squirrels, the population was decreasing in size, whereas if the juveniles comprised 71% of the kills, the population was increasing (ref. 29). It was suggested that this method should be tested for use with tassel-eared squirrel populations (ref. 28). In another method for aging squirrels, Hoffmeister in 1986 used squirrel teeth and considered squirrels to be adults when their Pm^3 (third premolars–upper jaw) were fully erupted and in their occluded positions (ref. 30).

Techniques for Marking Squirrels in the Field

A toe clipping technique was used to mark captured Kaibab squirrels. The technique involved clipping one toe per foot following a diagram on which each toe was assigned a particular number. Thus each squirrel would have a different number that could be used for field identification from tracks in the snow (ref. 31).

Ear tagging with small metal piercing tags, sometimes in combination with colored plastics discs, has been used successfully for identification after retrapping and in field observations when binoculars are used to identify a squirrel (ref. 8, 13, 16, 32, 33). Occasionally the tags are torn out in fighting bouts or caught in such a way that the tag is ripped out. Color-coded vinyl collars have been used to mark Kaibab squirrels for field identification but the collars have to be removed, which requires successfully retrapping the collared squirrels (ref. 7).

Hall used a dye consisting of picric acid and potassium permanganate to create different patterns on the snowy white tails of Kaibab squirrels; he also docked tail hairs in various patterns. Both of these techniques were useful for only about three weeks because the dye faded and the hairs grew back. However, Hall stated that the most useful field identifications were the natural marks that the squirrels had, such as white specks or patches that differed between squirrels (ref. 7). Other techniques involved marking squirrels with ear tattoos, dying patches of fur, and freeze-branding (ref. 34, 35).

Some of these techniques are used to identify captured squirrels by marking them and "recapturing" by observation rather than recapturing in a trap. Recapturing in live traps can provide additional data such as weight loss/gain and reproductive status, but when the researcher needs only to field-identify the squirrel, tags, collars, tattoos, and bleaching hair are adequate.

Trapping Squirrels

Wooden traps used in the early studies of tassel-eared squirrels were heavy and bulky, making them difficult to carry into the field, especially during the winter snows (ref. 1). Modified wooden traps were used in the first tassel-eared squirrel study at Fort Valley in Flagstaff, Arizona (ref. 32). In the 1950s, metal live traps constructed of heavy-gauge wire of various sizes were used. Numerous researchers have successfully used metal traps and described their techniques of placing, monitoring, handling, tagging, marking, measuring, releasing trapped squirrels, treating injuries sustained by trapped squirrels, determining reproductive status, and collecting fecal samples used in seasonal diet analyses (ref. 7, 8, 13, 33, 36, 37). Table 12.2 gives various baits used by researchers in their live traps. Other forest animals, including many mammals, birds, and reptiles, extract bait from traps and may unintentionally become trapped (table 12.3).

— TABLE 12.2 —
Bait used in live traps for tassel-eared squirrels

Researcher, year	Bait
Taylor, 1924a	bacon, walnuts, pinyon nuts, prunes, fresh meat, hazelnuts, apples, green corn (both of these last two are "best results")
Trowbridge and Lawson, 1942	various grains, nuts, and scents; found pinyon nuts to be best, especially if the nuts were crushed within the traps
Kufeld, 1965	mixture of oatmeal and honey; whole corn kernels ("no value as bait"), pinyon nuts
Brown and Evans, 1972	dry oatmeal with peanut butter
Ratcliff et al., 1975	unshelled peanuts, raw or roasted
Patton, 1975a	raw peanuts
Patton et al., 1976; 1985	raw or roasted unsalted unshelled peanuts
Hall, 1981	orange and watermelon slices, peanut butter, shelled English walnuts
Pederson et al., 1987	roasted peanuts, peanut butter
Austin, 1990	unshelled peanuts
Halloran and Bekoff, 1994	peanut butter and sunflower seeds
Lema, 2001	raw or roasted unsalted shelled peanuts
Dodd et al., 1998; 2003	raw or roasted unsalted shelled peanuts

– TABLE 12.3 –

Researcher, year	Animals
Trowbridge and Lawson, 1942	golden-mantled ground squirrels, chipmunks
Kufeld, 1965	chipmunks, red squirrels, Steller's jay
Gaud (personal communication)	juvenile cottontail rabbit, juvenile striped skunk, Steller's jay
Dodd et al., 1998	golden-mantled ground squirrel, rock squirrel, striped skunk, Mexican wood rat, chipmunk, ringtail, cottontail rabbit, red squirrel, gray fox, porcupine, Steller's jay, dark-eyed junco, acorn woodpecker, mountain chickadee, bull snake

In 2002, Koprowski described a cloth handling cone for restraining tree squirrels captured in live traps that greatly reduces mortality due to shock induced by stress (< 0.01% in handling 3,500 squirrels). The cloth cone covers the eyes and reduces stress, thus maintaining normal heart rate in the handled squirrel. The only part of the squirrel that is not accessible when using the handling cone is the mouth (ref. 38).

Radio Tracking

Patton used radio transmitters to track Kaibab squirrels in a home range study. After squirrels were live-trapped, they were anesthetized and fitted with radio transmitters as either backpack design or as collars. The 36-g transmitters did not seem to affect the squirrels' activities (ref. 36). Radio collars that weighed 20 g were used in a later Kaibab squirrel home range study (ref. 7). Lema used even lighter radio collars that weighed only 18 g with a battery life of ten and one-half months in an Abert's home range study. The location of each squirrel was stored in a GPS unit (ref. 39).

Planning for Squirrel Monitoring

In considering monitoring techniques, from field observations to live trapping, tagging, and tracking of squirrels, researchers must have the time; necessary equipment; and reliable, competent field assistants; and must be familiar with the accessibility of the areas to be sampled during inclement weather conditions. To reduce observer bias, researchers should train their crews to pay attention to details and follow protocols. Teams of crew members in the field should work together for safety reasons. Crew members should be trained in the proper care and treatment of trapped animals. Researchers need to plan carefully by asking the right questions before entering the field to conduct surveys, so that their data collections are structured and will not have to be repeated.

Because squirrels bite and have extremely sharp claws, it is strongly recommended that leather gloves be used when trapping and handling squirrels. Researchers who live-trap squirrels should have the proper permits and permissions from the agencies and institutions involved with the management area being trapped. Researchers should never leave traps open during the night. Traps should be checked at least twice daily if left open during daylight and more often in inclement weather. Traps must be placed so trapped squirrels are protected from direct sunlight and so squirrels cannot turn the trap over while inside.

Summary

Numerous methods and techniques have been developed, modified, and revised for conducting censuses of tassel-eared squirrels. Indirect squirrel-monitoring methods have been used extensively. During certain times of the year these methods produce reasonable estimates of squirrel densities, though at other times of the year there is little benefit other than to establish the presence or absence of squirrels. Capture-recapture techniques allow the researcher to follow individual squirrels over time. In purely observational studies, marking squirrels so they can be recognized at a distance can provide data on home range movements, especially if the squirrels have radio collars for tracking. Planning and paying attention to details during field projects involving live squirrel trapping are crucial for success.

Future Research

(1) Census data on the *S. a. kaibabensis* is completely lacking, even though the AZGFD allows a two-month hunting season within the North Kaibab National Forest; thus a census study is warranted. (2) Census studies on *S. a. chuscensis* in Arizona on the Navajo Reservation and on the two Mexican subspecies *S. a. durangi* and *S. a. barberi* should be conducted on these sky island populations. (3) There is a need for improvement of field techniques for developing a reliable population index for tassel-eared squirrels that could be validated by capture-mark-recapture methods (ref. 8).

References for Chapter Twelve

1. Taylor, W. P. 1924a. Memorandum for Major Goldman, handling Abert squirrels (*Sciurus aberti*), Flagstaff, Arizona. Smithsonian Institution archives, record unit 7176, box 29, folder 14.

2. Keith, J. O. 1965. The Abert squirrel and its dependence on ponderosa pine. *Ecology* 46:150–63.

3. Pederson, J. C., R. N. Hasenyager, and A. W. Heggen. 1976. Habitat Requirements of the Abert Squirrel (*Sciurus aberti navajo*) on the Monticello District, Manti-LaSal National Forest. Publication 76-9. Salt Lake City: Utah State Division of Wildlife.

4. Rasmussen, D. I., D. E. Brown, and D. Jones. 1975. Use of ponderosa pine by tassel-eared squirrels and a key to determine evidence of their use from that of red squirrels and porcupines. *In* Wildlife Digest. Phoenix: Arizona Game and Fish Department.

5. Brown, D. E. 1982. The use of "clippings" to index tassel-eared squirrel population levels. *Journal of Wildlife Management* 46 (2): 520–25.

6. Brown, D. E. 1986. Arizona's Tree Squirrels. Phoenix: Arizona Game and Fish Department.

7. Hall, J. G. 1981. A field study of the Kaibab squirrel in Grand Canyon National Park. *Wildlife Monographs* 75.

8. Dodd, N. L., S. S. Rosenstock, C. R. Miller, and R. E. Schweinsburg. 1998. Tassel-eared squirrel population dynamics in Arizona: Index techniques and relationships to habitat conditions. Research Branch Technical Report no. 27. Phoenix: Arizona Game and Fish Department.

9. Dodd, N. L. 2003a. Guidelines for applying a tassel-eared squirrel feeding sign index to estimate spring density. Unpublished file document. Phoenix: Arizona Game and Fish Department (copy in author's files).

10. Bumstead, R. 1958. Abert squirrel survey and hunt information. Completion Report. Project W-53-R-8, work plan 2 & 3, job 12. Phoenix: Arizona Game and Fish Department.

11. Smith, R. H. 1967. Hunt questionnaires—1966. Special Report. Project W-53-R-17, work plan 2 & 3, jobs 1–4. Phoenix: Arizona Game and Fish Department.

12. Stephenson, R. L., and D. E. Brown. 1980. Snow cover as a factor influencing mortality of Abert's squirrels. *Journal of Wildlife Management* 44 (4): 951–55.

13. Ratcliff, T. D., D. R. Patton, and P. F. Ffolliott. 1975. Ponderosa pine basal area and the Kaibab squirrel. *Journal of Forestry* 75:284–86.

14. Prather, J. W., N. L. Dodd, B. G. Dickson, H. M. Hampton, Y. Xu, E. N. Aumack, and T. D. Sisk. 2006. Landscape models to predict the influence of forest structure on tassel-eared squirrel populations. *Journal of Wildlife Management* 70 (3): 723–31.

15. Drennan, J. E., P. Beier, and N. L. Dodd. 1998. Use of track stations to index abundance of sciurids. *Journal of Mammalogy* 79:352–59.

16. Kufeld, R. C. 1965. Tree squirrel management information. Progress Report. Project W-53-R-15, work plan 3, job 3. Phoenix: Arizona Game and Fish Department.

17. Brown, D. E. 1969. Tree squirrel management information. Completion Report. Project W-53-R-19, work plan 3, job 3. Phoenix: Arizona Game and Fish Department.

18. Brown, D. E. 1970. Tree squirrel management information. Progress Report. Project W-53-R-20, work plan 3, job 3. Phoenix: Arizona Game and Fish Department.

19. Brown, D. E. 1971. Tree squirrel management information. Progress Report. Project W-53-R-21, work plan 3, job 3. Phoenix: Arizona Game and Fish Department.

20. Bumstead, R. 1956. Abert squirrel survey. Completion Report. Project W-53-R-6, work plan 3, job 12. Phoenix: Arizona Game and Fish Department.

21. Bumstead, R. 1957. Abert squirrel survey. Completion Report. Project W-53-R-7, work plan 3, job 12. Phoenix: Arizona Game and Fish Department.

22. Kufeld, R. C. 1963. Tree squirrel management information. Progress Report. Project W-53-R-13, work plan 3, job 3. Phoenix: Arizona Game and Fish Department.

23. Flyger, V. F. 1959. A comparison of methods for estimating squirrel populations. *Journal of Wildlife Management* 23 (2): 220–23.

24. Hayne, D. W. 1949. An examination of the strip census method for estimating animal populations. *Journal of Wildlife Management* 13 (2): 145–57.

25. Kufeld, R. C. 1964. Tree squirrel management information. Progress Report. Project W-53-R-14, work plan 3, job 3. Phoenix: Arizona Game and Fish Department.

26. Sharp, W. M. 1958. Aging gray squirrels by use of tail-pelage characteristics. *Journal of Wildlife Management* 22 (1): 29–34.

27. Carson, J. D. 1961. Epiphyseal cartilage as an age indicator in fox and gray squirrels. *Journal of Wildlife Management* 25 (1): 90–93.

28. Kufeld, R. C. 1962. Tree squirrel management information. Progress Report. Project W-53-R-12, work plan 3, job 3. Phoenix: Arizona Game and Fish Department.

29. Uhlig, H. G. 1957. Gray squirrel populations in extensive forested areas of West Virginia. *Journal of Wildlife Management* 21 (3): 335–41.

30. Hoffmeister, D. F. 1986. Mammals of Arizona. Tucson: University of Arizona Press.

31. Baumgartner, L. L. 1940. Trapping, handling, and marking fox squirrels. *Journal of Wildlife Management* 4 (4): 444–50.

32. Trowbridge, A. H., and L. L. Larson. 1942. Abert squirrel–ponderosa pine relationships at the Fort Valley Experimental Forest, Flagstaff, Arizona (copy in author's files).

33. Austin, W. J. 1990. The foraging ecology of Abert squirrels. PhD diss., Northern Arizona University.

34. Halloran, M. E., and M. Bekoff. 1994. Nesting behavior of Abert's squirrels. *Ethnology* 97:236–48.

35. Hadow, H. H. 1972. Freeze-branding: A permanent marking technique for pigmented mammals. *Journal of Wildlife Management* 36 (2): 645–49.

36. Patton, D. R. 1975a. Nest use and home range of three Abert squirrels as determined by radio tracking. Research Note RM-281. Fort Collins, CO: USDA Forest Service, Rocky Mountain Forest and Range Experiment Station.

37. Sanford, C. A. 1986. Food habits and related behavior of the Abert squirrel. MS thesis, Northern Arizona University.

38. Koprowski, J. L. 2002. Handling tree squirrels with a safe and efficient restraint. *Wildlife Society Bulletin* 30 (1): 101–3.

39. Lema, M. F. 2001. Dynamics of Abert squirrel populations: Home range, seasonal movements, survivorship, habitat use and sociality. MS thesis, Northern Arizona University.

13

MANAGEMENT AND CONSERVATION OF TASSEL-EARED SQUIRRELS

Results of research from several state and federal agencies confirm that squirrels need a certain size, density, and arrangement of ponderosa pine to survive and reproduce. In turn, there is evidence that squirrels and other small animals recycle nutrients that contribute to the health of ponderosa pine. The Abert's squirrel and other small rodents have not caused damage to the extent predicted by foresters in the early 1900s and both are part of an ecosystem that has been functioning for thousands of years. It appears, from what we now know, discounting dramatic climatic change, that future generations will continue to enjoy both the Abert's squirrels and ponderosa pine for another several thousand years.

—D. R. Patton, "The Fort Valley Experimental Forest,
Ponderosa Pine and Wildlife Habitat Research," 2008

Introduction

Ponderosa pine forests were deemed to be endangered ecosystems in a 1995 assessment of ecosystems conducted for the National Biological Survey (ref. 1). Almost twenty years earlier, Pederson and his colleagues in Utah recommended in a paper addressing habitat requirements of tassel-eared squirrels that "the forest should be managed solely for the propagation and enhancement of this unique animal" (ref. 2). David Brown emphatically declared in a 1986 Arizona Game and Fish Department publication, "Actually, it is the forester whose tree management threatens the squirrel" (ref. 3). Important benefits of tassel-eared squirrels with respect to forest management practices are: squirrels are watchable wildlife, squirrels are a prey species for northern goshawks, and squirrels spread spores of mycorrhizal fungi in their feces (ref. 4).

In the early 1960s, Abert's squirrels were dismissed as game animals or even forest pests (ref. 5). But by 1999, their importance was considerably more understood as tassel-eared squirrels were referred to as "ecological barometers" and "windows" that could be used to assist researchers in understanding the intricate relationships within the ponderosa pine forest ecosystem (ref. 6). And now tassel-eared squirrels are recognized as a management indicator species (MIS) because of their narrow habitat association with ponderosa pine forests and because they can be monitored to indicate the effects of a particular management practice (ref. 7, 8, 9).

Management of the southwestern ponderosa pine forests for recreation, maintaining all the floral and faunal components, livestock grazing, fire prevention, and timber harvesting, presents administrative and bureaucratic challenges. Conflicts occur when goals are contradictory. For example, thinning of the ponderosa pine forests in restoration efforts to reduce forest fires also reduces basal area and interlocking branches of the canopy. This forest management treatment alters those two components of squirrel habitat, thus affecting tassel-eared squirrel populations. This chapter reviews the practices, management studies, and current recommendations for habitat for tassel-eared squirrels in ponderosa pine forests.

Basal Area and Tree Density

Basal area is the cross-sectional measurement of trees in a given area (m²/ha). Basal area and the number of Kaibab squirrel nests in a virgin ponderosa pine forest were used to develop a model that predicted a top rating for habitat quality if the basal area was 40 m²/ha with eight nests and a poor rating for habitat quality if the basal area was 28 m²/ha with two nests (ref. 10). Another study recommended maintaining areas with basal areas of > 35 m²/ha, especially in areas with large trees (30.5–61.0 cm dbh), for preserving quality habitats for squirrels, because this "may reflect a threshold where further wide-scale reduction of squirrel habitat structural attributes and landscape diversity impact squirrel populations and genetic viability" (ref. 11).

Patton developed a squirrel habitat model, using data from two other tassel-eared squirrel studies that were conducted in Arizona (ref. 10, 12).

He rated the model from optimum quality class → poor quality class. To achieve a good quality class rating, there must be > 296 trees/ha with a stand dbh > 30 cm. The trees should be in groups of at least six with interlocking canopies with nest trees and have a dbh range of 28–41 cm dbh (ref. 13). Similar values of good habitat quality with respect to dbh (30–40 cm) were found in a study on tree and squirrel densities in the Carson National Forest in New Mexico (ref. 14).

Landscape Models

In 2006, Prather and his colleagues developed four landscape models that can be used to predict the influence of forest structure on tassel-eared squirrel populations by habitat. They mapped 800,000 ha of mostly ponderosa pine–forested land in northwestern Arizona. In their analyses they found that canopy cover of 40–50% has a very clear influence on squirrel recruitment and that tassel-eared squirrel recruitment was positively influenced with forested areas of 160–305 ha. They recommended that large-scale forest treatments focus on removal of smaller trees and keep areas with high basal areas to minimize impacts on tassel-eared squirrels. Uncut or moderately cut areas could serve as sources of squirrel recruitment and as corridors for travel. The real advantage to this model is that it is Global Positioning System (GPS) based and allows restoration planning to occur on a virtual landscape, which permits an immediate assessment of the restoration project on the habitat of tassel-eared squirrels (ref. 9).

Forest Restoration

Restoration treatments of ponderosa pine forests in the southwestern United States are forest management practices to restore forests to pre-Euro-American settlement conditions by using thinning and prescribed fires (ref. 15). Squirrel densities and habitat utilization by squirrels were examined, and the strongest relationship revealed was that in forested areas with high levels of interlocking canopies there were higher densities of squirrels. In the eight study sites involved, any site that had heavy even-aged tree harvesting with < 3 interlocking trees per sampling point demonstrated very low or inconsistent squirrel recruitment (ref. 11).

Ponderosa pine stands on Mt. Trumbull in northwestern Arizona were examined in a study in 1999 before any ecological restoration prescriptions were enacted, resulting in two approaches to diminish possible impacts on tassel-eared squirrel population levels: the individual tree approach (ITA) and the patch approach (PA). The ITA involved saving the most intensely used trees while trying to mitigate impacts on the restoration prescription. Adding 2–4 feed trees/ha could have the potential to reduce forest restoration impacts on squirrels by 50%. Squirrels have been known to abandon feed trees in areas that have been logged, and therefore retaining only feed trees could have future genetic implications within the forest (ref. 16).

The PA involved retaining trees used for inner bark within clumps with non-feed trees. The PA could benefit squirrels by providing more cover, nesting sites, and travel corridors. It would also benefit mycorrhizal associations that flourish beneath more dense canopies, thus providing additional food resources for squirrels. If restoration managers are not inclined to allow tree exclusions by designating clumps within the treatments, then perhaps they could reduce levels of tree thinning and/or understory thinning. It was concluded that wildlife managers and foresters will have to agree on an acceptable compromise between forest restoration practices and optimum squirrel habitat (ref. 16). Another study conducted in northern Arizona in 2009 found that tassel-eared squirrels selected untreated forests with high canopy cover during the winter. During the other times of the year, squirrels extended their home ranges into the treated areas that had the highest canopy cover. This research suggests that "untreated areas are important for winter ranges and nest sites and may be critical for the persistence of the squirrels in the treated landscapes" (ref. 17).

An investigation of squirrel habitat in northern Arizona with particular emphasis on the ratio of optimal to marginal patch area (ROMPA) found the threshold to be 35%. It was recommended that forest restoration treatments be above this ROMPA threshold and that patches of forests of at least 36 ha should be left untreated (ref. 18).

There is consensus that old trees that were growing prior to Euro-American settlement should not be removed during restoration treatments (ref. 19). However, Patton suggested that the best cover requirements for tassel-eared squirrels were found in uneven-aged stands of ponderosa pines (ref. 20). Saving just the old large trees during restoration treatments without maintaining a mixture of other age classes will not preserve the habitat best suited for squirrels.

Timber Harvest and Management Considerations

A multiyear study of the effects of logging on habitat quality and feeding by tassel-eared squirrels was conducted in Utah. The researchers compared squirrel feeding activities at a logged site with those at an unlogged site. Squirrels fed in only 26% of the sampled plots in the logged area compared with 43% of the sampled plots in the unlogged area. Squirrel recruitment was lower in the logged site. One conclusion reached was that clear-cut timber harvest prescriptions negatively affect tassel-eared squirrels (ref. 21). When trees are removed, canopy cover is reduced, causing squirrels to seek cover in the more densely forested areas surrounding the logged area, though they will return for seeds from ovulate cones (ref. 22, 23, 24).

Peter Ffolliott and David Patton developed a model to assist in decisions regarding the management of habitat for tassel-eared squirrels and for timber harvest. They proposed that if squirrels prefer certain sizes of trees for food and nesting, managers should allow trees to grow to at least those dbh values before harvesting (ref. 25).

A project using artificial nest boxes was conducted to determine if tassel-eared squirrels would use the boxes for nesting in areas that had been cut for timber. The hypothesis was that these nesting boxes would provide opportunities for squirrels to return to areas that had been harvested for timber or for new squirrel colonizations from the surrounding uncut areas. The project was begun in May 1974 with twelve nest boxes, and by October 1977 all twelve boxes had evidence of squirrel use. This is the only study conducted to artificially attract squirrels back into harvested areas (ref. 26).

It was reported in 1989 that in some timber harvests, guidelines for impacts on wildlife, specifically the northern goshawk and Abert's squirrel, were barely being met (ref. 27). In another study nine years later, Dodd and his colleagues explained that tassel-eared squirrels are sensitive to fragmentations and decreases in heterogeneity of ponderosa pine forests. Timber harvesting methods that result in an even-aged forest and that reduce interlocking canopies alter the squirrel habitat (ref. 11).

Forest managers who are concerned with timber yields as well as with forest wildlife issues should consider a compromise of leaving living Gambel oaks that are serving as den trees for Abert's squirrels (ref. 28). Ponderosa and Gambel oak snags should be left during timber harvesting activities since some of these snags are used by Abert's squirrels and cavity-nesting birds (ref. 20).

Heavy infections of dwarf mistletoe in ponderosa pine branches form tangled growths and distorted branches referred to as "witches' brooms." Abert's squirrels use these brooms as caching sites for food items, foraging sites for inner bark, and nest building sites (ref. 29, 30). A group of investigators recommended that forest managers making decisions about the removal of brooms or mistletoe-infected trees consider pruning the brooms to reduce wildfire risks and improve tree health while maintaining some brooms for squirrels. Trees with brooms that are not closed up enough to provide caching or nest sites and that are < 18 m above the ground could be harvested since they are not being selected by squirrels (ref. 29, 31).

Three different researchers have advocated that since several species depend on ponderosa pines for food, including tassel-eared squirrels, porcupines (*Erethizon dorsatum*), bark beetles (*Dendroctonus ponderosae*), and dwarf mistletoe, and since these specific species potentially offer multiple directions for selection within the forest stand, forest management practices should attempt to maintain the diversity of pines that these species require (ref. 32, 33, 34).

Ecological Considerations in Management

A "triangle-based relationship" between squirrel, ponderosa pine, and hypogeous fungi (see figure 11.1) was first described by J. S. States (ref. 35). The northern goshawk is now recognized as the fourth organism in this relationship, which could be viewed as a quadrangle. Goshawks are primarily found in ponderosa pine and spruce-fir forests in the southwestern United States (ref. 36). In ponderosa pine forests, goshawks feed on tassel-eared squirrels (ref. 36). Tassel-eared squirrels feed on the false truffles of the mycorrhizal fungi, which benefit the ponderosa pine trees, especially in environments with porous soils. The pine trees provide habitat for squirrels, goshawks, and hypogeous fungi. If one species is affected within this system, all are affected. John Muir said it best in his classic book *My First Summer in the Sierra*: "When we try to pick out anything by itself, we find it hitched to everything else in the universe" (ref. 37).

False truffles, sporocarps of mycorrhizal fungi, are specifically clustered under the more dense canopies of blackjack ponderosa pines rather than under the mature yellow pines (ref. 38). Squirrel recruitment is positively related to interlocking canopies and fungal inventories, and those relationships are positively linked to the basal area. This positive correlation with denser canopy cover and mycorrhizal fungi production should be considered with any timber management practices (ref. 24).

Logging activities that concentrate on intensive thinning practices can damage or destroy root systems of pines left standing after logging has ceased because the soil is disturbed (ref. 21, 24). Damaged roots, packed soil, and more intense drying conditions caused by the removal of the shady overstory can decrease false truffle production (ref. 38, 39). Higher diversity and abundance of false truffles in unthinned and unburned sites in ponderosa forests in northern Arizona were reported in a 2004 study. Thinning and prescription burns can negatively affect tassel-eared squirrels because of the reduction of the fungal component of their diet (ref. 40).

A positive relationship with squirrel winter survival and a diversity of fungi in the diet has been demonstrated (ref. 24). When snow cover limits squirrel recovery of false truffles and buried cones, squirrels must increase their consumption of inner bark, which has a marginal nutritional status (ref. 41, 42, 43).

Forest restoration projects should avoid concentrated thinning practices that reduce interlocking canopies and false truffle production, both necessary components of tassel-eared squirrel habitat (ref. 24). Instead, forest restoration projects should recognize the important aspects of the habitat of the tassel-eared squirrel in light of its designation as a MIS.

Conservation

Koprowski conducted a literature review pertaining to various tree squirrel responses to forest management practices. Recommendations from this review for the conservation of the squirrels are based on the management of the forests that provide the habitat for the squirrels. Optimum habitats for tree squirrels are dense patches of trees with high canopy cover with many interlocking canopies. Forest management practices should leave these dense patches while thinning surrounding areas. The thinned areas with low densities of trees could serve as firebreaks and travel corridors for squirrels and other wildlife (ref. 44).

Since *S. a. kaibabensis* and *S. a. chuscensis* have extremely small habitats when compared with *S. a. aberti* and *S. a. ferreus*, conservation efforts for these two subspecies are particularly important. *S. a. chuscensis* is afforded protection by the Navajo Nation as it lives within its boundaries, but logging activities have been allowed in the Chuska Mountains (ref. 45). *S. a. kaibabensis* is not protected within the Kaibab National Forest but does have federal protection within Grand Canyon National Park, 10% of its range. The two subspecies of tassel-eared squirrels in Mexico are considered rare and have a status of "species subject to special protection," but because of the paucity of research nothing is known of their population levels or what, if any, protection is really afforded them (ref. 46).

Management Conclusions

Interlocking canopies are an absolute requirement for cover, nest sites, and travel corridors for tassel-eared squirrels, and for shade for hypogeous fungi production. Uneven-aged stands of trees with a mixture of multiple dbh classes with a variable vertical structure and basal areas of at least > 35 m/ha are necessary for maintaining good-quality squirrel habitat. Forest managers should consider leaving cover trees around nest trees and providing corridors for squirrels to travel within fragmented areas. Reductions in the size of forested areas undergoing thinning treatments are consistently recommended. The range of tree dbh preferred by squirrels for feeding and nesting should be incorporated into management plans. Snags and mistletoe-infected trees are important for squirrels and other wildlife and should be considered in forest management planning.

Catastrophic forest fires resulting from years of fire suppression have ravaged the southwestern United States. Prescription fires to reduce fuel loads and forest thinning practices have been implemented to restore ponderosa pine forests to presettlement conditions. Tassel-eared squirrels, hypogeous fungi, goshawks, and the ponderosa pines have evolved together. Forest managers and wildlife biologists must work jointly to ensure that this ecosystem is removed from the endangered list.

Future Research

(1) Determine the impacts of hunting squirrels with emphasis on the age groups of the killed animals (ref. 11). (2) Determine the impacts of roads on squirrel population levels (ref. 11). (3) Develop a field test to determine the chemical composition of a tree, allowing immediate evaluation of its status as a FT or NFT. (4) Determine the maximum spacing between trees that would allow squirrels to remain within a restored site.

References for Chapter Thirteen

1. Noss, R. F., E. T. LaRoe II, and J. M. Scott. 1995. Endangered ecosystems of the United States: A preliminary assessment of loss and degradation. Biological Report 28. Washington, DC: U.S. Department of the Interior, National Biological Service.

2. Pederson, J. C., R. N. Hasenyager, and A. W. Heggen. 1976. Habitat Requirements of the Abert Squirrel (*Sciurus aberti navajo*) on the Monticello District, Manti-LaSal National Forest. Publication 76-9. Salt Lake City: Utah State Division of Wildlife.

3. Brown, D. E. 1986. Arizona's Tree Squirrels. Phoenix: Arizona Game and Fish Department.

4. Dodd, N. L. 1996. Taking tassel-eared squirrel management into the 21st century, a research status report. *In* Wildlife Views, November. Phoenix: Arizona Game and Fish Department.

5. Reynolds, H. G. 1966. Abert's squirrels feeding on pinyon pine. *Journal of Mammalogy* 47:550–51.

6. Dodd, N. L. 1999. Landscape-scale forest habitat relationships to tassel-eared squirrel population dynamics in north-central Arizona. Research Study Plan 1999–2002 (Draft). Phoenix: Arizona Game and Fish Department (copy in author's files).

7. Keith, J. O. 2003. The Abert's Squirrel (*Sciurus aberti*): A Technical Conservation Assessment. Golden, CO: USDA Forest Service, Rocky Mountain Region.

8. USDA Forest Service. 2005. Final Environmental Assessment. Management Indicator Species. Forest Plan Amendment 30. Pueblo, CO: USDA Forest Service.

9. Prather, J. W., N. L. Dodd, B. G. Dickson, H. M. Hampton, Y. Xu, E. N. Aumack, and T. D. Sisk. 2006. Landscape models to predict the influence of forest structure on tassel-eared squirrel populations. *Journal of Wildlife Management* 70 (3): 723–31.

10. Ratcliff, T. D., D. R. Patton, and P. F. Ffolliott. 1975. Ponderosa pine basal area and the Kaibab squirrel. *Journal of Forestry* 75:284–86.

11. Dodd, N. L., S. S. Rosenstock, C. R. Miller, and R. E. Schweinsburg. 1998. Tassel-eared squirrel population dynamics in Arizona: Index techniques and relationships to habitat conditions. Research Branch Technical Report no. 27. Phoenix: Arizona Game and Fish Department.

12. Patton, D. R. 1977. Managing southwestern ponderosa pine for the Abert squirrel. *Journal of Forestry* 75:264–67.

13. Patton, D. R. 1984. A model to evaluate Abert squirrel habitat in uneven-aged ponderosa pine. *Wildlife Society Bulletin* 12:408–14.

14. Frey, J. K. 2006. Abert's squirrel (*Sciurus aberti*) monitoring on Carson National Forest, New Mexico, 2006. Taos, NM: Carson National Forest.

15. Covington, W. W., P. Z. Fule, M. M. Moore, S. C. Hart, T. E. Kolb, J. N. Mast, S. S. Sackett, and M. R. Wagner. 1997. Restoring ecosystem health in ponderosa pine forests of the Southwest. *Journal of Forestry* 95:23–29.

16. Elson, M. T. 1999. Tassel-eared foraging patterns and projected effects of ecological restoration treatments at Mt. Trumbull, Arizona. MS thesis, Northern Arizona University.

17. Loberger, C. 2009. Tassel-eared squirrel home range and habitat selection within a restoration-treated ponderosa pine forest. MS thesis, Northern Arizona University.

18. Dodd, N. L. 2003b. Landscape-scale habitat relationships to tassel-eared squirrel population dynamics in north-central Arizona. Technical Guidance Bulletin 6. Phoenix: Arizona Game and Fish Department.

19. Abella, S. R., P. Z. Fule, and W. W. Covington. 2006. Diameter caps for thinning southwestern ponderosa pine forests: Viewpoints, effects, and tradeoffs. *Journal of Forestry* 104 (8): 407–14.

20. Patton, D. R. 1975b. Abert squirrel cover requirements in southwestern ponderosa pine. Research Paper RM-145. Fort Collins, CO: USDA Forest Service, Rocky Mountain Forest and Range Experiment Station.

21. Pederson, J. C., R. C. Farentinos, and V. M. Littlefield. 1987. Effects of logging on habitat quality and feeding patterns of Abert squirrels. *Great Basin Naturalist* 47 (2): 252–58.

22. Lema, M. F., W. S. Allred, W. S. Gaud, and N. L. Dodd. 1999. Social behavior of Abert's squirrels in ponderosa pine forests. *In* Proceedings of the Fourth Biennial Conference on Research on the Colorado Plateau, ed. C. van Riper III and M. A. Stuart, 105–12. Flagstaff: Northern Arizona University.

23. Lema, M. F. 2001. Dynamics of Abert squirrel populations: Home range, seasonal movements, survivorship, habitat use and sociality. MS thesis, Northern Arizona University.

24. Dodd, N. L., J. S. States, and S. S. Rosenstock. 2003. Tassel-eared squirrel population, habitat condition, and dietary relationships in north-central Arizona. *Journal of Wildlife Management* 67 (3): 622–33.

25. Ffolliott, P. F., and D. R. Patton. 1975. Production-rating functions for Abert squirrels in southwestern ponderosa pine. *Journal of Wildlife Management* 3:162–65.

26. Pederson, J. C., R. N. Hasenyager, and A. W. Heggen. 1978. Use of artificial nest boxes by Abert's squirrel. *Southwestern Naturalist* 23:700–702.

27. Dodd, N. L., and S. L. Adams. 1989. Integrating wildlife needs into national forest timber sale planning: A state agency perspective. *In* Proceedings, Multiresource Management of Ponderosa Pine Forests, ed. A. Tecle, W. W. Covington, and R. H. Hamre, 131–40. General Technical Report RM-185. Fort Collins, CO: USDA Forest Service.

28. Reynolds, H. G., W. P. Clary, and P. F. Ffolliott. 1970. Gambel oak for southwestern wildlife. *Journal of Forestry* 68:545–47.

29. Garnett, G. N., C. L. Chambers, and R. L. Mathiasen. 2006. Use of witches' brooms by Abert squirrels in ponderosa pine forests. *Wildlife Society Bulletin* 34 (2): 467–72.

30. Allred, W. S., and W. S. Gaud. 1994a. Characteristics of ponderosa pines and Abert squirrel herbivory. *Southwestern Naturalist* 39:89–90.

31. Garnett, G. N., R. L. Mathiasen, and C. L. Chambers. 2004. A comparison of wildlife use in broomed and unbroomed ponderosa pine trees in northern Arizona. *Western Journal of Applied Forestry* 19 (1): 42–46.

32. Linhart, Y. B., M. A. Snyder, and S. A. Habeck. 1989. The influence of animals on genetic variability within ponderosa pine stands, illustrated by the effects of Abert's squirrel and porcupine. *In* Proceedings, Multiresource Management of Ponderosa Pine Forests, ed. A. Tecle, W. W. Covington, and R. H. Hamre, 141–48. General Technical Report RM-185. Fort Collins, CO: USDA Forest Service.

33. Patton, D. R. 1989. Wildlife habitat concerns: Moderator's comments. *In* Proceedings, Multiresource Management of Ponderosa Pine Forests, ed. A. Tecle, W. W. Covington, and R. H. Hamre, 130. General Technical Report RM-185. Fort Collins, CO: USDA Forest Service.

34. Snyder, M. A. 1998. Abert's squirrel (*Sciurus aberti*) in ponderosa pine (*Pinus ponderosa*) forests: Directional selection, diversifying selection. *In* Ecology and Evolutionary Biology of Tree Squirrels, ed. M. A. Steele, J. F. Merritt, and D. A. Zegers, 195–201. Special Publications 6. Martinsville: Virginia Museum of Natural History.

35. States, J. S. Personal communication.

36. Reynolds, R. T., R. T. Graham, H. M. Reiser, R. L. Bassett, P. L. Kennedy, D. A. Boyce Jr., G. Goodwin, R. Smith, and E. L. Fisher. 1992. Management recommendations for the northern goshawk in the southwestern United States. General Technical Report RM-217. Fort Collins, CO: USDA Forest Service, Rocky Mountain Forest and Range Experiment Station.

37. Muir, J. 1911. My First Summer in the Sierra. Boston: Houghton Mifflin Co.

38. States, J. S. 1985. Hypogeous, mycorrhizal fungi associated with ponderosa pine: Sporocarp phenology. *In* Proceedings of the 6th North American Conference on Mycorrhizae, June 25–29, Bend, Oregon, ed. R. Molina, 271. Corvallis: Oregon State University, College of Forestry.

39. States, J., and W. S. Gaud. 1997. Ecology of hypogeous fungi associated with ponderosa pine. I. Patterns of distribution and sporocarp production in some Arizona forests. *Mycologia* 89:712–21.

40. Beiler, K., C. Gehring, and T. Theimer. 2004. Ectomycorrhizal fungal responses to restoration of southwestern ponderosa pine forest: Implications for tassel-eared squirrels. Poster Abstract Session 37: Forest Ecology, Ecological Society of America, Portland, Oregon.

41. Stephenson, R. L., and D. E. Brown. 1980. Snow cover as a factor influencing mortality of Abert's squirrels. *Journal of Wildlife Management* 44 (4): 951–55.

42. States, J. S., W. S. Gaud, W. S. Allred, and W. J. Austin. 1988. Foraging patterns of tassel-eared squirrels in selected ponderosa pine stands. *In* Proceedings, Management of Amphibians, Reptiles, and Small Mammals in North America, ed. R. C. Szaro, K. E. Severson, and D. R. Patton, 425–31. General Technical Paper RM-166. Fort Collins, CO: USDA Forest Service.

43. Patton, D. R. 1974a. Estimating food consumption from twigs clipped by the Abert squirrel. Research Note RM-272. Fort Collins, CO: USDA Forest Service, Rocky Mountain Forest and Range Experiment Station.

44. Koprowski, J. L. 2005. Management and conservation of tree squirrels: The importance of endemism, species richness, and forest condition. *In* Proceedings, Connecting Mountain Islands and Desert Seas: Biodiversity and Management of the Madrean Archipelago II. 2004, May 11–15, comp. G. J. Gottfried, B. S. Gebow, L.G. Eskew, and C. B. Edminster. RMRS-P-36. Tucson, AZ: USDA Forest Service.

45. Murphy, A. 1994. Graced by Pines. Missoula, MT: Mountain Press Publishing Co.

46. Ramirez-Pubido, J., J. Arroyo-Cabrales, and A. Castro-Campillo. 2005. Current status and relationship of nomenclatural land mammals of Mexico. *Zoological Record Mexicana*, n.s., 21 (1): 21–82.

END NOTES

Oone late summer morning, while walking through my study plots in the ponderosa pine forest at Lowell Observatory conducting a weekly census of squirrel herbivory activities, I noticed a young squirrel on the ground about 10 meters away. I stopped and we stared at each other. After a long minute of staring, the squirrel began to advance toward me in tiny bounds while I remained motionless. When the squirrel was within a meter of my location and just as I was ready to retreat to avoid being either bitten or scratched or both, the squirrel leaped onto the ponderosa pine adjacent to me and climbed quickly to my eye level. Though fearing being raked by the squirrel's sharp claws, I was intrigued by this behavior so I remained in place. The squirrel showed no signs of fear, aggression, or agitation—only curiosity. We simply stared at each other, one species to another species. After a minute of eye-to-eye contact, the squirrel swirled around the tree and climbed to a higher branch, flicked its tail, and dismissed me to my duties.

The future of the tassel-eared squirrels depends on *Homo sapiens*. We have contributed to the global warming of the Earth that affects the habitat of tassel-eared squirrels. Warmer temperatures in the southwestern United States coupled with drought conditions have led to an increase in bark beetle infestations that destroy the ponderosas. Large areas with standing dead trees provide excellent fuel sources for catastrophic wildfires, caused either by our carelessness or by lightning, that can destroy adjacent habitat. These landscape-size fires release even more carbon dioxide into the atmosphere, furthering the effects of global warming. We still allow the hunting of the Kaibab squirrels—yet to be counted! We have thinned forests in ways that do not leave essential canopy for tassel-eared squirrels. But, we now recognize the critical importance of the tassel-eared squirrel in management of forests, as harbingers of the healthy forest. The management indicator species designation of the squirrel gives foresters a gauge for management of the forest and consequently the squirrels. We can continue to petition for protection of squirrels whose numbers have not been identified. We now recognize the perils of global warming with respect to its cascading effects on the Earth.

> [T]he welfare of the forests of ponderosa pine is the welfare of this squirrel.
>
> —Joseph Hall, "White tails and yellow pines," 1967a

Taxonomy of Tassel-Eared Squirrels

Rodentia

The Order Rodentia contains 2,277 of the 5,416 named species of mammals, representing 42% of the mammalian biodiversity on the Earth (ref. 1). Descriptively named from the Latin *rodere*—to gnaw—rodents have a constant need to gnaw on surfaces to file down their ever-growing incisor teeth.

Examples of rodents include lemmings, voles, mice, rats, prairie dogs, chipmunks, marmots, woodchucks, porcupines, ground squirrels, flying squirrels, and tree squirrels. The largest member of this order, the capybara, lives in South America. The smallest rodent member is the jerboa, which lives in deserts of Asia and Africa.

The Order Rodentia contains five suborders and numerous families. The Family Sciuridae contains 278 species representing 51 genera. The genus *Sciurus* has 28 species, of which *S. aberti* is one (ref. 1, 2, 3).

The Hierarchical System of Nomenclature
of the Tassel-Eared Squirrels

Domain—Eukarya (eukaryotic)

Kingdom—Animalia (animals)

Phylum—Chordata (chordates)

Subphylum—Vertebrata (vertebrates)

Class—Mammalia[1] (mammals)

Subclass—Theria[2]

Infraclass—Eutheria[3]

Order—Rodentia[4] (rodents)

Suborder—Sciuromorpha[5] (squirrels)

Family—Sciuridae[6]

Subfamily—Sciurinae[7]

Tribe—Sciurini[8]

Genus—*Sciurus*[9] (tree squirrel—Latin for "shade tail")

Subgenus—*Otosciurus*[10] (tassel-eared squirrels)

species—*aberti* (in honor of John James Abert)

---

1 —Mammalia Linnaeus, 1758
2 —Theria–Parker and Haswell, 1897
3 —Eutheria–Gill, 1872
4 —Rodentia–Bowdich, 1821
5 —Sciuromorpha–Brandt, 1855

6 —Sciuridae–Fisher de Waldheim, 1817
7 —Sciurinae–Fischer de Waldheim, 1817
8 —Sciurni–Fischer de Waldheim, 1817
9 —Sciurus–Linnaeus, 1758
10 —Otosciurus–Nelson, 1899

(All information about the above taxa and the authors of those taxa was obtained from www.itis.usda.gov/servlet/SingleRpt?search_topic with the exception of Nelson, 1899.)

References for Appendix One

1. Carleton, M. D., and G. G. Musser. 2005. Order Rodentia. *In* Mammal Species of the World: A Taxonomic and Geological Reference, ed. D. E. Wilson and D. M. Reeder. 3rd ed. Vols. 1 and 2. Baltimore, MD: Johns Hopkins University Press.

2. Thorington, R. W., Jr., and R. S. Hoffmann. 2005. Family Sciuridae. *In* Mammal Species of the World: A Taxonomic and Geological Reference, ed. D. E. Wilson and D. M. Reeder. 3rd ed. Vols. 1 and 2. Baltimore, MD: Johns Hopkins University Press.

3. Myers, P., R. Espinosa, C. S. Parr, T. Jones, G. S. Hammond, and T. A. Dewey. 2008. The Animal Diversity Web. University of Michigan Museum of Zoology National Science Foundation Initiative. http://animaldiversity.org.

HISTORY OF
TASSEL-EARED SQUIRREL
NOMENCLATURE

The names of the accepted six subspecies are denoted with an asterisk*

Reporter	Scientific name	Year report	Location of discovery
S. W. Woodhouse	*S. abertii,* now *S. aberti aberti**	1853b	northern Arizona
S. F. Baird	*S. castanotus* Corrected to *castanonotus* due to typographical error	1855 1858	New Mexico–Mexican border
O. Thomas	*S. a. durangi** Also reported by Elliot 1905, called the common name Durango squirrel	1893	Mexico
F. W. True	*S. a. concolor* Name changed to *S. a. ferreus**	1894 1900	Colorado/ New Mexico
J. A. Allen	*S. a. barberi** and *S. a. phaeurus* Also reported by Elliot 1905, called the common name Barber's squirrel	1904	Mexico
C. Hart Merriam	*S. kaibabensis,* now *S. a. kaibabensis**	1904	Kaibab Plateau, northern Arizona
	S. a. mimus	1904	
E. A. Goldman	*S. a. chuscensis**	1931	Arizona/ New Mexico
S. D. Durant	*S. a. navajo*	1947	Utah

THE NATURALISTS AND THE SIX RECOGNIZED SUBSPECIES OF TASSEL-EARED SQUIRRELS

Sciurus aberti aberti

This truly elegant squirrel I procured in the San Francisco mountain, during the month of October, where I found it quite abundant, and after leaving which place I did not see it again. I have been informed lately by Major Backus, U.S. Army, that they are quite numerous near Fort Defiance, in the Navajoe country. When I first described this animal in the Academy's proceedings, last June, I called it *Sciurus dorsalis*, since when I have found that the specific name of dorsalis has been occupied by J. G. Gray for one of the same genus. In the Academy's proceedings of December I have called it *Sciurus Abertii*, in honor of Col. J. J. Abert, Chief of the Corps of Topographical Engineers, to whose exertions science is so much indebted.

—Samuel W. Woodhouse, in Sitgreaves, *Report of an Expedition down the Zuni and Colorado Rivers*, 1853

Samuel Washington Woodhouse (1821–1904) was an American physician and a knowledgeable naturalist who accompanied the Sitgreaves Expedition, serving in both capacities (ref. 1, 2). Woodhouse collected the first tassel-eared squirrel, in October 1851, from an area in the San Francisco Peaks, near present-day Flagstaff, Arizona, and named it *Sciurus dorsalis* (ref. 3). Woodhouse renamed this specimen *S. aberti* because *S. dorsalis* had already been used. The species was named in honor of Colonel John James Abert of the U.S. Corps of Topological Engineers (ref. 4).

Woodhouse, born in Philadelphia, developed an early interest in birds and in the techniques of their collection and mounting. In the 1840s Woodhouse entered the University of Pennsylvania Medical School. After a brief medical career he joined an expedition as the physician and naturalist, led by Colonel John James Abert. Woodhouse collected numerous plants and animals, some of which had never been reported. In 1851, Woodhouse joined a second expedition, again as physician and naturalist, led by Captain Sitgreaves. Their charge was to explore and assess the navigational potential of the Zuni and Little Colorado Rivers. This is the expedition on which he collected the first tassel-eared squirrel (ref. 1, 2).

Sciurus aberti durangi

In 1882 two squirrels sent from Durango, Central Mexico, by Mr. A. Forrer were referred by me to *Sciurus Aberti*, Woodh., a species previously known from Colorado, Arizona, and New Mexico, and which I presumed to extend southwards down the high lands of the Sierra Madre as far as the point at which Mr. Forrer found it. Some doubt has been recently thrown on this determination, and I have therefore now made a renewed examination of Mr. Forrer's beautiful skins.

—O. Thomas, "On the Mexican representative of *Sciurus aberti*," 1893

Michael Rogers Oldfield Thomas (1858–1929), a British zoologist and recognized expert on mammals, worked at the British Museum. He identified a squirrel skin sent to him by a collector from the Sierra Madre, Mexico. At first glance Thomas thought it might be *S. aberti* but, upon closer examination, recognized "sufficient difference" to name it *S. a. durangi* (ref. 5).

Sciurus aberti ferreus

In connection with certain studies of North American mammals which I have recently undertaken, I find it desirable to separate out a few forms under new names. . . . SCIURUS ABERTI CONCOLOR, new subspecies. Similar to *S. aberti*, but with no rufous area on the back, all the upper surfaces being gray throughout.

—F. W. True, "Diagnoses of new North American mammals," 1894

Frederick William True (1858–1914), an American naturalist and later an assistant director of the Smithsonian Institution, named a tassel-eared squirrel collected in Colorado *Sciurus aberti concolor* (ref. 6). Six years later, he found out that an Asiatic squirrel had been given the species name *concolor*, and to prevent any confusion renamed the squirrel *Sciurus aberti ferreus*.

True served as the curator of mammals and librarian at the National Museum and in the administration of the Smithsonian Institution throughout his career, which began in 1878. Several species of animals are named *truei* in his honor. Some examples are the pinyon mouse (*Peromyscus truei*), the Mindanao wood shrew (*Podogymnura truei*), and the tailed frog (*Ascaphus truei*). True wrote a twenty-two-page paper titled *Catalogue of Aquatic Mammals of the United States* in 1884. In 1885, True authored the paper *Suggestions to keepers of the U.S. life-saving stations, lighthouses, and light-ships; and to other observers, relative to the best means of collection and preserving specimens of whales and porpoises*. These publications reflected his interest in the natural history of marine mammals.

Sciurus aberti barberi

This form [*Sciurus aberti barberi*] is closely related to true *aberti*, it is considerably exceeding in size either *durangi* or *phaeurus*, from both of which it differs in having the under surface of the tail heavily washed with white, so that the gray basal portion of the hairs is thinly overlaid by white, while in *aberti* the hairs of the lower surface of the tail present a solid mass of white, the hairs of the whole lower surface being pure white at the base.

—J. A. Allen, "Further notes on mammals from northwestern Durango," 1904

Joel Asaph Allen (1838–1921), an American mammalogist and ornithologist, named the second tassel-eared squirrel from Mexico, this one from Chihuahua, Mexico, in honor of its collector C. M. Barber: *Sciurus aberti barberi*.

Allen's name has endured in biology because of Allen's Rule, proposed in 1877, relating climate temperatures to lengths of appendages of animals: Warm-blooded animals that live in colder climates have shorter appendages than corresponding animals from warmer climates. Allen served as curator of birds and mammals at the American Museum of Natural History and as the first editor of *The Auk*. Some of his books include *The American Bisons* (1876), *Ontogenetic and Other Variations in Musk-Oxen* (1913), and *Monographs of North American Rodentia* (1877), coauthored with E. Coues.

Sciurus aberti kaibabensis

Mr. John T. Stewart has recently sent me two specimens of a new squirrel collected by him in the pine forest on the Kaibab Plateau in northern Arizona. One of these, a female, was obtained in August; the other, a male, in December. They agree in essential characters and differ strikingly from the well known Abert['s] squirrel of the pine forest of the Arizona plateau south of Grand Canyon.

—C. H. Merriam, "Two new squirrels of the aberti group," 1904

Clinton Hart Merriam (1855–1942), like Woodhouse, was a physician before becoming a naturalist and ethnographer. J. T. Stewart, a collector, sent Merriam two specimens of tassel-eared squirrels collected from the Kaibab Plateau in Arizona. Merriam named the squirrel *Sciurus kaibabensis* (ref. 7). It is now recognized as a subspecies and named *S. a. kaibabensis* (ref. 8).

Merriam, born in New York City, was one of the founding members of the National Geographic Society. He developed the Life Zone Concepts that connected biomes in North America with elevation, temperatures, and latitude. Merriam has several mammals named in his honor: the extinct Merriam's elk, *Cervus elaphus merriami*; Merriam's wild turkey, *Meliagris gallopavo merriami*; and Merriam's chipmunk, *Tamias merriami*. He died in Berkeley, California, and the Bancroft Library at the University of California at Berkeley is the repository for his papers and numerous photographs.

Sciurus aberti chuscensis

S. a. chuscensis is a peripheral form of the *S. aberti* group which although restricted to yellow pine forests has a lengthy range as whole, along the backbone of the continent from Colorado to Durango. Few mammals are more closely associated with a single species of tree than are the squirrels of this group with the Rocky Mountain yellow pine . . .

—E. A. Goldman, "Three new rodents from Arizona and New Mexico," 1931

Edward Alphonso Goldman (1873–1946), a prominent American naturalist, described and named a subspecies of tassel-eared squirrel collected by Vernon Bailey from the Chusca Mountains, New Mexico, *Sciurus aberti chuscensis* (ref. 9). This is the last of the six recognized subspecies of tassel-eared squirrels (ref. 8).

In 1892 near Death Valley, E. W. Nelson, a renowned naturalist with the Bureau of Biological Survey, needed to have a singletree repaired for a buckboard wagon. While at the Goldman ranch waiting for the repair to be made, Nelson learned that Jacob Goldman's eighteen-year-old son, Edward, who was away in Fresno, had an interest in natural history. At the request of Nelson, young Goldman came home to the ranch and met with him, immediately becoming "personal assistant to Nelson . . . with a salary of $30 a month plus board. Nelson paid this out of his own salary, which at the time was $1,800 per annum." Nelson and Goldman became a natural history collecting team, together collecting more than 22,000 specimens. During his forty-four-year career, Goldman published more than two hundred papers and books. As he served in the U.S. Army during World War I, Goldman is buried at Arlington National Cemetery (ref. 10).

References for Appendix Three

1. Davis, G. P. 1986. Man and Wildlife in Arizona: The American Exploration Period. Phoenix: Arizona Game and Fish Department.
2. Wallace, A., and R. H. Hevly. 2007. From Texas to San Diego in 1851—the Overland Journal of Dr. S. W. Woodhouse, Surgeon-Naturalist of the Sitgreaves Expedition. Lubbock: Texas Tech University Press.
3. Woodhouse, S. W. 1853a. Description of a new species of *Sciurus*. *Proceedings Academy of Natural Sciences Philadelphia* 6:110.
4. Woodhouse, S. W. 1853b. Renaming for *S. dorsalis* Woodhouse, 1853. *Proceedings Academy of Natural Sciences Philadelphia* 6:200.
5. Thomas, O. 1893. On the Mexican representative of *Sciurus aberti*. *Annual Magazine of Natural History*, series 6 (11): 49–50.
6. True, F. W. 1894. Diagnoses of new North American mammals. *Proceedings of the United States National Museum* 17:241–43.
7. Merriam, C. H. 1904. Two new squirrels of the *aberti* group. *Proceedings of Biological Society of Washington* 17:129–30.

8. Hoffmeister, D. F., and V. Diersing. 1978. Review of the tassel-eared squirrels of the subgenus *Otosciurus*. *Journal of Mammalogy* 59:402–13.

9. Goldman, E. A. 1931. Three new rodents from Arizona and New Mexico. *Proceedings of Biological Society of Washington* 44:133–36.

10. Young, S. P. 1947. Edward Alphonso Goldman. *Journal of Mammalogy* 28 (2): 91–108.

FAUNAL REMAINS, AN
ARTIFACT, AND FOSSILS OF
TASSEL-EARED SQUIRRELS

Faunal Remains

Bones, teeth, claws, feathers, and pelts that are located upon excavation within arch-aeological sites are useful to scientists who reconstruct ecosystems from the past and discern cultural activities during those times. Faunal remains of tassel-eared squir-rels have been reported in numerous locations in the southwestern United States. Table A lists various ruins of ancient pueblos where these faunal remains have been located. Tassel-eared squirrels were food items for the pueblos, and they were either hunted near the pueblos or transported from another location to the pueblo for con-sumption. Squirrel pelts were also used for clothing and in ceremonies (ref. 1, 2).

An Artifact

In 1954, in the Needles area of what is now Canyonlands National Park, Mary Beckwith and Kent Frost discovered an artifact (plate 52) of scarlet macaw (*Ara macao*) feathers attached to braided yucca ropes, a buckskin strap, and a tassel-eared squirrel pelt. Based on designs found on Mimbres pottery from 1000 to 1250 AD, which depicted a woman and a man in a kiva mural with similar cloth-ing, it is likely this artifact was used as a ceremonial skirt. This artifact was found in a cave in Lavender Canyon, San Juan County, Utah. It is housed in the Edge of the Cedars State Park Museum in Monticello, Utah. The cave contained a few fragments of the black-on-white pottery shards characteristic of the Mesa Verde Anasazi during the Pueblo II/Pueblo III period (ref. 3, 4).

"It was probably manufactured in Mexico . . . and reached Utah through various trade routes where its owner cached it, in a folded position in a small cave," Lyndon Hargrave surmised in 1979 (ref. 3). The squirrel pelt caused interest because if the artifact was made in Mexico, it was possible that the squirrel skin might be of *S. a. durangi* or *S. a. barberi* origin, since those subspecies of tassel-eared squirrels live in Mexico. However, Hargrave concluded that the squirrel pelt was attached to the more than two thousand macaw feathers after the artifact arrived in Utah, point-ing to the tassel-eared subspecies *S. a. ferreus* as the pelt source (ref. 3).

TABLE A. Faunal remains and fossils reported of tassel-eared squirrels

Subspecies/Faunal Remains	Location	Researcher/year	Notes
S. aberti, fossil, well-preserved lower jaw	Quarry No. 1, Upper Snake Creek, NE	Matthew, 1924[1]	Middle Pliocene
S. aberti, not identified	LA 12069; 12066, Rio Arriba County, NM	Holbrook, 1975	
S. aberti, bones, unidentified	Tijeras Pueblo, southeast of Albuquerque, NM	Cordell, 1977	
S. aberti, bone, not identified	San Antonio de Padua, site LA 24, east of Albuquerque, NM	Jaradian, 1980	Early period
S. aberti, partial jaw and humerus	Flood pool excavations of Cochiti Lake, Bandelier, NM	Guthrie, 1982a	
S. aberti, 3 bones, not identified	Flood pool excavations of Cochiti Lake, Bandelier, NM	Guthrie, 1982b	
S. aberti, 45 bones, not identified	Arroyo Hondo Pueblo, Santa Fe County, NM	Lang and Harris, 1984	
S. aberti, three mandibles, two radii, one ulna, one femur, one fibula	Pueblo Alto, Chaco Canyon, NM	Akins, 1985; 1987	Most likely transported from Chuska Mountains, Mt. Taylor, Zuni Mountains
S. aberti, bone, not identified	Guadalupe Ruin, Sandoval County, NM	Pippin, 1987	
S. aberti, bone, not identified	Burnt Mesa Pueblo and Casa del Rito, Bandelier National Monument, NM	Trierweiler, 1992	
S. aberti, broken tooth M1 or M2	Papago Springs Cave, AZ	Czaplewski et al., 1999a; 1999b	
S. aberti, bone, not identified	Yellow Jacket Pueblo in southwestern CO	Muir and Driver, 2003	Abandoned, 1275 AD
S. aberti, bones, not identified	Antelope House, Canyon de Chelly National Monument, AZ	*	
S. aberti, bone, not identified	Abo, Mound J, Salinas Pueblo Missions National Monument, NM	*	

1 —"is not distinguishable from the jaw of S. aberti, but is almost equally like any other of the large western black squirrels . . ." (Matthew, 1924)

* —information from Western Archeological and Conservation Center, Tucson, AZ (in author files)

The subspecies of tassel-eared squirrel used in the pelt was determined by sampling the pelt for DNA and by radiocarbon analysis. The analysis concluded: (1) the squirrel pelt dated to 920 +/- 35 years before present (BP), and (2) the mitochondrial cytochrome b gene extracted from the DNA showed that the squirrel was more closely related to the *S. a. ferreus* subspecies of tassel-eared squirrels of the southwestern United States than either of the two tassel-eared squirrels of Mexico. This DNA evidence supported the hypothesis that the artifact was constructed entirely from materials found in the southwestern United States with the exception of the scarlet macaw feathers that were imported from Mexico (ref. 5). This finding contradicted Hargrave's hypothesis that the feathered artifact was constructed in Mexico and brought to the southwestern United States, and that then the squirrel pelt was attached to it (ref. 3).

Fossils

The first sciurid in North America appeared in the Oligocene Epoch (33.7–23.8 million years ago), and a fossil record of a species of *Protosciurus* has been found in Nebraska and Montana (ref. 6). An occurrence of the genus *Sciurus* in North America, Asia, and Europe during the Pleistocene (1.8 million years to 10,000 years BP) has also been demonstrated (ref. 6). An excellent family tree of the genus *Sciurus*, demonstrating the splitting during the Pleistocene of that genus into three subgenera—*Neosciurus* (gray squirrels), *Parasciurus* (fox squirrels), and *Otosciurus* (tassel-eared squirrels)—can be found in *Arizona's Tree Squirrels* (ref. 7).

A jaw found in a quarry in the Upper Snake Creek beds in Nebraska in 1924 was labeled as an *S. aberti* fossil. It was described as "A well-preserved lower jaw . . . not distinguishable from the jaw of the modern *S. aberti*, but is almost equally like any other of the large western black squirrels" (ref. 8). However, it is doubtful that this is *S. aberti* (ref. 9).

There are no fossils of the genus *Sciurus* in the Pleistocene deposits of Arizona. Tree squirrels of the genus *Sciurus* of any type are rare in the late Pleistocene fossil records of the southwestern United States (ref. 10, 11, 12). "The most obvious requirement of the genus is the presence of trees . . . these squirrels utilize tree products" (ref. 11).

In 1988, *Sciurus* sp. from three of seven localities within Porcupine Cave in South Park, Colorado, at an elevation of 2,900 m, were identified (ref. 13). Later, in 2004, *Sciurus* was revised to *Tamiasciurus*. Thus there were no *Sciurus* fossils found in Porcupine Cave (ref. 14).

No fossil *Sciurus* specimens are known from northwestern Mexico (ref. 15). Maxillary teeth fossils closely matching the size of teeth of *S. a. barberi* were reported from Papago Springs Cave near Sonoita in Santa Cruz County, southern Arizona. Papago Springs Cave is known for fossils of the late Pleistocene. These specimens represent the first fossil links "potentially referable to *S. aberti*" (ref. 16, 17).

Summary

Studies conducted in the southwestern United States have yielded little fossil evidence of tassel-eared squirrels. Faunal remains that have been identified as tassel-eared squirrels have been found in many of the ancient ruins scattered across the southwestern United States. Some of these ruins are within known ponderosa pine habitats or in close proximity, whereas other ruins are distant from ponderosa pine forests, leading researchers to believe that the squirrels were hunted and taken back to the settlement. One very fine artifact has been found with scarlet macaw feathers attached to a tassel-eared squirrel pelt. Researchers believe that this artifact was a type of ceremonial dress. Faunal remains reflect that some squirrels were used as food and their pelts used as clothing.

References for Appendix Four

1. Cordell, L. S. 1977. Late Anasazi farming and hunting strategies: One example of a problem in congruence. *American Antiquity* 42:449–61.
2. Sturdevant, G. E. 1927. The Kaibab and Abert squirrel. *Arizona Wild Life* 1 (8): 2–3.
3. Hargrave, L. L. 1979. A macaw feather artifact from southwestern Utah. *Southwestern Lore* 45 (4): 1–6.
4. Canbt, T. Y. 1982. The Anasazi. *National Geographic* 162 (5): 554–629.
5. Borson, N., F. Berdan, E. Stark, J. S. States, and P. J. Wettstein. 1998. Origins of an Anasazi scarlet macaw feather artifact. *American Antiquity* 63:131–42.
6. Black, C. C. 1972. Holarctic evolution and dispersal of squirrels (Rodentia: Sciuridae). *Evolutionary Biology* 6:305–22.
7. Brown, D. E. 1986. Arizona's Tree Squirrels. Phoenix: Arizona Game and Fish Department.
8. Matthew, W. D. 1924. Article II. Third Contribution to the Snake Creek Fauna. *Bulletin of the American Museum of Natural History* 50:59–210.
9. Goodwin, H. T. Personal communication.
10. Lindsay, E. H., and N. T. Tessman. 1974. Cenozoic vertebrates localities and faunas in Arizona. *Journal of the Arizona Academy of Science* 9:3–24.
11. Harris, A. H. 1985. Late Pleistocene Vertebrate Paleoecology of the West. Austin: University of Texas Press.
12. Harris, A. H. 1990. Fossil evidence bearing on southwestern mammalian biogeography. *Journal of Mammalogy* 71 (2): 219–29.
13. Barnosky, A. D., and D. L. Rasmussen. 1988. Middle Pleistocene arvicoline rodents and environmental changes at 2900-meters elevation, Porcupine Cave, South Park, Colorado. *Annals of Carnegie Museum* 57 (article 12): 267–92.
14. Barnosky, A. D. Personal communication.
15. Alvarez-Castaneda, S. T., and J. L. Patton. 1999. Mamiferos del noroeste de Mexico. La Paz, Baja California Sur, Mexico: Centro de investigaciones del Noroeste, S.C.

16. Czaplewski, N. J., W. D. Peachey, J. I. Mead, Teh-Lung Ku, and C. J. Bell. 1999. Papago Springs Cave revisited, Part I: geologic setting, cave deposits, and radiometric dates. *Occasional Papers of the Oklahoma Museum of Natural History* 5:1–41.

17. Czaplewski, N. J., J. I. Mead, C. J. Bell, W. D. Peachey, and Teh-Lung Ku. 1999. Papago Springs Cave revisited, Part II: Vertebrate paleofauna. *Occasional Papers of the Oklahoma Museum of Natural History* 3:1–25.

A Brief Evolutionary History of Tassel-Eared Squirrels

[W]e appear to have in the Tassel-eared Squirrels a fine example of evolution in its first stages, not yet well defined in its trends and not yet in operation for a very long period, but having definite opportunities to develop well isolated forms along independent lines.

—E. D. McKee, "Distribution of the Tassel-Eared Squirrels," 1941

Jefferson's squirrel, *Douglassciurus jeffersoni*, is recognized as the earliest fossil squirrel. This fossil is from the late Eocene, approximately thirty-six million years ago, and was found in Wyoming in 1975 (ref. 1). Evidence suggests that tree squirrels originated in the Northern Hemisphere (ref. 2) and expanded west into Asia and Europe (ref. 3). Members of the genus *Sciurus* have been found in North America and Europe dating from the early Miocene, approximately twenty-two million years ago, but the origin has not been determined (ref. 3). The genus *Sciurus* was described as a "living fossil" based on the distinct similarities in its osteology with the discovered fossil remains (ref. 4). The fossil record is "woefully inadequate" for following the dispersal of the numerous arboreal squirrels through the Tertiary period (ref. 5).

As the Wisconsin glacial stage ended about 35,000 years ago, ponderosa pine forests began advancing into higher elevations as the Southwest began experiencing higher aridity. It is not known from the fossil records if the range of ponderosa pine forests and the distribution of tassel-eared squirrels were continuous from Colorado to Mexico "but presumably this was the case" (ref. 6).

An excellent summation of the climatic conditions and the forest flora of North America during the middle of the late Tertiary, approximately fifteen million years ago, is given in *Arizona's Tree Squirrels*. Moisture and temperature regimes changed, causing much colder and drier climates. Northern forests became more restrictive within particular habitats based on their temperature and moisture requirements. Conifers, which tolerate snow and colder, drier climates, endured in the higher elevations. The present configuration of coniferous forests within the southwestern

United States was established about 11,000 years ago. An accurate account of the actual arrival of tree squirrels in the Southwest is inexact because of the paucity of the fossil record. However, based on climatic data, Brown argues that the range of tree squirrels was established within the Holocene, at least 4,000 years ago (ref. 7).

The distribution of tassel-eared squirrels across the southwestern United States and Mexico was studied in 1977 by examining mtDNA of the six subspecies. The data gathered in this research supported a post-Pleistocene (10,000 years ago to present) distribution hypothesis proposing that tassel-eared squirrels dispersed northward as the range of ponderosa pine expanded (ref. 8).

References for Appendix Five

1. Thorington, R. W., Jr., and K. Ferrell. 2006. Squirrels: The Animal Answer Guide. Baltimore, MD: Johns Hopkins University Press.
2. Mercer, J. M., and V. L. Roth. 2003. The effects of Cenozoic global change on squirrel phylogeny. *Science* 299:1568–71.
3. Gurnell, J. 1987. The Natural History of Squirrels. New York: Facts on File.
4. Emry, R. J., and R. W. Thorington Jr. 1984. The tree squirrel *Sciurus* (Sciuridae, Rodentia) as a living fossil. In Living Fossils, ed. N. Eldredge and S. M. Stanley. New York: Springer Verlag.
5. Black, C. C. 1972. Holarctic evolution and dispersal of squirrels (Rodentia: Sciuridae). *Evolutionary Biology* 6:305–22.
6. McKee, E. D. 1941. Distribution of the tassel-eared squirrels. *Plateau* 14:12–20.
7. Brown, D. E. 1986. Arizona's Tree Squirrels. Phoenix: Arizona Game and Fish Department.
8. Lamb, T., T. R. Jones, and P. J. Wettstein. 1997. Evolutionary genetics and phylogeography of tassel-eared squirrels (*Sciurus aberti*). *Journal of Mammalogy* 78 (1): 117–33.

Average Measurements of Tassel-Eared Squirrels (Not Segregated by Sex)

Weight (g) (n)	Length (cm) [n]	Length of Tail (mm)	Length of hind foot (mm)	Subspecies	Researcher, year
――――	54.0 [NG]	230 [NG]	76 [NG]	S. a. aberti	McKee, 1941
――――	47.7 [NG]	216 [NG]	69 [NG]	S. a. phaeurus[1]	
――――	507 [NG]	237 [NG]	72 [NG]	S. a. barberi	
――――	483 [NG]	211 [NG]	58 [NG]	S. a. ferreus	
――――	495 [NG]	218 [NG]	71 [NG]	S. a. mimus[2]	
――――	486 [NG]	235 [NG]	71 [NG]	S. durangi[3]	
624 (119) 692 (57)	――――	――――	――――	S. a. aberti S. a. aberti	Stephenson, 1975; Dodd et al., 1998
――――	46.3–58.4 [NG]	195–255	65–80	S. a. aberti	Hall and Kelson, 1959
――――	――――	――――	65	S. a. mimus[1]	Ramey and Nash, 1976a
――――	48.8–50.8 (110)	221–240 (110)	71–75 (110)	S. a. aberti	Hoffmeister and Diersing, 1978
――――	50.9 (19)	238 (19)	74 (19)	S. a. barberi	
――――	50.7 (11)	229 (11)	73 (11)	S. a. chuscensis	
――――	46.0–47.8 (33)	223–225 (33)	68–71 (33)	S. a. durangi	
――――	48.1–48.8 (42)	217–219 (42)	70–74 (42)	S. a. kaibabensis	
――――	52.5 (16)	218 (16)	73 (16)	S. a. ferreus	
550–750	――――	――――	――――	S. a. aberti	Fitzgerald et al., 1994

1 —S. a. durangi since revision by Hoffmeister and Diersing (1978)

2 —S. a. aberti since revision by Hoffmeister and Diersing (1978)

3 —now S. a. durangi

NG—not given

TASSEL-EARED SQUIRREL EMBRYO MEASUREMENTS

Researcher, year	Month (n)	Average crown-rump measurements (mm)	Weight (g)
Hall, 1967b[1]	July (3)	25–30	NG
Leopold, 1972[2]	May (3)	NG	NG
Stephenson, 1975[3]	NG (2)	46	13
Pogany et al., 1998; Allred and Pogany[3] (unpublished data)	various (25)	29.3–57.3 $\overline{X}$ = 47.16	NG

1 —*S. a. kaibabensis*

2 —*S. aberti* (Mexico), subspecies name not given

3 —*S. a. aberti*

NG—not given

Changes in Weights of Developing Young Abert's Squirrels

(modified from Keith, 1956)

Age	Females (g)	Males (g)	Females (n)	Males (n)
At birth	11.4	12.7	5	2
2 days	13	13	2	1
5 days	12	14	2	1
8 days	10	13	2	1
11 days	11	12	2	1
5 weeks	169	170	2	2
6 weeks	197	192	5	3
7 weeks	241	244	5	3
9 weeks	343	365	2	1

Standard Mammal Measurements at Birth and Six Weeks of Young Abert's Squirrels

(modified from Keith, 1956)

Age	Sex	Total Length (cm)	Tail (mm)	Hind foot (mm)	Ear (mm)
At birth	Both	60	NG	NG	NG
Six weeks	Female	360	150	62	29
	Male	360	150	73	30

NG—not given

BIBLIOGRAPHY

Literature Cited

Abella, S. R., P. Z. Fule, and W. W. Covington. 2006. Diameter caps for thinning southwestern ponderosa pine forests: Viewpoints, effects, and tradeoffs. *Journal of Forestry* 104 (8): 407–14.

Akins, N. J. 1985. Prehistoric faunal utilization in Chaco Canyon Basketmaker III through Pueblo III. *In* Environment and Subsistence of Chaco Canyon, New Mexico, ed. F. J. Mathien, 305–445. Publication in Archeology A8E, Chaco Canyon Studies. Albuquerque, NM: National Park Service.

———. 1987. Faunal Remains from Pueblo Alto. *In* Investigations at Pueblo Alto Complex, Chaco Canyon, New Mexico 1975–1979. Vol. 3, pt. 2: Artifactual and Biological Analyses, ed. J. M. Mathien and T. C. Windes, 445–649. Publications in Archeology 18F. Santa Fe, NM: National Park Service.

Allen, G. M. 1941. Our rarer mammals. *Audubon Magazine* 43 (March–April): 151–60.

Allen, J. A. 1895. On a collection of mammals from Arizona and Mexico, made by Mr. W. W. Price, with field notes by the collector. *Bulletin of the American Museum Natural History* 7:193–258.

———. 1904. Further notes on the mammals from Northwestern Durango. *Bulletin of the American Museum Natural History* 20:205–10.

Allred, W. S. 1989. The effects of Abert squirrel herbivory on ponderosa pines. PhD diss., Northern Arizona University.

———. 1995. Black-bellied form of an Abert squirrel (*Sciurus aberti aberti*) from the San Francisco Peaks area, Arizona. *Southwestern Naturalist* 40:420.

Allred, W. S., and W. S. Gaud. 1993. Green foliage losses from ponderosa pines induced by Abert squirrels and snowstorms: A comparison. *Western Journal of Applied Forestry* 8:16–18.

———. 1994a. Characteristics of ponderosa pines and Abert squirrel herbivory. *Southwestern Naturalist* 39:89–90.

———. 1994b. Effects of Abert squirrel herbivory on foliage and nitrogen losses in ponderosa pine. *Southwestern Naturalist* 39:350–53.

———. 1999. Abert squirrel (*Sciurus aberti*) as a soil excavator. *Southwestern Naturalist* 44:88.

Allred, W. S., and G. Pogany. 1996. Early estrus in a female Abert squirrel (*Sciurus aberti aberti*). *Southwestern Naturalist* 41:90.

Allred, W. S., W. S. Gaud, and J. S. States. 1994. Effects of herbivory by Abert squirrels (*Sciurus aberti*) on cone crops of ponderosa pine. *Journal of Mammalogy* 75:700–703.

Allred, W. S., W. S. Gaud, J. S. States, and W. J. Austin. 1987. Abert squirrel herbivory: Implications for nutrient cycling. Abstract no. 134. American Society of Mammalogists, 67th annual meeting, University of New Mexico, Albuquerque.

Alvarez-Castaneda, S. T., and J. L. Patton. 1999. Mamiferos del noroeste de Mexico. La Paz, Baja California Sur, Mexico: Centro de investigaciones del Noroeste, S.C.

American Society of Mammalogists. 1965. Report of Conservation of Land Mammals Committee, 45th annual meeting, Winnipeg, Manitoba, Canada (copy in author's files).

Arizona Game and Fish Commission. 1964a. Minutes and proceedings, May 23 (copy in author's files).

———. 1964b. Minutes and proceedings, August 15 (copy in author's files).

———. 1984. Minutes and proceedings, April 28 (copy in author's files).

Arizona Game and Fish Department. 2008. 2008–2009 Arizona Hunting and Trapping Regulations. Phoenix: AZGFD.

Armstrong, D. M. 1972. Distribution of Mammals in Colorado. Monograph no. 3 of the Museum of Natural History. Lawrence: University of Kansas.

———. 1987. Rocky Mountain Mammals. Boulder: Colorado Associated University Press.

Assault on common sense. 1964. *National Parks Magazine* 38 (August): 16.

Austin, W. J. 1990. The foraging ecology of Abert squirrels. PhD diss., Northern Arizona University.

Bailey, A. M., and R. J. Niedrach. 1965. Birds of Colorado. Vol. 1. Denver: Denver Museum of Natural History.

Bailey, F. M. 1932. Abert squirrel burying pine cones. *Journal of Mammalogy* 13:154–66.

———. 1939. Among the Birds in the Grand Canyon Country. U.S. Department of the Interior. Washington, DC: U.S. Government Printing Office.

Bailey, V. 1929. Handwritten field notes on *Sciurus aberti*. Smithsonian Institution's Archives, record unit 7176, box 22, folder 8.

———. 1931. Mammals of New Mexico. North American Fauna no. 53. U.S. Department of Agriculture, Bureau of Biological Survey. Washington, DC: U.S. Government Printing Office.

———. 1935. Mammals of the Grand Canyon Region. Natural History Bulletin no. 1. Grand Canyon, AZ: Grand Canyon Natural History Association.

Baird, S. F. 1855. Characteristics of some new species of mammalia, collected by the U.S. and Mexican Boundary Survey, Major W. H. Emery, U.S.A. Commissioner. *Proceedings Academy of Natural Sciences Philadelphia* 7:331–36.

Baker, R. H., and J. K. Greer. 1962. Mammals of the Mexican State of Durango. Publication of the Museum. *University of Michigan Biological Series* 2:25–154.

Barnes, I. R. 1964. Arizona gambles with the Kaibab squirrel. Naturalist. *Washington Post–Times Herald*, June 28.

Barnosky, A. D., ed. 2004. Biodiversity Response to Climatic Change in the Middle Pleistocene: The Porcupine Cave Fauna from Colorado. Berkeley: University of California Press.

Barnosky, A. D., and D. L. Rasmussen. 1988. Middle Pleistocene arvicoline rodents and environmental changes at 2900-meters elevation, Porcupine Cave, South Park, Colorado. *Annals of Carnegie Museum* 57 (article 12): 267–92.

Baumgartner, L. L. 1940. Trapping, handling, and marking fox squirrels. *Journal of Wildlife Management* 4 (4): 444–50.

Beiler, K., C. Gerhring, and T. Theimer. 2004. Ectomycorrhizal fungal responses to restoration of southwestern ponderosa pine forest: Implications for tassel-eared squirrels. Poster Abstract Session 37: Forest Ecology, 2004 Ecological Society of America, Portland, Oregon.

Black, C. C. 1972. Holarctic evolution and dispersal of squirrels (Rodentia: Sciuridae). *Evolutionary Biology* 6:305–22.

Bolen, E. G., and W. L. Robinson. 2002. Wildlife Ecology and Management. 5th ed. Upper Saddle River, NJ: Prentice Hall.

Booth, E. S. 1982. How to Know the Mammals. 4th ed. Dubuque, IA: William C. Brown Co.

Borson, N., F. Berdan, E. Stark, J. States, and P. J. Wettstein. 1998. Origins of an Anasazi scarlet macaw feather artifact. *American Antiquity* 63:131–42.

Brown, D. E. 1969. Tree squirrel management information. Completion Report. Project W-53-R-19, work plan 3, job 3. Phoenix: Arizona Game and Fish Department.

———. 1970. Tree squirrel management information. Progress Report. Project W-53-R-20, work plan 3, job 3. Phoenix: Arizona Game and Fish Department.

———. 1971. Tree squirrel management information. Progress Report. Project W-53-R-21, work plan 3, job 3. Phoenix: Arizona Game and Fish Department.

———. 1982. The use of "clippings" to index tassel-eared squirrel population levels. *Journal of Wildlife Management* 46 (2): 520–25.

———. 1986. Arizona's Tree Squirrels. Phoenix: Arizona Game and Fish Department.

Brown, D. E., and J. W. Evans. 1972. Kaibab squirrel stocking. Progress Report. Project W-53-R-22, work plan 6, job 4. Phoenix: Arizona Game and Fish Department.

———. 1974. Kaibab squirrel stocking. Progress Report. Project W-53-R-24, work plan 6, job 4. Phoenix: Arizona Game and Fish Department.

Brown, J. H., and A. C. Gibson. 1983. Biogeography. St. Louis, MO: C. V. Mosby Co.

Brown, L. N. 1965. Abert's squirrel in southern Wyoming. *Journal of Mammalogy* 46:516.

Bryant, M. D. Phylogeny of Nearctic Sciuridae. 1945. *American Midland Naturalist* 33:275–390.

Buchheister, C. W. 1964. Why shoot the Kaibab squirrel? *Audubon Magazine*, November–December, 359–60.

Bumstead, R. 1956. Abert squirrel survey. Completion Report. Project W-53-R-6, work plan 3, job 12. Phoenix: Arizona Game and Fish Department.

———. 1957. Abert squirrel survey. Completion Report. Project W-53-R-7, work plan 3, job 12. Phoenix: Arizona Game and Fish Department.

———. 1958. Abert squirrel survey and hunt information. Completion Report. Project W-53-R-8, work plan 2 & 3, job 12. Phoenix: Arizona Game and Fish Department.

Burt, W. H. 1940. Territorial behavior and population of small mammals in southern Michigan. *Miscellaneous Publication of the Museum of Zoology, University of Michigan* 45:1–58.

Burton, J. A. 1987. The Collins Guide to the Rare Mammals of the World. Lexington, MA: Stephen Greene Press.

Cahalane, V. H. 1947. Mammals of North America. New York: Macmillan Co.

Canbt, T. Y. 1982. The Anasazi. *National Geographic* 162 (5): 554–629.

Capretta, P. J., and R. C. Farentinos. 1979. Determinants of selective herbivory in tassel-eared squirrels (*Sciurus aberti*). *In* Preference Behavior and Chemoreception, ed. J. H. A. Kroeze. London: Information Retrieval, Ltd.

Capretta, P. J., R. C. Farentinos, V. M. Littlefield, and R. M. Potter. 1980. Feeding preferences of captive tassel-eared squirrels (*Sciurus aberti*) for ponderosa pine twigs. *Journal of Mammalogy* 61:734–37.

Carleton, M. D., and G. G. Musser. 2005. Order Rodentia. *In* Mammal Species of the World: A Taxonomic and Geological Reference, ed. D. E. Wilson and D. M. Reeder. 3rd ed. Vols. 1 & 2. Baltimore, MD: Johns Hopkins University Press.

Carson, J. D. 1961. Epiphyseal cartilage as an age indicator in fox and gray squirrels. *Journal of Wildlife Management* 25 (1): 90–93.

Cary, M. 1911. North American Fauna no. 33. U.S. Department of Agriculture, Bureau of Biological Survey. Washington, DC: U.S. Government Printing Office.

Chambers, C. L., and S. S. Germaine. 2003. Vertebrates. *In* Ecological Restoration of Southwestern Ponderosa Pine Forests, ed. P. Friederici. Washington, DC: Island Press.

Chapman, J. A., and G. A. Feldhamer. 1982. Wild Mammals of North America. Baltimore, MD: Johns Hopkins University Press.

Clark, T. W., and M. R. Stromberg. 1987. Mammals of Wyoming. Lawrence: Museum of Natural History, University of Kansas.

Cockrum, E. L. 1960. The Recent Mammals of Arizona: Their Taxonomy and Distribution. Tucson: University of Arizona Press.

———. 1982. Mammals of the Southwest. Tucson: University of Arizona Press.

Coconino County Health Department. 2008. Cases: 08-6093 and 08-6094. Reports of West Nile Virus infected Abert's squirrels. Flagstaff, AZ: Coconino County Health Department (copies in author's files).

Cooper, D. J. 1987. Abert's squirrel above treeline on the San Francisco Peaks, Arizona. *Southwestern Naturalist* 32 (4): 507.

Cordell, L. S. 1977. Late Anasazi farming and hunting strategies: One example of a problem in congruence. *American Antiquity* 42:449–61.

Coues, E. 1867. The quadrupeds of Arizona. *American Naturalist* 1:281–92, 351–63, 393–400, 531–41.

Coues, E., and J. A. Allen. 1877. Monographs of North American Rodentia. Department of the Interior. Report of the U.S. Biological Survey of the Territories, F. V. Hayden, U.S. Geologist in charge. Vol. 11. Washington, DC: U.S. Government Printing Office.

Coughlin, L. E. 1938. The case against the tuft-eared squirrel. U.S. Forest Service. *Rocky Mountain Region Bulletin* 21 (4): 10–12.

Covington, W. W., P. Z. Fule, M. M. Moore, S. C. Hart, T. E. Kolb, J. N. Mast, S. S. Sackett, and M. R. Wagner. 1997. Restoring ecosystem health in ponderosa pine forests of the Southwest. *Journal of Forestry* 95:23–29.

Creed, W. A., and W. M. Sharp. 1958. Melanistic gray squirrels in Cameron County, Pennsylvania. *Journal of Mammalogy* 39 (4): 532–37.

Czaplewski, N. J., J. I. Mead, C. J. Bell, W. D. Peachey, and Teh-Lung Ku. 1999a. Papago Springs Cave revisited. Part II: Vertebrate Paleofauna. *Occasional Papers of the Oklahoma Museum of Natural History* 3:1–25.

Czaplewski, N. J., W. D. Peachey, J. I. Mead, Teh-Lung Ku, and C. J. Bell. 1999b. Papago Springs Cave revisited. Part I: Geologic setting, cave deposits, and radiometric dates. *Occasional Papers of the Oklahoma Museum of Natural History* 5:1–41.

Dartt, M. 1879. On the Plains and Among the Peaks, or How Mrs. Maxwell Made Her Natural History Collection. Philadelphia: Claxton, Remen, and Haffelfinger.

Davis, G. P. 1986. Man and Wildlife in Arizona: The American Exploration Period. Phoenix: Arizona Game and Fish Department.

Davis, R., and S. J. Bissell. 1989. Distribution of Abert's squirrel (*Sciurus aberti*) in Colorado: Evidence for a recent expansion of range. *Southwestern Naturalist* 34 (2): 306–9.

Davis, R., and D. E. Brown. 1988. Documentation of the transplanting of Abert's squirrels. *Southwestern Naturalist* 33 (4): 490–92.

———. 1989. Role of post-Pleistocene dispersal in determining the modern distribution of Abert's squirrel. *Great Basin Naturalist* 49 (3): 425–34.

Dodd, N. L. 1996. Taking tassel-eared squirrel management into the 21st century, a research status report. *In* Wildlife Views, November. Phoenix: Arizona Game and Fish Department.

———. 1999. Landscape-scale forest habitat relationships to tassel-eared squirrel population dynamics in north-central Arizona. Research Study Plan 1999–2002 (Draft). Phoenix: Arizona Game and Fish Department (copy in author's files).

———. 2003a. Guidelines for applying a tassel-eared squirrel feeding sign index to estimate spring density. Unpublished file document. Phoenix: Arizona Game and Fish Department (copy in author's files).

———. 2003b. Landscape-scale habitat relationships to tassel-eared squirrel population dynamics in north-central Arizona. Technical Guidance Bulletin 6. Phoenix: Arizona Game and Fish Department.

Dodd, N. L., and S. L. Adams. 1989. Integrating wildlife needs into national forest timber sale planning: A state agency perspective. *In* Proceedings, Multiresource Management of Ponderosa Pine Forests, ed. A. Tecle, W. W. Covington, and R. H. Hamre, 131–40. General Technical Report RM-185. Fort Collins, CO: USDA Forest Service.

Dodd, N. L., S. S. Rosenstock, C. R. Miller, and R. E. Schweinsburg. 1998. Tassel-eared squirrel population dynamics in Arizona: Index techniques and relationships to habitat conditions. Research Branch Technical Report no. 27. Phoenix: Arizona Game and Fish Department.

Dodd, N. L., J. S. States, and S. S. Rosenstock. 2003. Tassel-eared squirrel population, habitat condition, and dietary relationships in north-central Arizona. *Journal of Wildlife Management* 67 (3): 622–33.

Dodge, N. N. 1965. Whitetail squirrel. *Pacific Discovery* 18:23–26.

Drennan, J. E., and P. Beier. 2003. Forest structure and prey abundance in winter habitat of northern goshawks. *Journal of Wildlife Management* 67 (1): 177–85.

Drennan, J. E., P. Beier, and N. L. Dodd. 1998. Use of track stations to index abundance of sciurids. *Journal of Mammalogy* 79:352–59.

Durrant, S. D. 1947. The Abert squirrel in Utah. *Journal of Mammalogy* 28:66.

Durrant, S. D., and K. R. Kelson. 1947. A new Abert squirrel from Utah. *Proceedings of Biological Society of Washington* 60:79–82.

Dutton, C. E. 1882. Tertiary History of the Grand Canyon, with Atlas. Washington, DC: U.S. Geological Survey.

Edelman, A. J., and J. L. Koprowski. 2005a. Selection of drey sites by Abert's squirrels in an introduced population. *Journal of Mammalogy* 86 (6): 1220–26.

———. 2005b. Diet and tree use of Abert's squirrels (*Sciurus aberti*) in a mixed-conifer forest. *Southwestern Naturalist* 50 (4): 461–65.

———. 2006a. Characteristics of Abert's squirrel (*Sciurus aberti*) cavity nests. *Southwestern Naturalist* 51 (1): 64–70.

———. 2006b. Seasonal changes in home range of Abert's squirrels: Impact of mating season. *Canadian Journal of Zoology* 84:404–11.

———. 2006c. Introduced Abert's squirrels in the Pinaleño Mountains: A review of their natural history and potential impacts on the red squirrel. *In* Proceedings of the Endangered Mount Graham Red Squirrel Symposium: Ecology, Conservation, and Management, Safford, Arizona, May 20–22, 2003, ed. H. R. Sanderson and J. L. Koprowski. Tucson: University of Arizona Press.

———. 2006d. Communal nesting in asocial Abert's squirrels: the role of social thermoregulation and breeding strategy. *Ethology* 112:147–54.

———. 2009. Introduced Abert's squirrels in the Pineleño Mountains: A review of their natural history and potential impacts on the red squirrel. *In* The Last Refuge of the Mt. Graham Red Squirrel, ed. H. R. Sanderson and J. L. Koprowski, 358–76. Tucson: University of Arizona Press.

Edelman, A. J., J. L. Koprowski, and S. R. Bertelsen. 2009. Potential for nest site competition between native and exotic tree squirrels. *Journal of Mammalogy* 90 (1): 167–74.

Edelman, A. J., J. L. Koprowski, and J. L. Edelman. 2005c. Kleptoparasitic behavior and species richness at Mt. Graham red squirrel middens. *In* Connecting Mountain Islands and Desert Seas: Biodiversity and Management of the Madrean Archipelago II, 2004 May 11–15, comp. G. J. Gottfried, B. S. Gebow, L. G. Eskew, and C. B. Edminster. Proceedings, RMRS-P-36. Tucson, AZ: USDA Forest Service.

Elliot, D. G. 1905. Check List of Mammals of the North American Continent, the West Indies, and the Neighboring Seas. Vol. 6, Publication 105, Zoological Series. Chicago: Field Columbian Museum.

Elson, M. T. 1999. Tassel-eared foraging patterns and projected effects of ecological restoration treatments at Mt. Trumbull, Arizona. MS thesis, Northern Arizona University.

Emmons, R. W. 1988. Ecology of Colorado tick fever. *Annual Review of Microbiology* 42:49–64.

Emry, R. J., and R. W. Thorington Jr. 1984. The tree squirrel *Sciurus* (Sciuridae, Rodentia) as a living fossil. *In* Living Fossils, ed. N. Eldredge and S. M. Stanley. New York: Springer Verlag.

Executive Order of the President [Theodore Roosevelt] of the United States to create the Kaibab National Forest, July 2, 1908. Monthly Catalogue, July. United States Public Documents, no. 163. Washington, DC: U.S. Government Printing Office.

Exit the Kaibab squirrel. *Washington Post–Times Herald*, editorial, July 5.

Farentinos, R. C. 1972a. Nests of tassel-eared squirrels. *Journal of Mammalogy* 53:900–903.

———. 1972b. Social dominance and mating activity in the tassel-eared squirrel (*Sciurus aberti ferreus*). *Animal Behavior* 20:316–26.

———. 1972c. Observations on the ecology of the tassel-eared squirrel. *Journal of Wildlife Management* 36 (4): 1234–39.

———. 1974. Social communication of the tassel-eared squirrel (*Sciurus aberti*): A descriptive analysis. *Z. Tierpsychology* 34:441–58.

———. 1979. Seasonal changes in home range size of tassel-eared squirrels (*Sciurus aberti*). *Southwestern Naturalist* 24:49–62.

———. 1980. Sexual solicitation of subordinate males by female tassel-eared squirrels (*Sciurus aberti*). *Journal of Mammalogy* 61 (2): 337–41.

Farentinos, R. C., P. J. Capretta, R. E. Kepner, and V. M. Littlefield. 1981. Selective herbivory in tassel-eared squirrels: Role of monoterpenes in ponderosa pines chosen as feeding trees. *Science* 213:1273–75.

Feldhamer, G. A., L. C. Drickamer, S. H. Vessey, and J. F. Merritt. 2004. Mammalogy. 2nd ed. Dubuque, IA: McGraw-Hill.

Ferner, J. W. 1974. Habitat relationships of *Tamiasciurus hudsonicus* and *Sciurus aberti* in the Rocky Mountains. *Southwestern Naturalist* 18:470–73.

Ffolliott, P. F. 1975. Production-rating functions for Abert squirrels in southwestern ponderosa pine. *Journal of Wildlife Management* 3:162–65.

———. 1978. Abert squirrel use of ponderosa pine as feed trees. Research Note RM-362. Fort Collins, CO: USDA Forest Service.

———. 1990. Small game habitat use in southwestern ponderosa pine forests. *In* Proceedings of Managing Wildlife in the Southwest, ed. P. R. Krausman and N. S. Smith, 107–17. Phoenix: The Wildlife Society, Arizona Chapter.

Findley, J. S. 1987. The Natural History of New Mexican Mammals. Albuquerque: University of New Mexico Press.

Findley, J. S., and S. Anderson. 1956. Zoogeography of the montane mammals of Colorado. *Journal of Mammalogy* 37 (1): 80–82.

Findley, J. S., A. H. Harris, D. E. Wilson, and C. Jones. 1975. Mammals of New Mexico. Albuquerque: University of New Mexico Press.

Fisher, J., N. Simon, and J. Vincent. 1969. The Red Book—Wildlife in Danger. London: Collins.

Fitzgerald, J. P., C. A. Meaney, and D. M. Armstrong. 1994. Mammals of Colorado. Denver: Denver Museum of Natural History.

Flyger, V. F. 1959. A comparison of methods for estimating squirrel populations. *Journal of Wildlife Management* 23 (2): 220–23.

Forsyth, D. R. 1991. A comparative cytogenetic investigation of *Sciurus aberti aberti* and *Sciurus aberti kaibabensis*. MS thesis, Northern Arizona University.

Fowells, H. A., and G. H. Schubert. 1956. Seed crops of forest trees in the pine region of California. Technical Bulletin 1150. Washington, DC: U.S. Department of Agriculture.

Frey, J. F., and T. L. Yates. 1996. Mammalian diversity in New Mexico. *New Mexico Journal of Science* 36:4–37.

Frey, J. K. 2003. Initiation of Abert's squirrel (*Sciurus aberti*) monitoring on Carson National Forest, New Mexico. Taos, NM: Carson National Forest.

———. 2004. Abert's squirrel (*Sciurus aberti*) monitoring and habitat analysis on Carson National Forest, New Mexico, 2004. Final report. Taos, NM: Carson National Forest.

———. 2006. Abert's squirrel (*Sciurus aberti*) monitoring on Carson National Forest, New Mexico, 2006. Taos, NM: Carson National Forest.

Galliziolli, S. 1953. Investigation of the Mt. Graham area. Completion Report. Project W-53-R-3, work plan 5, job 1. Phoenix: Arizona Game and Fish Commission.

Garnett, G. N., C. L. Chambers, and R. L. Mathiasen. 2006. Use of witches' brooms by Abert squirrels in ponderosa pine forests. *Wildlife Society Bulletin* 34 (2): 467–72.

Garnett, G., N., R. L. Mathiasen, and C. L. Chambers. 2004. A comparison of wildlife use in broomed and unbroomed ponderosa pine trees in northern Arizona. *Western Journal of Applied Forestry* 19 (1): 42–46.

Gaud, W. S., W. S. Allred, and J. S. States. 1991. Tree selection by tassel-eared squir-
rels of the ponderosa pine forests of the Colorado Plateau. *In* Proceedings,
First Biennial Conference on Research in Colorado Plateau National Parks, ed.
G. Rowlands, C. van Riper III, and M. K. Sogge, 56–64. Flagstaff, AZ: Northern
Arizona University.

Goldman, E. A. 1924. Report on conditions affecting the Kaibab squirrel (August
16–26, 1924). Smithsonian Institution Archives, record unit 7176, box 25,
folder 4.

———. 1925. Memorandum concerning the Kaibab squirrel (June 6–18, 1925).
Smithsonian Institution Archives, record unit 7176, box 25, folder 9.

———. 1928. The Kaibab or white-tailed squirrel. *Journal of Mammalogy* 9:127–29.

———. 1931. Three new rodents from Arizona and New Mexico. *Proceedings of
Biological Society of Washington* 44:133–36.

Golightly, R. T., and R. D. Ohmart. 1978. Heterothermy in free-ranging Abert's
squirrels (*Sciurus aberti*). *Ecology* 59:897–909.

Green, R. G., C. L. Larson, and J. F. Bell. 1939. Shock disease as the cause of the periodic decimation of the snowshoe hare. *American Journal of Hygiene* 30:83–102.

Gurnell, J. 1987. The Natural History of Squirrels. New York: Facts on File.

Guthrie, D. A. 1982a. Faunal remains. *In* Bandelier Excavations in the Flood Pool
of Cochiti Lake, New Mexico, ed. L. Hubbell and D. Traylor, 370–81. U.S.
GPO: 1982-578-880/298. Washington, DC: National Park Service, Southwest
Cultural Resource Center.

———. 1982b. Analysis of faunal remains from LA 13569 and LA 12117. *In*
Bandelier Excavations in the Flood Pool of Cochiti Lake, New Mexico, ed.
L. Hubbell and D. Traylor, 577–58. U.S. GPO: 1982-578-880/298. Washington,
DC: National Park Service, Southwest Cultural Resource Center.

Guzman, D. 1997. A histological analysis of the female Abert squirrel, *Sciurus
aberti aberti*, reproductive cycle. MS thesis, Northern Arizona University.

Hadow, H. H. 1972. Freeze-branding: A permanent marking technique for pigmented mammals. *Journal of Wildlife Management* 36 (2): 645–49.

Hall, E. R., and K. R. Kelson. 1959. The Mammals of North America. 2 vols. New
York: Ronald Press.

Hall, J. G. 1967a. White tails and yellow pines. *National Parks Magazine* 41:9–11.

———. 1967b. The Kaibab squirrel in Grand Canyon National Park—a seven seasons summary—1960–1967. Grand Canyon, AZ: Grand Canyon National Park.

———. 1972. The Kaibab squirrel. *In* Symposium on Rare and Endangered Wildlife
of the Southwestern United States, 18–21. Santa Fe: New Mexico Game and
Fish Department.

———. 1981. A field study of the Kaibab squirrel in Grand Canyon National Park.
Wildlife Monographs 75.

Halloran, M. E. 1993. Social behavior and ecology of Abert squirrels (*Sciurus
aberti*). PhD diss., University of Colorado.

Halloran, M. E., and M. Bekoff. 1994. Nesting behavior of Abert's squirrels. *Ethnology* 97:236–48.

———. 1995. Cheek rubbing as grooming by Abert's squirrels. *Animal Behavior* 50:987–93.

Hancock, D. C., Jr., and D. J. Nash. 1982. Dorsal hair length and coat color in Abert's squirrel (*Sciurus aberti*). *Great Basin Naturalist* 42:597–98.

Hargrave, L. L. 1979. A macaw feather artifact from southwestern Utah. *Southwestern Lore* 45 (4): 1–6.

Harlow, W. M., and E. S. Harrar. 1941. Textbook of Dendrology. American Forestry Series. New York: McGraw-Hill.

Harris, A. H. 1985. Late Pleistocene Vertebrate Paleoecology of the West. Austin: University of Texas Press.

———. 1990. Fossil evidence bearing on southwestern mammalian biogeography. *Journal of Mammalogy* 71 (2): 219–29.

Hawbecker, A. C. 1944. General notes: The use of a road by mammals. *Journal of Mammalogy* 25:196.

Hawksworth, F. G. 1977. The 6-class mistletoe rating system. General Technical Report RM-48. Fort Collins, CO: USDA Forest Service.

Hayne, D. W. 1949. An examination of the strip census method for estimating animal populations. *Journal of Wildlife Management* 13 (2): 145–57.

Heaney, L. R. 1984. Climatic influences of life-history tactics and behavior of North American tree squirrels. *In* The Biology of Ground-Dwelling Squirrels, ed. J. O. Murie and G. R. Michener, 43–78. Lincoln: University of Nebraska Press.

Hight, M. E. 1972. The use of serum proteins in studying phylogenetic relationships of the Sciuridae. PhD diss., Wayne State University.

Hill, J. E. 1942. Notes on mammals of northeastern New Mexico. *Journal of Mammalogy* 23:75–82.

Hill, T. P., and D. W. Duszynski. 1986. Coccidia (Apicomplexa: Eimeriidae) from Sciurid rodents (*Eutamias, Sciurus, Tamiasciurus* spp.) from the western United States and northern Mexico with descriptions of two new species. *Journal of Protozoology* 33 (2): 282–88.

Hoffmeister, D. F. 1956. Mammals of the Graham (Pinaleño) Mountains, Arizona. *American Midland Naturalist* 55 (2): 257–88.

———. 1971. Mammals of the Grand Canyon. Chicago: University of Illinois Press.

———. 1986. Mammals of Arizona. Tucson: University of Arizona Press.

Hoffmeister, D. F., and V. Diersing. 1978. Review of the tassel-eared squirrels of the subgenus *Otosciurus*. *Journal of Mammalogy* 59:402–13.

Holbrook, S. J. 1975. Prehistoric paleoecology of northeastern New Mexico. PhD diss., University of California, Berkeley.

Hough, E. 1921. The president's forest. *Saturday Evening Post* 194:6–7.

Hurst, W. D. 1967. Memorandum—wildlife habitat management. U.S. Department of Agriculture, Forest Service (copy in author's files provided by William Hurst).

———. 1971. Memorandum—Kaibab squirrel study. U.S. Department of Agriculture, Forest Service (copy in author's files provided by William Hurst).

———. 1972. Timber management plan, North Kaibab block, Kaibab National Forest, Region 3 (copy in author's files).

Huang, Feng-Hou, Song-Gen Huang, Po-Han Hsu, and Yen-Li Chung. 1982. A preliminary study by peroxidase analysis of two genotypes of China fir (*Cunninghamia lanceolata*) differing in their susceptibility to squirrel damage. *Quarterly Journal of Chinese Forestry* 15 (4): 21–22.

Hutton, K. A., J. L. Koprowski, V. I. Greer, M. I. Alanen, C. A. Schauffert, and P. J. Young. 2003. Use of mixed conifer and spruce-fir forests by an introduced population of Abert's squirrels (*Sciurus aberti*). *Southwestern Naturalist* 48:257–60.

Inventory of sensitive species and ecosystems in Utah. 1997. Salt Lake City: Utah Division of Wildlife Resources.

Jaradian, G. 1980. Faunal analysis and interpretation. *In* Archaeological Investigations at San Antonio de Padua, LA 24, Bernalillo County, New Mexico, ed. A. Dart, 244–93. Laboratory of Anthropology Note no. 167. Santa Fe: Museum of New Mexico.

Jarne, P., and P. J. L. Lagoda. 1996. Microsatellites, from molecules to populations and back. *Trends in Ecology and Evolution* 11:424–29.

Jordan, K. 1925. New Siphonaptera. *Novitates Zoologicae* 32:96–112.

Kaibab National Forest. 2009. News release. Kaibab National Forest celebrates special squirrel, www.fs.fed.us/r3/kai.

Kaibab National Forest Map. 1960. Washington, DC: USDA, U.S. Forest Service.

Keith, J. O. 1956. The Abert squirrel (*Sciurus aberti aberti*) and its relation to the forests of Arizona. MS thesis, University of Arizona.

———. 1965. The Abert squirrel and its dependence on ponderosa pine. *Ecology* 46:150–63.

———. Assessment. Golden, CO: USDA Forest Service, Rocky Mountain Region.

Koprowski, J. L. 2002. Handling tree squirrels with a safe and efficient restraint. *Wildlife Society Bulletin* 30 (1): 101–3.

———. 2005. Management and conservation of tree squirrels: The importance of endemism, species richness, and forest condition. *In* Connecting Mountain Islands and Desert Seas: Biodiversity and Management of the Madrean Archipelago II, 2004, May 11–15, Proceedings, comp. G. J. Gottfried, B. S. Gebow, L. G. Eskew, and C. B. Edminster. RMRS-P-36. Tucson, AZ: USDA Forest Service.

Kotter, M. M., and R. C. Farentinos. 1984a. Formation of ponderosa pine ectomychorrhizae after inoculation with feces of tassel-eared squirrels. *Mycologia* 76:758–60.

———. 1984b. Tassel-eared squirrels as spore dispersal agents of hypogeous mycorrhizal fungi. *Journal of Mammalogy* 65:684–87.

Krauch, H. 1934. Diameter growth of ponderosa pine as related to age and crown development. *Journal of Forestry* 32:68–71.

Kufeld, R. C. 1962. Tree squirrel management information. Progress Report. Project W-53-R-12, work plan 3, job 3. Phoenix: Arizona Game and Fish Department.

——. 1963. Tree squirrel management information. Progress Report. Project W-53-R-13, work plan 3, job 3. Phoenix: Arizona Game and Fish Department.

——. 1964. Tree squirrel management information. Progress Report. Project W-53-R-14, work plan 3, job 3. Phoenix: Arizona Game and Fish Department.

——. 1965. Tree squirrel management information. Progress Report. Project W-53-R-15, work plan 3, job 3. Phoenix: Arizona Game and Fish Department.

Lamb, T., T. R. Jones, and P. J. Wettstein. 1997. Evolutionary genetics and phylogeography of tassel-eared squirrels (*Sciurus aberti*). *Journal of Mammalogy* 78 (1): 117–33.

Lang, R. W., and A. H. Harris. 1984. The faunal remains from Arroyo Hondo Pueblo, New Mexico, a study in short term subsistence change. Arroyo Hondo Archaeological Series. Vol. 5. Santa Fe: School of American Research Press.

Lange, K. I. 1960. Mammals of the Santa Catalina Mountains, Arizona. *American Midland Naturalist* 64 (2): 436–58.

Larson, M. M., and G. H. Schubert. 1970. Cone crops of ponderosa pine in central Arizona. Research Note RM-58USDA. Fort Collins, CO: USDA Forest Service.

Lauckhart, J. Burton. 1957. Animal cycles and food. *Journal of Wildlife Management* 21 (2): 230–34.

Lechleitner, R. R. 1969. Wild Mammals of Colorado—Their Appearance, Habits, Distribution, and Abundance. Boulder, CO: Pruett Publishing Co.

Lema, M. F. 2001. Dynamics of Abert squirrel populations: Home range, seasonal movements, survivorship, habitat use and sociality. MS thesis, Northern Arizona University.

Lema, M. F., W. S. Allred, W. S. Gaud, and N. L. Dodd. 1999. Social behavior of Abert's squirrels in ponderosa pine forests. *In* Proceedings of the Fourth Biennial Conference on Research on the Colorado Plateau, ed. C. van Riper III and M. A. Stuart, 105–12. Flagstaff: Northern Arizona University.

Leopold, A. S. 1972. Wildlife of Mexico: The Game Birds and Mammals. Berkeley: University of California Press.

Lindsay, E. H., and N. T. Tessman. 1974. Cenozoic vertebrates localities and faunas in Arizona. *Journal of the Arizona Academy of Science* 9:3–24.

Linhart, Y. B., M. A. Snyder, and S. A. Habeck. 1989. The influence of animals on genetic variability within ponderosa pine stands, illustrated by the effects of Abert's squirrel and porcupine. *In* Proceedings, Multiresource Management of Ponderosa Pine Forests, ed. A. Tecle, W. W. Covington, and R. H. Hamre, 141–48. General Technical Report RM-185. Fort Collins, CO: USDA Forest Service.

Ligon, J. S. 1927. Wild Life of New Mexico—Its Conservation and Management. Santa Fe, NM: State Game Commission, Department of Game and Fish.

Linnaeus, C. 1758. Systema Naturae. 10th ed.

Littlefield, V. M. 1984. Habitat interrelationships of Abert squirrels (*Sciurus aberti*) and fox squirrels (*Sciurus niger*) in Boulder County, Colorado. PhD diss., Miami University.

Loberger, C. 2009. Tassel-eared squirrel home range and habitat selection within a restoration-treated ponderosa pine forest. MS thesis, Northern Arizona University.

Lomolino, M. V., J. H. Brown, and R. Davis. 1989. Island biogeography of montane forest mammals in the American Southwest. *Ecology* 70 (1): 180–94.

MacClintock, D. 1970. Squirrel of North America. New York: Van Nostrand Reinhold Co.

Marchand, P. J. 2001. Riding the witches' broom. *Natural History Magazine*, May, 40–41.

Maser, C., and Z. Maser. 1988. Interactions among squirrels, mycorrhizal fungi, and coniferous forests in Oregon. *Great Basin Naturalist* 48 (3): 358–69.

Maser, C., J. M. Trappe, and R. A. Nussbaum. 1978. Fungal–small mammal interrelationships with emphasis on Oregon coniferous forests. *Ecology* 59 (4): 799–809.

Matthew, W. D. 1924. Article II. Third contribution to the Snake Creek fauna. *Bulletin of the American Museum of Natural History* 50:59–210.

McCartney, E. S. 1937. Calling on the Kaibab squirrel. *Nature Magazine* 29 (5): 271–72.

McKee, B. H. 1934. Raven vs. squirrel. *Grand Canyon Nature Notes* 8 (11): 247.

McKee, E. D. 1941. Distribution of the tassel-eared squirrels. *Plateau* 14:12–20.

Mearns, E. A. 1907. Mammals of the Mexican Boundary of the United States. Pt. 1. U.S. National Museum Bulletin 56. Washington, DC: Smithsonian Institution.

Mellott, R. S., and J. R. Choate. 1984. *Sciurus aberti* and *Microtus montanus* on foothills of the Culebra Range in southern Colorado. *Southwestern Naturalist* 29:135–37.

Mercer, J. M., and V. L. Roth. 2003. The effects of Cenozoic global change on squirrel phylogeny. *Science* 299:1568–71.

Merriam, C. H. 1890. Results of a biological survey of the San Francisco Mountain region and desert of the Little Colorado, Arizona. U.S. Bureau of the Biological Survey. *North American Fauna* 3.

———. 1894. Laws of temperature control of the geographic distribution of terrestrial animals and plants. *National Geographic* 6:229–38.

———. 1898. Life Zones and Crop Zones of the United States. U.S. Department of Agriculture Bulletin no. 10. Washington, DC: U.S. Government Printing Office.

———. 1904. Two new squirrels of the *aberti* group. *Proceedings of Biological Society of Washington* 17:129–30.

Miller, G. S., and R. Kellogg. 1955. List of North American Recent Mammals. U.S. National Museum Bulletin 205. Washington, DC: Smithsonian Institution.

Miller, R. 1996. History of the intent and management of the Grand Canyon Game Preserve. Unpublished report prepared for Arizona Game and Fish Department, Flagstaff (copy in author's files).

Minard, A. 2000. Morphological and genetic investigations of Abert squirrels (*Sciurus aberti aberti*). MS thesis, Northern Arizona University.

Minard, A., and W. S. Allred. 1999. Analyses of Road-Killed Abert Squirrels in Northern Arizona. April. Flagstaff: Arizona/Nevada Academy of Science.

Minckley, W. L. 1968. Possible extirpation of the spruce squirrel from the Pinaleño (Graham) Mountains, south-central Arizona. *Journal of the Academy of Science* 5:110.

Moore, J. C. 1959. Relationships among the living squirrels of the Sciurinae. *Bulletin of the American Museum of Natural History* 118 (4): 153–206.

Moore, T. D., L. E. Spense, and C. E. Dugnolle. 1974. Identification of Dorsal Guard Hairs of Some Mammals of Wyoming. Laramie: Wyoming Game and Fish Department.

Morrell, T. E., E. A. Point, and J. C. deVos Jr. 1999. Nest site characteristics of sympatric Mount Graham red squirrels and Abert's squirrels in the Pinaleño Mountains, Arizona. Final Report. Department of Biology Technical Report 2. Muncie, IN: Ball State University.

———. 2009. Nest site characteristics of sympatric Mt. Graham red squirrels and Abert's squirrels in the Pinaleño Mountains. *In* The Last Refuge of the Mt. Graham Red Squirrel, ed. H. R. Sanderson and J. L. Koprowski, 339–57. Tucson: University of Arizona Press.

Muir, J. 1911. My First Summer in the Sierra. Boston: Houghton Mifflin Co.

Muir, R. J., and J. C. Driver. 2003. Faunal Remains. *In* The Archaeology of Yellow Jacket Pueblo (Site 5MT5): Excavations at a Large Community Center in Southwestern Colorado, ed. K. A. Kuckelman. www.crowcanyon.org/yellowjacket.

Murphy, A. 1994. Graced by Pines. Missoula, MT: Mountain Press Publishing Co.

Murphy, S. M., and Y. B. Linhart. 1999. Comparative morphology of the gastrointestinal tract in the feeding specialist *Sciurus aberti* and several generalist congeners. *Journal of Mammalogy* 80 (4): 1325–30.

Myers, P., R. Espinosa, C. S. Parr, T. Jones, G. S. Hammond, and T. A. Dewey. 2008. The Animal Diversity Web. University of Michigan Museum of Zoology National Science Foundation Initiative. http://animaldiversity.org.

Nadler, C. F., and D. A. Sutton. 1967. Chromosomes of some squirrels (mammalia —Sciuridae) from the genera *Sciurus* and *Glaucomys*. *Experientia* 23:249–51.

Nash, D. J., and R. N. Seaman. 1977. Mammalian Species no. 80. *Sciurus aberti*. N.p.: American Society of Mammalogists.

National History Museum, London. 2008. http://www.nhm.ac.uk/nature-online/online-exhibitions/art-themes/caught_in_oils/more/thomas_more_info.htm.

Navajo Nation. 2008. Sensitive Species List. Window Rock, AZ: Division of Natural Resources, Department of Fish and Wildlife. www.navajofishand wildlife.org.

Nelson, E. W. 1899. Revision of the squirrels of central Mexico and Central America. *Proceedings of the Washington Academy of Sciences* 1:15–110.

———. 1918. Smaller North American Mammals. *National Geographic* 18 (5).

Noss, R. F., E. T. LaRoe II, and J. M. Scott. 1995. Endangered ecosystems of the United States: A preliminary assessment of loss and degradation. Report 28. Washington, DC: National Biological Survey.

Olin, G. 1961. Mammals of the Southwestern Mountains and Mesas. Globe, AZ: Southwestern Monuments Association.

Patrick, M. J., and W. D. Wilson. 1995. Parasites in the Abert's squirrel (*Sciurus aberti*) and red squirrel (*Tamiasciurus hudsonicus*) of New Mexico. *Journal of Parasitology* 81 (2): 321–24.

Patton, D. R. 1974a. Estimating food consumption from twigs clipped by the Abert squirrel. Research Note RM-272. Fort Collins, CO: USDA Forest Service, Rocky Mountain Forest and Range Experiment Station.

———. 1974b. Characteristics of ponderosa pine stands selected by Abert's squirrels for cover. PhD diss., University of Arizona.

———. 1975a. Nest use and home range of three Abert squirrels as determined by radio tracking. Research Note RM-281. Fort Collins, CO: USDA Forest Service, Rocky Mountain Forest and Range Experiment Station.

———. 1975b. Abert squirrel cover requirements in southwestern ponderosa pine. Research Paper RM-145. Fort Collins, CO: USDA Forest Service, Rocky Mountain Forest and Range Experiment Station.

———. 1977. Managing southwestern ponderosa pine for the Abert squirrel. *Journal of Forestry* 75:264–67.

———. 1984. A model to evaluate Abert squirrel habitat in uneven-aged ponderosa pine. *Wildlife Society Bulletin* 12:408–14.

———. 1989. Wildlife habitat concerns: Moderator's comments. *In* Proceedings, Multiresource Management of Ponderosa Pine Forests, ed. A. Tecle, W. W. Covington, and R. H. Hamre, 130. General Technical Report RM-185. Fort Collins, CO: USDA Forest Service.

———. 1997. Wildlife Habitat Relationships in Forested Ecosystems. 2nd ed. Portland, OR: Timber Press.

Patton, D. R., and W. Green. 1970. Abert's squirrels prefer mature ponderosa pine. Research Note RM-169. Fort Collins, CO: USDA Forest Service, Rocky Mountain Forest and Range Experiment Station.

Patton, D. R., T. D. Ratcliff, and K. J. Rogers. 1976. Weights and temperatures of the Abert and Kaibab squirrels. *Southwestern Naturalist* 21:236–38.

Patton, D. R., R. L. Wadleigh, and H. G. Hudak. 1985. The effects of timber harvesting on the Kaibab squirrel. *Journal of Wildlife Management* 49 (1): 14–19.

Pearson, G. A. 1950. Management of Ponderosa Pine in the Southwest. Agriculture Monograph 6. Washington, DC: USDA Forest Service.

Pederson, J. C., and B. L. Welch. 1985. Comparison of ponderosa pines as feed and non-feed trees for Abert squirrels. *Journal of Chemical Ecology* 11:149–57.

Pederson, J. C., R. C. Farentinos, and V. M. Littlefield. 1987. Effects of logging on habitat quality and feeding patterns of Abert squirrels. *Great Basin Naturalist* 47 (2): 252–58.

Pederson, J. C., R. N. Hasenyager, and A. W. Heggen. 1976. Habitat Requirements of the Abert Squirrel (*Sciurus aberti navajo*) on the Monticello District, Manti-LaSal National Forest. Publication 76-9. Salt Lake City: Utah State Division of Wildlife.

————. 1978. Use of artificial nest boxes by Abert's squirrel. *Southwestern Naturalist* 23:700–702.

Pippin, L. C. 1987. Prehistory and Paleoecology of Guadalupe Ruin. Anthropological Papers no. 112. Salt Lake City: University of Utah Press.

Pogany, G. C., and W. S. Allred. 1992. Sperm morphology as a tool for taxonomy. *In* Proceedings Fifth U.S./Mexico Border States Conference on Recreation, Parks, and Wildlife. Las Cruces, New Mexico, September 17–19, pp. 44–47. Tucson: University of Arizona.

————. 1995. Abert's squirrels of the Colorado Plateau: Their reproductive cycle. *In* Proceeding of the Second Biennial Conference of Research in Colorado Plateau National Parks, ed. C. van Riper III, 293–305. NPS/NRNAU/NKTP-95/11. Flagstaff: Northern Arizona University.

Pogany, G. C., W. S. Allred, and T. Barnes. 1998. The reproductive cycle of Abert's squirrel. *In* Ecology and Evolutionary Biology of Tree Squirrels, ed. M. A. Steele, J. F. Merritt, and D. A. Zegers, 53–59. Special Publications 6. Martinsville: Virginia Museum of Natural History.

Potter, R. M. 1980. The development of ponderosa pine cone processing ability in young tassel-eared squirrels (*Sciurus aberti*). PhD diss., Miami University.

Prather, J. W., N. L. Dodd, B. G. Dickson, H. M. Hampton, Y. Xu, E. N. Aumack, and T. D. Sisk. 2006. Landscape models to predict the influence of forest structure on tassel-eared squirrel populations. *Journal of Wildlife Management* 70 (3): 723–31.

Presnall, C. C. 1938. Mammals of Zion, Bryce and Cedar Breaks. Zion-Bryce Bulletin no. 2. N.p.: Zion-Bryce Natural History Association.

Proclamation by the President [Benjamin Harrison] of the United States to create the Grand Canyon Forest Preserve, February 20, 1893. http://memory.loc.gov/ammem/amrvhtml/conshome.html.

Proclamation by the President [Theodore Roosevelt] of the United States to create the Grand Canyon Game Reserve, November 28, 1906. U.S. Statutes at Large 34:3263. http://memory.loc.gov/ammem/amrvhtml/conshome.html.

Ramey, C. A. 1972. Squirrels with tassel ears. *Colorado Outdoors* 21:36–38.

————. The movement patterns and coat color polymorphism of Abert's squirrel, *Sciurus aberti ferreus*. PhD diss., Colorado State University.

Ramey, C. A., and D. J. Nash. 1971. Abert's squirrel in Colorado. *Southwestern Naturalist* 16:125–26.

————. 1976a. Geographic variation in Abert's squirrel (*Sciurus aberti*). *Southwestern Naturalist* 21 (2): 135–39.

————. 1976b. Coat color polymorphism of Abert's squirrel, *Sciurus aberti*, in Colorado. *Southwestern Naturalist* 21 (2): 209–17.

Ramirez-Pubido, J., J. Arroyo-Cabrales, and A. Castro-Campillo. 2005. Current status and relationship of nomenclatural land mammals of Mexico. *Zoological Record Mexicana*, n.s., 21 (1): 21–82.

Rasmussen, D. I. 1929. The Kaibab squirrel (copy in author's files provided by William Hurst).

———. 1941. Biotic communities of the Kaibab Plateau, Arizona. *Ecological Monographs* 11:229–75.

———. 1971. National and international interest in the Kaibab squirrel: A problem analysis. Rough draft (copy in author's files).

Rasmussen, D. I., D. E. Brown, and D. Jones. 1975. Use of ponderosa pine by tassel-eared squirrels and a key to determine evidence of their use from that of red squirrels and porcupines. *In* Wildlife Digest. Phoenix: Arizona Game and Fish Department.

Ratcliff, T. D., D. R. Patton, and P. F. Ffolliott. 1975. Ponderosa pine basal area and the Kaibab squirrel. *Journal of Forestry* 75:284–86.

Raught, R. W. 1967. Tree squirrels. *In* New Mexico Wildlife Management, 95–100. Santa Fe: New Mexico Game and Fish Department.

Redburn, R. 1931. A mother squirrel transports its young. *Grand Canyon Nature Notes* 5 (8): 80–81.

———. 1932. A Kaibab squirrel family. *Grand Canyon Nature Notes* 6:66–68.

Reynolds, H. G. 1963. Western goshawk takes Abert squirrel in Arizona. *Journal of Forestry* 61:551.

———. 1966. Abert's squirrels feeding on pinyon pine. *Journal of Mammalogy* 47:550–51.

Reynolds, H. G., W. P. Clary, and P. F. Ffolliott. 1970. Gambel oak for southwestern wildlife. *Journal of Forestry* 68:545–47.

Reynolds, R. T., R. T. Graham, H. M. Reiser, R. L. Bassett, P. L. Kennedy, D. A. Boyce Jr., G. Goodwin, R. Smith, and E. L. Fisher. 1992. Management recommendations for the northern goshawk in the southwestern United States. General Technical Report RM-217. Fort Collins, CO: USDA Forest Service, Rocky Mountain Forest and Range Experiment Station.

Rice, D. W. 1957. Sexual behavior of tassel-eared squirrels. *Journal of Mammalogy* 38 (1): 129.

Roeser, J., Jr. 1941. Some aspects of flower and cone production in ponderosa pine. *Journal of Forestry* 39:534–36.

Rose, M. D. 1997. Histological examination of the male reproductive cycle in the Abert squirrel, *Sciurus aberti*. MS thesis, Northern Arizona University.

Rutledge, R. H. 1924. Statement of policy for the administration of the Kaibab National Forest (copy in author's files).

Salyer, J. C. 1962. Kaibab squirrel—Kaibab Plateau pine forest, Arizona. Evaluation for natural landmark designation. Washington, DC: U.S. Fish and Wildlife Service.

Sanford, C. A. 1986. Food habits and related behavior of the Abert squirrel. MS thesis, Northern Arizona University.

Schmid, J. M., J. C. Mitchell, and S. A. Mata. 1986. Ponderosa pine conelet and cone mortality in central Arizona. *Great Basin Naturalist* 46 (3): 445–48.

Schubert, G. H. 1974. Silviculture of the southwestern ponderosa pine: The status of our knowledge. Research Paper RM-123. Fort Collins, CO: USDA Forest Service.

Seaman, R. N., and D. J. Nash. 1977. An electrophoretic description of five species of squirrel. *Comparative Biochemical Physiology* 58B:309–11.

Searle, A. G. 1968. Comparative Genetics of Coat Colour in Mammals. London: Academic Press.

Seton, E. T. 1953. Lives of Game Animals. Vol. 4, pt. 1. Boston: Charles T. Branford Co.

Sharp, W. M. 1958. Aging gray squirrels by use of tail-pelage characteristics. *Journal of Wildlife Management* 22 (1): 29–34.

Short, H. L., and W. B. Duke. 1971. Seasonal food consumption and body weights of captive tree squirrels. *Journal of Wildlife Management* 35:425–39.

Sieg, M. J. 2002. Landscape composition and Abert squirrel survivorship, predator-based mortality, home range size and movement. MS thesis, Northern Arizona University.

Sitgreaves, L. 1853. Report of an Expedition Down the Zuni and Colorado Rivers. United States Army Corps of Topographical Engineers. Washington, DC: R. Armstrong.

Skinner, T. H. 1976. Contribution of Abert squirrel to nutrient transfer through litterfall in ponderosa pine ecosystem. MS thesis, University of Arizona.

Skinner, T. H., and J. O. Klemmedson. 1978. Abert squirrels influence nutrient transfer through litterfall in a ponderosa pine forest. Research Note RM-353. Fort Collins, CO: USDA Forest Service, Rocky Mountain Research Station.

Smith, R. H. 1967. Hunt questionnaires—1966. Special Report. Project W-53-R-17, work plan 2, 3, jobs 1–4. Phoenix: Arizona Game and Fish Department.

Smith, C. C. 1970. The coevolution of pine squirrels (*Tamiasciurus*) and conifers. *Ecological Monographs* 40:349–71.

Snyder, M. A. 1992. Selective herbivory by Abert's squirrel mediated by chemical variability in ponderosa pine. *Ecology* 73:1730–41.

———. 1993. Interactions between Abert's squirrel and ponderosa pine: The relationship between selective herbivory and host plant fitness. *American Naturalist* 141:866–79.

———. 1998. Abert's squirrel (*Sciurus aberti*) in ponderosa pine (*Pinus ponderosa*) forests: Directional selection, diversifying selection. *In* Ecology and Evolutionary Biology of Tree Squirrels, ed. M. A. Steele, J. F. Merritt, and D. A. Zegers, 195–201. Special Publications 6. Martinsville: Virginia Museum of Natural History.

Snyder, M. A., and Y. B. Linhart. 1994. Nest-site selection by Abert's squirrel: Chemical characteristics of nest trees. *Journal of Mammalogy* 75:136–41.

———. 1998. Subspecific selectivity by mammalian herbivore: Geographical differentiation of interactions between two taxa of *Sciurus aberti* and *Pinus ponderosa*. *Evolutionary Ecology* 12:755–65.

Soderquist, T. R. 1987. The impact of tassel-eared squirrel defoliation on ecotonal ponderosa pine. *Journal of Mammalogy* 68 (2): 398–401.

Spicer, R. B. 1985. Status of the Mt. Graham Red Squirrel, *Tamiasciurus hudsonicus grahamensis*, of Southeastern Arizona. Phoenix: Arizona Game and Fish Department.

States, J. S. 1985. Hypogeous, mycorrhizal fungi associated with ponderosa pine: Sporocarp phenology. *In* Proceedings of the 6th North American Conference on Mycorrhizae, June 25–29, Bend, Oregon, ed. R. Molina, 271. Corvallis: Oregon State University, College of Forestry.

States, J. S., and W. S. Gaud. 1997. Ecology of hypogeous fungi associated with ponderosa pine. I. Patterns of distribution and sporocarp production in some Arizona forests. *Mycologia* 89:712–21.

States, J. S., and P. J. Wettstein. 1998. Food habits and evolutionary relationships of the tassel-eared squirrel (*Sciurus aberti*). *In* Ecology and Evolutionary Biology of Tree Squirrels, ed. M. A. Steele, J. F. Merritt, and D. A. Zegers, 185–94. Special Publications 6. Martinsville: Virginia Museum of Natural History 6.

States, J. S., W. S. Gaud, W. S. Allred, and W. J. Austin. 1988. Foraging patterns of tassel-eared squirrels in selected ponderosa pine stands. *In* Proceedings, Management of Amphibians, Reptiles, and Small Mammals in North America, ed. R. C. Szaro, K. E. Severson, and D. R. Patton, 425–31. General Technical Paper RM-166. Fort Collins, CO: USDA Forest Service.

Stephenson, R. L. 1975. Reproductive biology and food habits of Abert's squirrels in central Arizona. MS thesis, Arizona State University.

Stephenson, R. L., and D. E. Brown. 1980. Snow cover as a factor influencing mortality of Abert's squirrels. *Journal of Wildlife Management* 44 (4): 951–55.

Stone, W. 1904. Dr. Samuel W. Woodhouse's obituary. Alumni Register, University of Pennsylvania. December.

Sturdevant, G. E. 1927. The Kaibab and Abert squirrel. *Arizona Wild Life* 1 (8): 2–3.

———. 1934. Observations from *Grand Canyon Nature Notes*. In The Best of Grand Canyon Nature Notes, 1926–1935, ed. Susan Lamb. Grand Canyon, AZ: Grand Canyon Natural History Association, 1994.

Sutton, A., and M. Sutton. 1970. The Wilderness World of the Grand Canyon. Philadelphia: J. B. Lippincott Co.

Tallon, J. 1983. Photograph. *Arizona Highways* 59 (8): 38.

Tamarin, R. 1998. Principles of Genetics. 6th ed. Dubuque, IA: McGraw-Hill.

Taylor, W. P. 1916. Field notes: Arizona—Jerome and Mingus Mountain. U.S. Fish and Wildlife Service, Field Reports, 1860–1961. Smithsonian Institution Archives, record unit 7176, box 28, folder 26.

———. 1924a. Memorandum for Major Goldman, handling Abert squirrels (*Sciurus aberti*), Flagstaff, Arizona. Smithsonian Institution Archives, record unit 7176, box 29, folder 14.

———. 1924b. Memorandum for Major Goldman, summary of work, field season 1924, Tucson, Arizona. Smithsonian Institution Archives, record unit 7176, box 29, folder 15.

————. 1924c. Progress report on animal forest work, Division of Biological Investigations, Bureau of Biological Survey: Conducted in cooperation with the Southwestern Forest Experiment Station, Flagstaff, Arizona. Smithsonian Institution Archives, record unit 7176, box 29, folder 14.

————. 1925a. Report of winter work at the Southwestern Forest Experiment Station, especially on the life habits and control of the porcupine (*Erethizon epixanthum couesi*), Flagstaff, Arizona. Smithsonian Institution Archives, record unit 7176, box 29, folder 18.

————. 1925b. Report of winter work at the Southwestern Forest Experiment Station. The Abert squirrel, Flagstaff, Arizona. Smithsonian Institution Archives, record unit 7176, box 29, folder 18.

————. 1926a. Narrative report, Tucson Office, Division of Biological Investigations, Bureau of Biological Survey, United States Department of Agriculture. Smithsonian Institution Archives, record unit 7176, box 29, folder 22.

————. 1926b. Memorandum of the White-Tailed Squirrel (*Sciurus kaibabensis*) of the Grand Canyon National Game Preserve, Division of Biological Investigations, Bureau of Biological Survey, United States Department of Agriculture. Smithsonian Institution Archives, record unit 7176, box 29, folder 19.

————. 1927. The biological side of business of forest and forage production. *Journal of Forestry* 25:386–414.

Thomas, G. R. 1979. The role of phloem sugars in the selection of ponderosa pine by the Kaibab squirrel. MS thesis, San Francisco State University.

Thomas, O. 1893. On the Mexican representative of *Sciurus aberti*. *Annual Magazine of Natural History*, series 6 (11): 49–50.

Thomson, W. G. 1940. A growth rate classification of southwestern ponderosa pine. *Journal of Forestry* 38:547–53.

Thorington, R. W., Jr., and K. Ferrell. 2006. Squirrels: The Animal Answer Guide. Baltimore, MD: Johns Hopkins University Press.

Thorington, R. W., Jr., and R. S. Hoffmann. 2005. Family Sciuridae. *In* Mammal Species of the World: A Taxonomic and Geological Reference, ed. D. E. Wilson and D. M. Reeder. 3rd ed. Vols. 1 and 2. Baltimore, MD: Johns Hopkins University Press.

Tinnin, R. O., F. G. Hawksworth, and D. M. Knutson. 1982. Witches' broom formation in conifers infected by *Arceuthobium* spp.: An example of parasitic impact upon community dynamics. *American Midland Naturalist* 107:351–59.

Trierweiler, W. N. 1992. Faunal analysis. *In* Bandelier Archaeological Excavation Project: Summer 1990 Excavations at Burnt Mesa Pueblo and Casa del Rito, ed. T. Kohler and M. Root, 135–46. Reports of Investigation 64. Pullman: Washington State University, Department of Anthropology.

Trowbridge, A. H., and L. L. Larson. 1942. Abert squirrel–ponderosa pine relationships at the Fort Valley Experimental Forest, Flagstaff, Arizona (copy in author's files).

True, F. W. 1894. Diagnoses of new North American mammals. *Proceedings of the United States National Museum* 17:241–43.

———. 1900. New name for North American squirrel. *Proceedings of the Biological Society of Washington* 13:183.

Turbak, G. 1987. Prisoner of geography. *National Wildlife* 25 (2): 14–16.

Turkowski, F. J. 1980. Carnivora food habits and habitat use in ponderosa pine forests. Research Paper RM-215. Fort Collins, CO: USDA Forest Service.

Uhlig, H. G. 1957. Gray squirrel populations in extensive forested areas of West Virginia. *Journal of Wildlife Management* 21 (3): 335–41.

Ure, D. C., and C. Maser. 1982. Mycophagy of red-backed voles in Oregon and Washington. *Canadian Journal of Zoology* 60:3307–15.

USDA Forest Service. 1976. Cooperative Agreement with Arizona Game and Fish Commission (copy in author's files).

———. 2005. Final Environmental Assessment. Management Indicator Species. Forest Plan Amendment 30. Pueblo, CO: USDA Forest Service.

U.S. Department of the Interior. 1973. Threatened Wildlife of the United States. Resource Publication 114 (Revised Resource Publication 34). Washington, DC: U.S. Government Printing Office.

Vireday, C. C. 1982. Mycophagy in tassel-eared squirrels (*Sciurus aberti aberti* and *S. a. kaibabensis*) in northern Arizona. MS thesis, Northern Arizona University.

Wade, O. 1935. Notes on the northern tuft-eared squirrel *Sciurus aberti ferreus* True, in Colorado. *American Midland Naturalist* 16 (2): 201–2.

Wade, O., and P. T. Gilbert. 1935. The baculum of some Sciuridae and its significance in determining relationships. *Journal of Mammalogy* 16:52–62.

Wallace, A., and R. H. Hevly. 2007. From Texas to San Diego in 1851—the Overland Journal of Dr. S. W. Woodhouse, Surgeon-Naturalist of the Sitgreaves Expedition. Lubbock: Texas Tech University Press.

Warren, E. R. 1910. The Mammals of Colorado. New York: G. P. Putnam's Sons.

Wettstein, P. J., and J. States. 1986a. The major histocompatibility complex of tassel-eared squirrels. I. Genetic diversity associated with Kaibab squirrels. *Immunogenetics* 24:230–41.

———. 1986b. The major histocompatibility complex of tassel-eared squirrels. II. Genetic diversity associated with Abert squirrels. *Immunogenetics* 24:242–50.

Wettstein, P. J., R. Chakraborty, J. S. States, and G. Ferrari. 1990. T-cell receptor genes in tassel-eared squirrels (*Sciurus aberti*) I. Genetic polymorphism and divergence in the Abert and Kaibab subspecies. *Immunogenetics* 32:219–30.

Wettstein, P. J., P. Lager, L. Jin, J. S. States, T. Lamb, and R. Chakraborty. 1994. Phylogeny of mitochondrial DNA clones in tassel-eared squirrels *Sciurus aberti*. *Molecular Ecology* 3:541–50.

Wettstein, P. J., M. Strausbauch, T. Lamb, J. States, R. Chakraborty, L. Jin, and R. Riblet. 1995. Phylogeny of six *Sciurus aberti* subspecies based on nucleotide sequences of cytochrome b. *Molecular Phylogenetics and Evolution* 4 (2): 150–62.

Woodhouse, S. W. 1853a. Description of a new species of *Sciurus*. *Proceedings Academy of Natural Sciences Philadelphia* 6:110.

———. 1853b. Renaming for *S. dorsalis* Woodhouse, 1853. *Proceedings Academy of Natural Sciences Philadelphia* 6:200.

Wyoming Game and Fish Department. http://gf.state.wy.us/.

Young, S. P. 1947. Edward Alphonso Goldman. *Journal of Mammalogy* 28 (2): 91–108.

Zeveloff, S. I. 1988. Mammals of the Intermountain West. Salt Lake City: University of Utah Press.

Zhang, X., and J. S. States. 1991. Selective herbivory of ponderosa pine by Abert squirrels: A re-examination of the role of terpenes. *Biochemical Systematics and Ecology* 19:111–15.

Additional References Consulted

Adams, S., and S. Mallman. 2007. Arizona Wildlife Viewing Guide. Cambridge, MN: Adventure Publishing.

Aleshire, P. 1991. Suit shines light on ecosystem, logging fight over more than trees. *Arizona Republic*, September 3, B2–B3.

Allen, J. A. 1893. List of mammals collected by Mr. Charles P. Rowley in the San Juan Region of Colorado, New Mexico and Utah, with descriptions of new species. *Bulletin of the American Museum Natural History* 5:69–84.

Allen, J. A. 1899. The North American arboreal squirrels. *American Naturalist* 33 (8): 635–42.

Allen, J. A., C. Lumholtz, F. Robinette, and A. D. Meeds. 1893. List of mammals and birds collected in northeastern Sonora and northwestern Chihuahua, Mexico, on the Lumholtz Archaeological Expedition, 1890–1892. *Bulletin of the American Museum of Natural History* 5:27–42.

Allred, W. S. 1996. The unique tassel-eared squirrels. *Grand Canyon Association Member Newsletter* 11 (2): 7.

———. 2002. What's that sound coming from above? Arizona's tassel-eared squirrels—three unique subspecies. *Canyon Echo, Grand Canyon Chapter of the Sierra Club* 38 (3): 8.

———. 2007. Rascal, the Tassel-Eared Squirrel. Grand Canyon, AZ: Grand Canyon Association.

———. 2010. Tassel-eared squirrels of Arizona. *Arizona Wild*, newsletter of the Arizona Wilderness Coalition, Phoenix. Spring–Summer.

Amberlyn, J. C. 2005. Drawing Wildlife. New York: Watson-Guptill.

Anderson, S. 1961. Mammals of Mesa Verde National Park, Colorado. *University of Kansas Publications, Museum of Natural History* 14 (3): 29–67.

———. 1972. Mammals of Chihuahua: Taxonomy and distribution. *Bulletin of the American Museum of Natural History* 148, article 2:151–410.

Arizona Game and Fish Department. 2006. Arizona's Comprehensive Wildlife Conservation Strategy: 2005–2015. Phoenix: AZGFD.

Arizona Natural History Association, Flagstaff. www.aznaturalhistory.org.

Armstrong, D. M. 1982. Mammals of the Canyon Country: A Handbook of Mammals of Canyonlands National Park and Vicinity. Moab, UT: Canyonlands Natural History Association.

Arrington, O. N. 1943. Completion Report: Project 11-d. July 1, 1942, to June 30, 1943. Phoenix: Arizona Game and Fish Commission, Federal Aid Division.

———. 1946. The status of restoration areas stocked with game species under Federal Aid in Wildlife Restoration in Arizona. Phoenix: Arizona Game and Fish Commission.

Aubry, K. B., J. P. Hayes, B. L. Biswell, and B. G. Marcot. 2003. The ecological role of tree-dwelling mammals in western coniferous forests. *In* Mammal Community Dynamics—Management and Conservation in the Coniferous Forests of Western North America, ed. C. J. Zabel and R. G. Anthony, 405–44. New York: Cambridge University Press.

Banks, J. C. 2009. Kaibab National Forest celebrates special squirrel. *Grand Canyon Association Member Newsletter* 15 (1).

Bassett, R. L., D. A. Boyce Jr., M. H. Reiser, R. T. Graham, and R. T. Reynolds. 1994. Influence of site quality and stand density on goshawk habitat in southwestern forests. *Studies in Avian Biology* 16:41–45.

Bayless, M., and M. Ingraldi. 2004. Estimation of tassel-eared squirrel abundance on Camp Navajo prior to a forest restoration treatment. Flagstaff: Arizona Game and Fish Department, Research Branch.

Bayless, M., M. Ingraldi, and S. Partridge. 2006. Estimation of tassel-eared squirrel abundance on Camp Navajo prior to a forest restoration treatment. Flagstaff: Arizona Game and Fish Department, Research Branch.

Bernard, S. R., and K. F. Brown. 1977. Distribution of Mammals, Reptiles, and Amphibians by BLM Physiographic Regions and A. W. Kuchler's Associations for the Eleven Western States. Technical Note 301. Washington, DC: U.S. Department of the Interior, Bureau of Land Management.

Betancourt, J. L., T. R. Van Devender, and P. S. Martin. 1990. Synthesis and prospectus. *In* Packrat Middens: The last 40,000 years of biotic change, 435–48. Tucson: University of Arizona Press.

Bieri, J. G., G. S. Stoewsand, G. M. Briggs, R. W. Phillips, J. C. Woodard, and J. J. Knapka. 1977. Report of the American Institute of Nutrition ad hoc committee on standards for nutritional studies. *Journal of Nutrition* 107:1340–48.

Black, C. C. 1963. A review of the North American Tertiary Sciuridae. *Bulletin of the Museum of Comparative Zoology, Harvard University* 130 (3): 109–248.

Bosworth, W. R., III. 2003. Vertebrate Information. Publication no. 03-45. Salt Lake City: Utah Division of Wildlife Resources.

Brown, D. E. 1972. Tree squirrel management information. Progress Report. Project W-53-R-22, work plan 3, job 3. Phoenix: Arizona Game and Fish Department.

———. 1973. Kaibab squirrel stocking. Progress Report. Project W-53-R-23, work plan 6, job 4. Phoenix: Arizona Game and Fish Department.

———. 1973. Tree squirrel management information. Performance Report. Project W-53-R-23, work plan 3, job 3. Phoenix: Arizona Game and Fish Department.

———. 1974. Tree squirrel management information. Performance Report. Project W-53-R-24, work plan 3, job 3. Phoenix: Arizona Game and Fish Department.

———. 1975. Tree squirrel investigations. Performance Report. Project W-53-R-25, work plan 2, job 1. Phoenix: Arizona Game and Fish Department.

———. 1976. Tree squirrel. Performance Report. Project W-53-R-26, work plan 2, job 1. Phoenix: Arizona Game and Fish Department.

———. 1977. Tree squirrel. Performance Report. Project W-53-R-27, work plan 2, job 1. Phoenix: Arizona Game and Fish Department.

———. 1978. Tree squirrel. Performance Report. Project W-53-R-28, work plan 2, job 1. Phoenix: Arizona Game and Fish Department.

———. 1979. Tree squirrel. Performance Report. Project W-53-R-29, work plan 2, job 1. Phoenix: Arizona Game and Fish Department.

———. 1980. Tree squirrel. Performance Report. Project W-53-R-30, work plan 2, job 1. Phoenix: Arizona Game and Fish Department.

———. 1980. Management history of Abert squirrels. *Wildlife News*, December, 6–7. Arizona Game and Fish Department.

———. 1981. Tree squirrel. Performance Report. Project W-53-R-31, work plan 2, job 1. Phoenix: Arizona Game and Fish Department.

Brown, D. E., and T. Britt. 1975. Kaibab squirrel stocking. Performance Report. Project W-53-R-25, work plan 6, job 4. Phoenix: Arizona Game and Fish Department.

Brown, D. E., T. Britt, and J. O'Neil. 1975. Tree squirrel investigations. Performance Report. Project W-53-R-25, work plan 3, job 5. Phoenix: Arizona Game and Fish Department.

Brown, D. E., J. Evans, and T. Britt. 1976. Kaibab squirrel stocking. Performance Report. Project W-53-R-26, work plan 6, job 4. Phoenix: Arizona Game and Fish Department.

———. 1977. Kaibab squirrel stocking. Performance Report. Project W-53-R-27, work plan 6, job 4. Phoenix: Arizona Game and Fish Department.

Bumstead, R. 1959. Abert squirrel hunt information and Abert squirrel survey information. Completion Report. Project W-53-R-9, work plan 2, job 12; work plan 3, job 12. Phoenix: Arizona Game and Fish Department.

Burt, W. H. 1964. A Field Guide to the Mammals. Boston: Houghton Mifflin Co.

Carey, A. B. 2000. Effects of new forest management strategies on squirrel populations. *Ecological Applications* 10 (1): 248–57.

Carey, A. B., J. Kershner, B. Biswell, and L. Dominguez de Toledo. 1999. Ecological scale and forest development: Squirrels, dietary fungi, and vascular plants in managed and unmanaged forests. *Wildlife Monographs* 142.

Casey, S. J., and A. M. Casey. 2003. Squirrel Rehabilitation Handbook. Evergreen, CO: WildAgain Wildlife Rehabilitation.

Coconino National Forest celebrates 100 years. Coconino National Forest. www. fs.fed.us/r3/Coconino/about/index.shtml.

Colby, C. B. 1967. Wild Rodents. New York: Meredith Press.

Colton, H. 1932. The first naturalist to visit northern Arizona. Museum of Northern Arizona, Flagstaff. *Museum Notes* 5 (1): 1–4.

Cooper, C. F. 1960. Changes in vegetation, structure, and growth of southwestern pine forests since white settlement. *Ecological Monographs* 30 (2).

Coues, E., and H. C. Yarrow. 1875. Report upon Geographical and Geological Explorations and Surveys West of the One Hundredth Meridian. Vol. 5. Report upon the Collection of Mammals Made in Portions of Nevada, Utah, California, New Mexico, and Arizona, During the Years 1871, 1872, 1873, and 1874. Washington, DC: U.S. Government Printing Office, pp. 116–17.

Covington, W. W., and M. M. Moore. 1994. Southwestern ponderosa forest structure —changes since Euro-American settlement. *Journal of Forestry* 92:39–47.

Covington, W., and P. K. Wagner, technical coordinators. 1996. Conference on Adaptive Ecosystem Restoration and Management: Restoration of Cordilleran Conifer Landscapes of North America. Flagstaff: Northern Arizona University.

Critters get nod on National Squirrel Day. 2010. *Grand Canyon News* (Williams, AZ), January 20.

Crook, B., W. F. Andelt, and S. Hopper. 1995. Life History, Status, and Effect of Hunting on Abert's Squirrels in Colorado. Fort Collins: Colorado State University.

Crumbo, K., and R. George. 2005. Protecting and Restoring the Greater Grand Canyon Ecoregion: Finding Solutions for an Ecoregion at Risk. Flagstaff, AZ: Grand Canyon Wildlands Council.

Davis, R., and R. Sidner. 1962. Mammals of Woodland and Forest Habitats in the Rincon Mountains of Saguaro National Monument, Arizona. Tucson: University of Arizona, Cooperative National Park Resources Studies Unit.

Day, R. 2008. Abert's squirrel. Wildlife Field Notes. Arizona Wildlife News. Arizona Game and Fish Department. Phoenix. September–October.

Dodd, N. L., R. E. Schweinsburg, and S. Boe. 2006. Landscape-scale forest habitat relationships to tassel-eared squirrel populations: Implications for ponderosa pine forest restoration. *Restoration Ecology* 14 (4): 537–47.

Durrant, S. D. 1952. Mammals of Utah. Taxonomy and distribution. *Museum of Natural History Publication* 6:94–95. Lawrence: University of Kansas.

Edelman, A. J. 2004. The ecology of an introduced population of Abert's squirrel in a mixed conifer forest. MS thesis, University of Arizona.

Engel-Wilson, R. 1985. Tree squirrel. Performance Report. Project W-53-R-35, work plan 2, job 1. Phoenix: Arizona Game and Fish Department.

———. 1986. Tree squirrel. Performance Report. Project W-53-R-36, work plan 2, job 1. Phoenix: Arizona Game and Fish Department.

———. 1987. Tree squirrel. Performance Report. Project W-53-R-37, work plan 2, job 1. Phoenix: Arizona Game and Fish Department.

———. 1988. Blue grouse, chukar, quail, cottontail rabbit, and tree squirrel. Performance Report. Project W-53-R-38, work plan 2, job 1. Phoenix: Arizona Game and Fish Department.

———. 1989. Blue grouse, chukar, quail, cottontail rabbit, and tree squirrel. Performance Report. Project W-53-R-39, work plan 2, job 1. Phoenix: Arizona Game and Fish Department.

Ezell, P., and G. Ezell. 1941. Animal fair. *Region III Quarterly* 3 (1). http://www.nps.gov/history/history/online_books/region_111/vol3–1e.htm.

Farentinos, R. C. 1971. Social dominance and mating activity in the tassel-eared squirrel (*Sciurus aberti ferreus*). PhD diss., University of Colorado.

Ffolliott, P. F. 1997. Guidelines for managing wildlife habitats in southwestern ponderosa pine forests of the United States. *Journal of Forestry Research* 8 (2): 108–10.

Finch, D. M. 1992. Threatened, Endangered, and Vulnerable Terrestrial Vertebrates in the Rocky Mountain States. General Technical Report RM-215. Fort Collins, CO: USDA Forest Service.

Findley, J. S. 1999. Abert's squirrel / *Sciurus aberti*. *In* The Smithsonian Book of North American Mammals, ed. D. E. Wilson and S. Ruff, 449–50. Washington, DC: Smithsonian Institution.

Fitter, R. 1968. Vanishing Wild Animals of the World. New York: Franklin Watts.

Fogel, R. R., and J. M. Trappe. 1958. Fungus consumption (mycophagy) by small animals. *Northwest Science* 52:1–31.

Forbes, R. E. 1997. Subnivean foraging by Abert's squirrels. *In* Life Among the Muses: Papers in Honor of James S. Findley, ed. T. Yates, W. L. Gannon, and D. E. Wilson, 287–90. Albuquerque: University of New Mexico, Museum of Southwestern Biology.

Fowells, H. A. 1965. Silvics of Forest Trees of the United States. Agriculture Handbook no. 271. Washington, DC: USDA Forest Service.

Frey, J. K. 1996. Mammalian type localities in New Mexico. Occasional Papers no. 7. Albuquerque: University of New Mexico, Museum of Southwestern Biology.

Garnett, G. N. 2002. Wildlife use of witches' brooms induced by dwarf mistletoe in ponderosa pine forests of northern Arizona. MS thesis, Northern Arizona University.

Grand Canyon Wildlands Council. Forthcoming. Appendix 5—Proposed Theodore Roosevelt Wildlife Conservation Area. *In* Safe Havens, Safe Passages: Protecting Wild Nature in the Grand Canyon Ecoregion. http://www.grandcanyonwildlands.org/libraryWritings.html.

Gray, J. E. 1867. Synopsis of the species of American squirrels in the collection of the British Museum. *Annuals and Magazine of Natural History* 20 (serial 3): 415–36.

Gray, M. T. 1992. Colorado Wildlife Viewing Guide. Helena, MT: Falcon Press.

Grinnell, H. W. 1943. Bibliography of Clinton Hart Merriam. *Journal of Mammalogy* 24 (4): 436–57.

Hafner, D. J. 1984. Evolutionary relationships of the Nearctic Sciuridae. *In* The Biology of Ground-Dwelling Squirrels, ed. J. O. Murie and G. R. Michener, 3–23. Lincoln: University of Nebraska Press.

Hall, E. R. 1957. Vernacular Names for North American Mammals North of Mexico. Topeka: University of Kansas, Museum of Natural History.

Harju, H. 1978. Make room for the tassel-eared squirrel. *Wyoming Wildlife* 42 (2): 12–13.

Hawksworth, F. G., and D. Wiens. 1996. Dwarf mistletoes: Biology, pathology, and systematics. Agriculture Handbook 709. Washington, DC: USDA Forest Service.

Healthy Forest Restoration Act of 2003. Title 1. Hazardous Fuel Reduction on Federal Land. H.R. 1904–3. 108th Cong., 1st sess.

Heidmann, L. J. 1992. An initial assessment of mammal damage in the forests of the Southwest. Research Note RM-219. Fort Collins, CO: USDA Forest Service.

Hendron, J. W. 1946. Atomic man in the haunts of the ancient cave man. *Desert Magazine* 9 (12): 5–9.

Hirsch, B. 1997. Squirrel hunting offers back-to-basics approach. *Arizona Republic* (Phoenix), October 16.

Hobbs, D. E. 1980. The effect of habitat sound properties on alarm calling behavior in two species of tree squirrels, *Sciurus nayaritensis* and *Sciurus arizonensis*. PhD diss., University of Arizona.

Hodge, C. 1983. High, wild, and lonesome. *Arizona Highways* 59 (8): 38–46.

Houk, R. 1993. Tree, squirrel, bird, and truffle. *In* The Magnificent Ponderosa. *Plateau Magazine*, pp. 12–15. Flagstaff: Museum of Northern Arizona, Flagstaff.

Hurst, W. D. 1969. Memorandum—Agencies plan Kaibab squirrel studies. USDA Forest Service (copy in author's files provided by William Hurst).

Hyatt, F., and S. Hyatt. 1952. A tuft-eared white-tail. *Natural History* 61 (10): 456.

Jellison, W. L. 1939. *Opisodasys* Jordan 1933, a genus of Siphonapteran. *Journal of Parasitology* 25:413–20.

Julyan, R., and M. Stuever. 2005. *Field Guide to the Sandia Mountains*. Albuquerque: University of New Mexico Press.

Kearsley, M. J. C., and J. G. Hall. 2000. Return to Walhalla: 25 years of forest development and effects on Kaibab squirrels. Ecological Society of America, 85th annual meeting, Snowbird, Utah, August (abstract). http://www.esa.org/meetings/archivedabstracts.php.

———. 2004. A reassessment of Kaibab squirrel activity and habitat quality on the Walhalla Plateau, Grand Canyon National Park. Final Report. Research Permit GRCA-2000-SCI-0057. Submitted to Grand Canyon Science Center, Grand Canyon National Park (copy in author's files).

Kopp, A. 1998. A bright-eyed, bushy tale. *New Mexico Magazine*, April, 30–33.

Koprowski, J. L. 1998. Conflict between the sexes: A review of social and mating systems of the tree squirrels. *In* Ecology and Evolutionary Biology of

Tree Squirrels, ed. M. A. Steele, J. F. Merritt, and D. A. Zegers, 33–41. Special Publications 6. Martinsville: Virginia Museum of Natural History.

Kotter, M. M. 1981. Interrelationships of tassel-eared squirrels, ponderosa pine and hypogeous mycorrhizal fungi. MS thesis, Ohio State University.

Kruse, W. H. 1992. Quantifying wildlife habitats within Gambel oak/forest/woodland vegetation associations in Arizona. *In* Ecology and Management of Oak and Associated Woodlands: Perspectives in the Southwestern United States and Northern Mexico, tech. coord. G. J. Gottfried, D. A. Bennett, V. M. Hernandez, C. A. Ortega-Rubio, and R. H. Hamre, 182–86. General Technical Report RM-218. Fort Collins, CO: USDA Forest Service.

Kufeld, R. C. 1966. Tree squirrel management information. Progress Report. Project W-53-R-16, work plan 3, job 3. Phoenix: Arizona Game and Fish Department.

Lamb, S. 1994. Observations. The Best of *Grand Canyon Nature Notes* 1926–1935. Grand Canyon, AZ: Grand Canyon Natural History Association.

Lanner, R. M. 1981. The Piñon Pine—A Natural and Cultural History. Reno: University of Nevada Press.

Lawson, L. 1941. Survey of Abert squirrel population in the state, June 13, 1941, to June 19, 1941. Phoenix: Arizona Game and Fish Commission, Federal Aid Division.

Lindenmayer, D. B., and J. F. Franklin. 2002. Conserving Forest Biodiversity: A Comprehensive Multiscaled Approach. Washington, DC: Island Press.

Long, K. 1995. Squirrels: A Wildlife Handbook. Boulder, CO: Johnson Books.

Manno, T. G. 2009. Pearl of a squirrel—tourists and park service celebrate peculiar rodent. *Earth Odyssey* 1 (11).

Matthews, W. H., III. 1968. A Guide to the National Parks—Their Landscape and Geology. Vol. 1, The Western Parks. Garden City, NY: Natural History Press.

McKee, E. N.d. Service fellows at Yale. *Regional Review* 5 (2 & 3). http://www.nps.gov/history/history/online_books/regional_review/rr-title.htm.

McTague, J. P., and D. R. Patton. 1989. Stand density index and its application in describing wildlife habitat. *Wildlife Society Bulletin* 17:58–62.

Messmer, T., R. Drake, and A. McElrone. 1998. Endangered and Threatened Animals of Utah. Salt Lake City: Utah Department of Natural Resources, Division of Wildlife Resources.

Mitchell, L. G., J. A. Mutchmor, and W. D. Dolphin. 1988. Zoology. Menlo Park, CA: Cummings Publishing Co.

Morehouse, B. J. 1996. A Place Called Grand Canyon. Tucson: University of Arizona Press.

Mossman, H. W., J. W. Lawlah, and J. A. Bradley. 1932. The male reproductive tract of the Sciuridae. *American Journal of Anatomy* 51 (1): 89–141.

Mount Graham red squirrel: An expanded biological assessment of impacts. 1988. *In* Coronado National Forest Land Management Plan and University of Arizona Proposal for Mt. Graham Astrophysical Development. Section 3.1. Tassel-eared/red squirrel overlap (copy in author's files).

Murie, O. J. 1998. A Field Guide to Animal Tracks. Boston: Houghton Mifflin Harcourt.

Nelson, L. 1992. A thriving . . . dying forest. Northern Arizona University *Horizons*, 1992–1993, 6–9.

Nowak, R. M. 1991. Walker's Mammals of the World. 5th ed. Vol. 1. Baltimore, MD: Johns Hopkins University Press.

O'Connell, M. 1991. Tracing nature's pattern purpose of squirrel study. *Arizona Daily Sun* (Flagstaff), May 4, 1.

Parchman, T. L., and C. W. Benkman. 2008. The geographic selection mosaic for ponderosa pine and crossbills: A tale of two squirrels. *Evolution* 62 (2): 348–60.

Partridge, S. T., and M. F. Ingraldi. 2007. Estimation of tassel-eared squirrel abundance at selected sites within the Lakeside Ranger District, Apache-Sitgreaves National Forest. Phoenix: Arizona Game and Fish Department.

———. 2007. 2006/2007 tassel-eared squirrel density on the west buffer of Camp Navajo. Flagstaff: Arizona Game and Fish Department, Research Branch.

Patton, D. R. 2008. The Fort Valley Experimental Forest, ponderosa pine and wildlife habitat research. *In* Fort Valley Forest—A Century of Research 1908–2008, tech. coord. S. D. Olberding and M. M. Moore, 81–88. Proceedings RMRS-P-55. Fort Collins, CO: USDA Forest Service, Rocky Mountain Research Station.

Pederson, J. C., and A. L. Pederson. 1976. Tassel-Eared Squirrels of North America: A Bibliography. Publication no. 76-14. Salt Lake City: Utah Department of Natural Resources, Division of Wildlife.

Peterson, W. 1965. The story of Arizona's own Kaibab squirrel. *Arizona Highways* 41:1–11.

Pollock, R. T. 1981. The squirrel with tassel ears . . . a handsome animal. *Colorado Outdoors* 30 (May–June): 35–37.

Ponderosa pine (*pinw ponderosa*). 2007. Library of Trees. Arbor Day Foundation. Nebraska City, NE. 8 pp (copy in author's files).

Pratt, H. S. 1935. A Manual of Land and Fresh Water Vertebrate Animals of the United States (Exclusive of Birds). 2nd ed. Philadelphia: P. Blakiston's Son and Co.

Quaintance, C. W. 1934. Mammals of the San Francisco Mountain region—no. 1, daytime rodents. Museum of Northern Arizona, Flagstaff. *Museum Notes* 7 (1): 1–4.

Ratcliff, T. D. 1974. Kaibab squirrel activities in relation to forest characteristics. MS thesis, University of Arizona.

Ridgeway, R. 1912. Color Standards and Color Nomenclature. Baltimore, MD: A. Hoen and Co.

Rockwell, R. B. 1916. The Squirrels, Chipmunks, and Gophers of Colorado. Publication no. 5. Denver: Colorado Mountain Club.

Sanderson, L. R., and J. L. Koprowski, eds. 2009. The Last Refuge of the Mt. Graham Red Squirrel. Tucson: University of Arizona Press.

Seaman, R. N. 1975. A re-evaluation of Nearctic sciurid phylogeny based upon biochemical, immunological and numerical taxonomic analyses. PhD diss., Colorado State University.

Sidener, J. 1991. Ecosystem strategy: Slow timber cutting has chain of effects. *Arizona Republic*, June 1, AZ (copy in author's files).

Sisk, T. 2005. Tassel-eared squirrel density and recruitment. www.forestera.nau.edu/docs/Products/WMPALA/WMPALADataAtlas.pdf.

Small game profile: Rabbits and tree squirrels. 1988. Arizona Game and Fish Department *Wildlife Views*, April, 16–17.

Smith, C. C., and R. P. Balda. 1979. Competition among insects, birds, and mammals for conifer seeds. *American Zoologist* 19:1065–83.

Snyder, M., and Y. B. Linhart. 1993. Barking up the right tree. *Natural History* 102:45–49.

Southwest Forest Alliance. 2000. Why the Flagstaff restoration model should not be applied to public forest land (copy in author's files).

Southwest Forest Health and Wildlife Prevention Act of 2004. Public Law 108–317. October 5, 2004.

Squillace, A. E. 1953. Effects of squirrels on the supply of ponderosa pine seed. Missoula, MT: Northern Rocky Mountain Forest and Range Experiment Station.

Squirrels may hold the key to reducing forest fire risks while protecting wildlife. 2005. http://www.azgfd/gov/artman/publish/printer_413.shtml.

Squirrels stable. 1979. Arizona Game and Fish Department *Wildlife Views* 22 (9): 9.

Squirrel numbers down. 1980. Arizona Game and Fish Department *Wildlife Views*, September.

Stair, J. L. Tree squirrel management information. 1960. Completion Report. Project W-53-R-10, work plan 3, job 3. Phoenix: Arizona Game and Fish Department.

———. Tree squirrel management information. 1961. Completion Report. Project W-53-R-11, work plan 3, job 3. Phoenix: Arizona Game and Fish Department.

States, J. S. 1990. Mushrooms and Truffles of the Southwest. Tucson: University of Arizona Press.

———. 2002. Ghosts in the trees. *Cerca Magazine*. www.cercamagazine.com.

Steele, M. A. 2008. Evolutionary interactions between tree squirrels and trees: A review and synthesis. *Current Science* 95 (7): 871–76.

Steele, M. A., and J. L. Koprowski. 2003. North American Tree Squirrels. Washington, DC: Smithsonian Institution Press.

Steffen, N. 2007. Effects of ecological restoration treatment on the home range sizes of tassel-eared squirrels (*sciurus aberti*) within the wildland urban interface surrounding Flagstaff, Arizona (Copy in author's files).

Stephenson, R. L. 1974. Seasonal food habits of Abert's squirrel, *Sciurus aberti*. *Journal of the Arizona Academy of Science*, 9:8.

Stevens, B. 2009. Holiday kisses or kiss of death? *Arizona Daily Sun*, December 21.

Stonoff, B. 1970. Giant squirrels of the high country. *Sports Afield*, August, 122–25.

Taylor, W. P. 1925a. Summary of field work, Southwestern Forest Experiment Station, the Abert squirrel. Flagstaff, Arizona. Smithsonian Institution Archives, record unit 7176, box 29, folder 18.

————. 1925b. Memorandum for Dr. E. W. Nelson, chief of bureau, project summary, Division of Biological Investigations, Bureau of Biological Survey. Tucson, Arizona. Smithsonian Institution Archives, record unit 7176, box 29, folder 17.

————. 1926. Work of the Division of Biological Investigations, Bureau of Biological Survey, in the Southwest, United States Department of Agriculture. Tucson, Arizona. Smithsonian Institution Archives, record unit 7176, box 29, folder 22.

————. 1930. Outlines for studies of mammalian life histories. Miscellaneous publication no. 86. Washington, DC: U.S. Department of Agriculture.

Theobald, D. P. 1982. Tree squirrel. Performance Report. Project W-53-R-32, work plan 2, job 1. Phoenix: Arizona Game and Fish Department.

Thornburg, R., and F. Thornburg. 1946. Tuft-eared squirrels. *Nature Magazine* 39:523–24.

Tighe, K. 2003. Shy sprites of the ponderosa pine forests. *Arizona Highways* 79 (2): 36–37.

Tolan, M. 1992–93. A thriving . . . or dying forest. Northern Arizona University *Horizons*, pp. 6–9.

Tree squirrel. 1990. Performance Report. Project W-53-R-40, work plan 2, job 5. Phoenix: Arizona Game and Fish Department.

Tree squirrel. 1991. Performance Report. Project W-53-R-41, work plan 2, job 5. Phoenix: Arizona Game and Fish Department.

Tree squirrel. 1992. Performance Report. Project W-53-R-42, work plan 2, job 5. Phoenix: Arizona Game and Fish Department.

Tree squirrel. 1993. Performance Report. Project W-53-R-43, work plan 2, job 5. Phoenix: Arizona Game and Fish Department.

Tree squirrel. 1994. Performance Report. Project W-53-R-44, work plan 2, job 5. Phoenix: Arizona Game and Fish Department.

Trouessart, E. L. 1880. Revision of the Sciuridae. *Le Naturaliste: Journal des échanges et des nouvelles* 37:290–93, 315.

Truffles, squirrels, goshawks, and chainsaws—the ecology and destruction of a forest. 1996. *In* Forest Forever! p.11. Flagstaff, AZ: Southwest Forest Alliance.

Turback, G. 1987a. The squirrel time forgot. *Arizona Highways* 63 (7): 12–13.

Unique Kaibab squirrel gets special honor. 2010. *Daily Courier* (Prescott. Arizona), January 20.

USDA Forest Service. 1986. Environmental Impact Statement. Carson National Forest Plan. Albuquerque, NM: USDA Forest Service, Southwestern Region (copy in author's files).

————. 2003. Management Indicator Species Assessment. Carson National Forest. Albuquerque, NM: USDA Forest Service, Southwestern Region (copy in author's files).

Vandermeer, J. 1981. Elementary Mathematical Ecology. New York: John Wiley and Sons.

Webb, P. M. 1967. Tree squirrel management information. Completion Report. Project W-53-R-17, work plan 3, job 3. Phoenix: Arizona Game and Fish Department.

———. 1968. Tree squirrel management information. Completion Report. Project W-53-R-18, work plan 3, job 3. Phoenix: Arizona Game and Fish Department.

Wheeler, G. M., H. C. Yarrow, and E. D. Cope. 1875. Report upon Geographical and Geological Explorations and Surveys West of the One Hundredth Meridian. Vol. 5, Zoology. Reports upon the Zoological Collections Obtained from Portions of Nevada, Utah, California, Colorado, New Mexico, and Arizona, During the Years 1871, 1872, 1873, and 1874. Washington, DC: U.S. Government Printing Office.

Wightman, C. 2006. The balancing act: What squirrel research tells us about forest health. Arizona Game and Fish Department. *Arizona Wildlife Views*, July–August, 28–32.

Williams, T. 2008. Pillar of the forest. *Audubon Magazine, Earth Almanac*, May–June edition.

Wilson, D. E., and S. Ruff. 1999. The Smithsonian Book of North American Mammals. Washington, DC: Smithsonian Institution Press.

Wood, D. J., J. L. Koprowski, and P. W. W. Lurz. 2007. Three squirrel introduction: A theoretical approach with population viability analysis. *Journal of Mammalogy* 88 (5): 1271–79.

Worden, K. J., and C. Kleier. 2009. Impact of ponderosa pine thinning on Abert's squirrel (*sciurus aberti*) populations in Boulder County, CO. PS 41–190 poster presented at 94th Ecological Society of America Meeting, Albuquerque, NM.

Yeager, L. E. 1956. Colorado squirrels. *Colorado Outdoors* 5 (40): 16–17.

INDEX

false truffles, 134–35; as dietary component, 38, 39, 134, 162, 163; and squirrel immune systems, 109–10

Farentinos, Robert, 57, 60, 69–70, 82, 95

faunal remains, 97, 179, 181, 182

feed trees: forest restoration efforts and, 160; growth rates of, 46; and nitrogen cycling, 133–34; rotation of, 45–46, 132–33; selection of, 42–44; terminal shoots of, 39–42, 45, 132, 133, 144–45. *See also* ponderosa pine trees

feet, 12–13, 15

Ffolliott, Peter, 161

Findley, James, 31

food. *See* diet

food caching, 51–52, 162

foraging, 66–67, 74

forest fires, 113, 158, 164

forest management, 157–64; and canopy cover, 135, 159, 162, 163–64; habitat preservation, 123, 124, 163; landscape models, 159; prescription fires, 163, 164; protection measures, 98, 118–19, 123–24, 163–64; removal of dwarf mistletoe, 162; restoration efforts, 113, 158, 159–60, 163; tree thinning practices, 113, 158, 161, 163, 164. *See also* ponderosa pine trees

Forsyth, David, 106

fossils, 179, 180, 181, 183

Frost, Kent, 178

future research areas: body temperature, 18; communal nesting, 76; forest ecology, 139–40; forest management practices, 164; genetics, 113–14; habitat and home range, 34; Kaibab squirrel, 124; mortality, 101; population census, 153; reproductive physiology, 89–90

Galliziolli, Steve, 32

gastrointestinal (GI) tract, 41–42, 98

geographic distribution, 21, 30–31, 34, 111–12, 113; of subspecies, 23, 25. *See also* home range

Gilbert, Paul, 87

glaciation, 112, 183

global warming, 81, 169

Goldman, Edward Alphonso, 9, 118, 120, 177

goshawks, 28, 95, 162

Grand Canyon, 2; National Game Preserve, 33, 118, 119; National Park, 117, 119, 123, 136, 164

gray squirrels, 7–8, 105, 106, 149–50

guard hair, 5, 10

Gurnell, John, 11, 72

Guzman, Deborah, 86

habitat, 21–27; characteristics, 24–27; and

home range, 28, 29–30, 34; loss of, 96, 123; optimal, 22, 25–26, 163; ponderosa pine as, 3, 21, 24, 27, 34, 162; preservation efforts, 123, 124; ROMPA comparison of, 25–26, 28, 160; sink, 22

Hall, Joseph G., 67, 74, 97, 116; on diet and feeding, 40, 47, 52; estimates Kaibab squirrel population, 146; on habitat, 124; marking methods of, 150; on nests, 57, 74; opposes hunting of Kaibab squirrels, 122–23; on pelage color, 110–11; on tree defoliation, 130–31

Halloran, Margaret, 28

Hargrave, Lyndon, 179

Harrison, Benjamin, 118

Heaney, Lawrence, 81

Hill, James, 84, 129

Hoffmeister, Donald, 32, 117, 150

home range, 21, 27–30, 34; seasonal variation in, 29. *See also* geographic distribution

Hough, E., 117

hunting: authorizations of, 119, 121, 122, 123; and census methods, 145, 146–47; restrictions on, 98, 118, 119, 123; and squirrel mortality, 97–98

Hurst, William D., 97, 119, 123

hypogeous fungi, 134–35, 162; as dietary component, 27, 29, 31, 38–39, 47–48, 52

immune system, 108–10, 113

individual tree approach (ITA), 160

inner bark, 29, 38, 39–42, 52, 144, 163; caloric content of, 41; digestion of, 41–42

interaction with other animals, 135–38

Jordan, Karl, 98

Kaibab National Forest, 117, 119, 164

Kaibab Plateau, 116–17

Kaibab squirrel. See *S. a. kaibabensis*

karyotypes, 105–7, 108–9, 113

Keith, Jim, 1, 11, 73, 95, 97; on age determination, 16; on diet and feeding, 39, 43–44, 49; on nests, 58, 60; on reproduction, 83, 87

Koprowski, John, 100, 152, 163

Kufeld, Robert, 149

lactation, 86

Larson, M. M., 131–32

lateral stripes, 10

leaping, 73–74, 100

Lema, Melissa, 28–29

Leopold, Aldo, 82

life span, 100–102

litters: maternal care of, 84–85; number of in year, 82, 87; sizes, 81, 85

logging, 29–30, 163, 164
Lomolino, Mark, 33

major histocompability compolex (MHC), 110
Mammals of North America (Cahalane), 93
Mammals of the Grand Canyon
   (Hoffmeister), 117
management indicator species (MIS), 3, 158,
   169–70
*Management of the Ponderosa Pine in the
   Southwest* (Pearson), 131
marking, 28, 150, 151, 153
mating, 70–72; bouts, 69, 71–72, 80; fighting
   among males, 71; and food availability, 81;
   and home range, 28, 30; seasonal factors,
   79, 80–81, 88
McKee, Ed, 6, 105
Mearns, Edgar, 79
melanism, 7
Merriam, Clinton Hart, 6, 117, 176
microsatellites, 112–13
mitochondrial DNA (mtDNA), 111–12, 184
molting, 11, 12
monitoring techniques, 144–53; age determination, 16–17, 149–50; body temperature, 17;
   determining home range, 28; feed tree
   characteristics, 43–44; litter count, 85;
   planning for, 152–53; social interaction,
   69–70. *See also* census methods
Monographs of North American Rodentia
   (Coues and Allen), 7
mortality, 28, 93, 100, 101; from automobiles, 97;
   from habitat loss, 96; from hunting, 97–98;
   juvenile survival rates, 81; from parasites,
   98–99; from predation, 28, 93–96; in winter, 96–97, 138
Mt. Graham, 32, 49, 135–36
Mt. Logan, 33, 119, 124
Muir, John, 162
My First Summer in the Sierra (Muir), 162

Nadler, Charles, 105
National Natural Landmark program, 119, 124
National Parks Magazine, 121, 122
Natural History of Squirrels, The (Gurnell), 72
natural range expansion, 31–32, 34
Navajo Nation, 98, 163–64
Nelson, Edward W., 74, 177
nests, 56–63; bolus, 57–60, 63; broom, 56, 57,
   60–61, 63; communal, 72–73; construction,
   57–59, 62, 63; counting of, 147; durability,
   60, 63; maintenance, 60, 72; multiple, 60,
   63; placement, 56, 59–60, 61–63; protection of, 74; in tree cavities, 57, 61, 63; uses
   of, 56–57
Niedrach, Robert, 95

oogenesis, 86–87
Order Rodentia, 14, 171
ovulate cone seeds, 29, 38–39, 46–47

parasites, 98–99
patch approach (PA), 160
Patton, David, 95, 157, 138; on body temperature,
   17; on diet, 41; on habitat, 24–25, 158–59,
   160, 161; on nests, 60, 61
Pearson, G. A., 131
Pederson, Jordan, 145, 157
pelage, 6–11, 17, 149; coloration, 110–11
Pinaleño Mountains, 49, 73, 135–36
polymorphism, 9, 105, 110, 111, 114, 133
ponderosa pine trees: age, 67–68; basal areas,
   22, 24, 25, 30, 147, 158–59; canopy cover,
   26–27, 30, 62–63, 135, 159, 162, 164; characteristics for squirrel nests, 27, 61–62; chemistry of, 43, 45, 46, 61–62; density of, 27, 34,
   113, 158–59; dwarf mistletoe infection, 49,
   162, 164; and elevation, 31; as habitat for
   tassel-eared squirrel, 3, 21, 24, 34, 162; inner
   bark composition, 39–42; mortality, 130–32;
   mycorrhizal fungi and, 134–35; and natural
   selection, 133; and nitrogen cycling, 133;
   ovulate cone development in, 46; as source
   of squirrel diet, 38–49, 52; in southwestern
   U.S., 22, 24, 183; squirrel contribution to
   ecology of, 129–30, 131–35, 157–58, 169–70.
   See also feed trees; forest management
population: calculating, 145–48; density, 26,
   138, 146, 159; of Kaibab squirrels, 119–20,
   123, 146
postnatal development, 84–85, 188
Potter, Randall, 47
Prather, J. W., 159
predation, 93–94; avian, 28, 94–95, 162;
   terrestrial, 96
protection of squirrels, 98, 118, 119, 122–23, 163–64

radio tracking, 152
Rasmussen, Donald, 49, 95, 116
Ratio of Optimum to Marginal Patch Area
   (ROMPA), 25–26, 28, 160
Red Book—Wildlife in Danger, The, 123
Redburn, R. A., 85
red squirrels, 51, 98; competition with, 30,
   135–36
reproduction. *See* copulation; mating
reproductive organs: female, 86, 89; male, 16,
   87–88, 89
Rice, Dale, 70
road kills, 97
Roosevelt, Theodore, 118
Rose, Michael D., 79, 87
Rutledge, R. H., 119